THE MYSTERY OF THE SHROUD OF TURIN

THE MYSTERY OF
THE SHROUD OF TURIN

New Scientific Evidence

John C. Iannone

ALBA·HOUSE   NEW·YORK

SOCIETY OF ST. PAUL, 2187 VICTORY BLVD., STATEN ISLAND, NEW YORK 10314

S

232.966
IAN

ST PAULS

Library of Congress Cataloging-in-Publication Data

Iannone, John C.
     The mystery of the shroud of Turin: new scientific evidence /
John C. Iannone.
          p.   cm.
     Includes bibliographical references.
     ISBN 0-8189-0804-1
     1. Holy Shroud.   I. Title.
     BT587.S4I19   1998
     232.96'6—dc21   97-31297
                                                          CIP

Produced and designed in the United States of America by the
Fathers and Brothers of the Society of St. Paul,
2187 Victory Boulevard, Staten Island, New York 10314,
as part of their communications apostolate.

ISBN: 0-8189-0804-1

Printing Information:

Current Printing - first digit   1   2   3   4   5   6   7   8   9   10

Year of Current Printing - first year shown

1998   1999   2000   2001   2002   2003   2004   2005

Dedication

This book is dedicated

to my Mom and Dad, Marie and John,
whom I barely knew but greatly loved;

to my wife, Kim;

to my precious children,
John Paul and Samantha Jo;

to my brothers and sisters,
William, Eugene, Kathryn, Elaine, Kris,
their spouses and children;

to my friends, especially
Herbert Hall and Richard Burke,
for their treasured support over the years.

Table of Contents

Foreword ix

Announcement xi

Acknowledgments xiii

Introduction xv

Chapter 1: What is the Shroud of Turin? 1

Chapter 2: Pollen, Mites and Flowers — A Unique Cloth 19

Chapter 3: Ancient Roman Coins Over the Eyes 33

Chapter 4: The Signature of Roman Crucifixion: Matching
the Words, the Weapons and the Wounds 47

Chapter 5: The Shroud and Ancient Jewish Burial Practices 73

Chapter 6: Tracing the Historical Journey: The First
Thousand Years 97

Chapter 7: The Journey Continues: The Second
Thousand Years 119

Chapter 8: Art and the Shroud 145

Chapter 9: Credibly Discrediting the Carbon-14 Test
on the Shroud 159

Chapter 10: How Were the Mysterious Images Formed? 177

Chronology...193

Epilogue 197

Appendix 199

Endnotes 203

Bibliography 215

Name Index 221

Subject Index 225

Foreword

Welcome to the intriguing world of Sindonology! If you are a neophyte, you will be blessed as you discover the truly amazing facts concerning the Shroud of Turin. If you are a Shroud enthusiast you will be brought current to some exciting new discoveries in this ever changing area of scholarship.

Having had the privilege to preview this excellent treatise, it was a double honor to be asked to write this Foreword. John Iannone has done a masterful job of synthesizing the many sources of research on this enigmatic artifact into a fascinating and thoroughly engrossing work. As a result, you will be rewarded with an excellent comprehensive understanding of the current status of the Shroud issue.

It has been my pleasure to work with John Iannone for a number of years in the field of Shroud studies. He strives tirelessly to maximize public awareness of the facts. That same unswerving devotion is reflected clearly in the pages that follow. In my opinion, John brings a sensitivity and sincerity to the Shroud story that makes this an interesting as well as thought-provoking addition to any library.

In my twenty years of Sindonology, I've read many books on the Shroud of Turin. Some books are vague, some downright boring, still others play loose and fast with the facts in order to justify pet theories about this unusual relic. Very few will ever qualify as valuable references. *The Mystery of the Shroud of Turin: New Scientific Evidence* will occupy a key place in my study and hopefully yours for years to come.

Dr. Kenneth Stevenson
New York
January 6, 1996

* * *

Dr. Stevenson was a member of the original Shroud of Turin Research Project — a scientific team that investigated the Shroud of Turin first-hand in 1978. He is a noted author and lecturer on the Shroud and has written two books on the subject: *Verdict on the Shroud* and *The Shroud and The Controversy*. He also edited the *Proceedings of the 1977 U.S. Conference of Research on the Shroud of Turin*.

ANNOUNCEMENT

On September 5, 1995 Cardinal Giovanni Saldarini, Archbishop of Turin, Italy and Papal Custodian of the Holy Shroud appeared on Italian television to state that the image on the Shroud is that of Jesus Christ and "no one else." The Cardinal indicated that he spoke for the Shroud's legal owner, Pope John Paul II.

At the same time, he announced public expositions of the Shroud of Turin from April 18 to May 31, 1998 (the 100th Anniversary of the photographic findings of Secondo Pia discussed in this book — photographs which triggered major scientific studies) and from April 29 to June 11, 2000 — the anniversary celebrating the birth of Jesus Christ.

We welcome the Cardinal's announcement and leave it to your judgment in reading this book as to whether the image on the Shroud of Turin is, in fact, that of Jesus Christ and "no one else."

Acknowledgments

I am indebted to a number of individuals who took the time to read the manuscript and add their considerable expertise and experience to refining its contents. Among these are my wife, Kim, for many hours of careful review and correction of the text; my brother Bill, chemist par excellence, for his suggestions; Manny Deren, whose intimate knowledge of Judaism helped assure accuracy; Fr. Albert Dreisbach who laboriously edited the manuscript, providing much updated information, and who wrote the Epilogue; to Fr. Joseph Marino, O.S.B., for his thorough review and refinements; to Reverend Kenneth Stevenson, whose personal dedication and two wonderful books on the Holy Shroud inspired me and who wrote the Foreword; to Reverend Aram Berard, S.J., who, as Chairman of the Holy Shroud Task Force offered me continued encouragement and support; to Dan McPherson — member of the H.S.T.F. who carefully read and edited my text; to Reverend Robert Dinegar, PhD, original member of the Shroud of Turin Research Project (S.T.U.R.P.) team who made several important corrections; to Dr. Daniel Scavone — Shroud author and Professor of History at the University of Indiana, for his guidance on the historical chapters; to Reverend Frederick Brinkmann, C.Ss.R., and Reverend Adam Otterbein, C.Ss.R., of the Holy Shroud Guild for their photographs and access to the Weunschel Collection; to Vernon Miller for the generous use of his photographs of the Holy Shroud; to the late Reverend Peter M. Rinaldi, S.D.B., for his personal inspiration and support; and to my friends Herbert Hall, Terri

Christopher, Mary Donaldson, Judy Chissel and B.J. Schwartz for their thoughtful reading and comments. Finally, I wish to thank Dr. Alan Whanger for his encouraging telephone conversations and Ian Wilson for the inspiration of his writings.

Introduction

*"There are more things in heaven and earth, Horatio,
than are dreamed of in your philosophy."*

Hamlet, Act I, Scene 5

The Shroud of Turin is considered the most precious relic in all Christendom. Millions of people believe it is the actual burial cloth of Jesus and that this linen cloth mysteriously bears His imprints and bloodstains. In 1978, over three million people viewed the Shroud at a rare exposition in Turin, Italy — its home for over four centuries. Undoubtedly, the Shroud is the most studied relic of all times. Very few ancient artifacts could withstand the scrutiny to which the Shroud has been subjected. Although the Catholic Church as owner of this precious cloth has withheld official recognition, the Church now encourages study of the Shroud and over thirty-five pontiffs have privately acknowledged their personal belief in the Shroud's authenticity, including John Paul II. The Church has legally owned the Shroud since 1983 when King Umberto II of Italy (House of Savoy) died and willed the Shroud to the Vatican.

The Shroud of Turin has been analyzed by surgeons and forensic pathologists who carefully examined the wounds imprinted on the cloth; by archaeologists, scriptural experts, historians, artists, physicists, chemists, biologists and photographers — all seeking clues to its antiquity and authenticity. Scientists continue to be intrigued by the imprints of a crucified body, alleged to be that of Jesus Christ, and seek to understand how such images may have been formed on the linen cloth. Sindonologists (from the New Testament Greek *sindon*, or shroud) consist of Christians, Jews and even agnostics.

What is the source of this fascination and why do we study this cloth so intently? Believers venerate it, not for itself as a cloth, but because of its powerful ramifications. For if it is the actual burial cloth of Jesus, it mysteriously bears images of His physical appearance and witnesses His earthly existence, graphically portraying His passion, death and resurrection. In this regard, it has been called the "Fifth Gospel" and the "Silent Witness," for in its fabric millions believe that Jesus has left a record of the glorious and historic moment when Christians believe He rose from the dead — a photograph, if you will — of an event that altered the course of history. Some authors note that the Shroud and its mysteries seem to have been created providentially for the scientific, analytical and searching minds of the twentieth century now in possession of the tools and instrumentation along with the medical and scientific knowledge to appreciate the fascinating clues contained in the cloth.

To some, the examination of the Shroud reads like a detective story as they piece together these many clues. The "preponderance of evidence," as Atlanta sindonologist Father Albert Dreisbach calls it, points to a startling and momentous conclusion: namely, that this is the actual burial cloth of Jesus Christ who lived some two thousand years ago. The tiny mites and ancient pollen found on the Shroud from the Dead Sea area; the discovery of Roman *lepton* coins over the eyes of the Man of the Shroud; the microscopic traces of dirt (travertine argonite) found on the heel, knee and tip of the nose; the calcium carbonate (limestone) dust — characteristic of the tombs of Jerusalem — found on the cloth; the three-dimensional image of the Man of the Shroud recorded by the space-age VP-8 Image Analyzer used by NASA; the identification of real human male blood by chemists and many more fascinating details: all provide clues that defy efforts by skeptics to portray the Shroud as the work of a forger or artist from the Medieval or Renaissance period.

In this regard, Lynn Picknett and Clive Prince in their book *Turin Shroud: In Whose Image?* (1994) have claimed the Shroud to be a forgery of the great master Leonardo da Vinci. We will address this issue in this book and refute the "Leonardo" theory as simply incorrect. Indeed, as several scientists point out, the burden of proof now falls on the skeptics to disprove the mounting and compelling evidence regarding the Shroud's authenticity.

To others, the story of the Shroud reads like a sweeping epic novel with a fascinating history that encompasses both reverence and intrigue. This linen cloth — claimed by millions to have witnessed the passion, death and resurrection of Jesus — was later transported in secrecy by His disciples to King Abgar in the city of Edessa. It was sealed up in the walls of Edessa to protect it during a persecution, only to be rediscovered five hundred years later when it was identified as the Image of Edessa and the model for Eastern and Western art. It became known as the *acheiropoietas,* or "image not made by human hands." Many miracles have been attributed to it in the course of its long history. After acquiring the shroud from the Moslems, the Byzantine army transported it from Edessa to Constantinople in 944. Here it was carried in procession with great pageantry and revered in the incredibly sumptuous Chapel of the Pharos, only to be stolen from the Eastern Emperors by the French and Venetian Crusaders of the infamous Fourth Crusade of 1204 and brought in secrecy to Europe.

Recent authors have pointed out evidence that the precious cloth inspired the earliest legends of the Holy Grail in Europe and was secretly protected and venerated for one hundred and fifty years by the "warrior monks" — the Knights Templar — and then displayed in France publicly in 1357 by a knight, Geoffroy de Charny. After having survived a terrible fire in 1532 that damaged parts of the Shroud, it was brought to Turin by the Dukes of Savoy, who later became the ruling family of Italy. In Turin, the beautiful Cathedral of John the Baptist was built to protect it. In 1978 it was subjected to five days of intensive scientific study by a team of over forty scientists — including agnostics, Jews and Christians — known as S.T.U.R.P. (Shroud of Turin Research Project), who have produced many scientific papers in support of its authenticity over the past years. The Shroud is the most studied relic of all times and to this day this enigmatic relic continues to baffle the minds of our greatest scientists.

In 1988 Shroud studies suffered a severe setback when the international press, overlooking the vast body of scientific evidence that had been accumulated, announced that Carbon-14 testing performed on samples of the Shroud dated it as a medieval cloth. The results of that Carbon-14 test have, however, been seriously challenged by many in the scientific community, and the position of the Shroud as the ancient burial cloth of Jesus has been reaffirmed, as we shall attempt to demonstrate. The mysterious Shroud has emerged once again out of the shadows.

I have attempted to provide in these pages a synthesis of the best work of sindonologists and to introduce the reader in a systematic way to the vast panorama of scientific, historical and artistic information surrounding the Shroud of Turin. There is an exciting synergy created as the pieces of the puzzle come together. My objective in this book is to demonstrate that the Shroud of Turin is, in fact, the actual burial cloth of Jesus of Nazareth and bears His crucified and possibly resurrected image. I will do this in four basic steps:

First, we will examine together the evidence about the Shroud of Turin itself to demonstrate that this cloth is, in fact, an ancient linen cloth which can be scientifically and historically linked with the Jerusalem of Jesus' time.

Second, we will examine the images on the cloth to demonstrate that the Shroud bears images of a Semitic male — initially referred to as the Man of the Shroud — who was crucified in the Roman style and laid out in death according to Jewish burial practices of the time.

Third, we will attempt to demonstrate that this Man of the Shroud can be identified with none other than the historic Jesus of Nazareth.

Fourth, we will attempt to show that the images are not a painting or forgery, but were created by a mysterious process which we will examine in detail.

As we now delve into the mystery and examine the evidence, I will leave it to you, the reader, to make your own judgment. Whatever your predisposition to this precious cloth, I ask only that you keep an open mind. I hope that you will find the study of the Shroud of Turin as fascinating, inspiring and thought provoking as I have.

THE MYSTERY OF THE SHROUD OF TURIN

CHAPTER ONE

What is the Shroud of Turin?

"For those who believe, no proof is necessary.
For those who do not believe, no proof will suffice."
(Quoted from Franz Werfel, *The Song of Bernadette*)

The Shroud Defined

The Shroud, often called the "Holy Shroud," is most commonly referred to as the Shroud of Turin because it has been physically located in the Cathedral of St. John the Baptist in Turin, Italy for over 400 years. This precious cloth is considered by millions of Christians throughout the world to be the actual burial cloth of Jesus Christ — a direct witness to His passion, death and resurrection 2,000 years ago. The Shroud is the holiest relic in Christianity.

Physically, the Shroud is a remarkably well-preserved oblong piece of linen cloth 14'3" long (4.36 meters) and 3'7" wide (1.1 meters), weighing approximately 5 1/2 lbs. (2.45 kgs.). The linen fibers are woven in a three-to-one herringbone twill with a Z-twist and consist of a fairly heavy yarn (34/100 of a millimeter thick) of Near Eastern or Mediterranean basin flax.[1] Down the left side of the Shroud is a border approximately 3 1/2 inches wide (8 centimeters from the edge) running the full length of the linen cloth. Once thought to be a side-strip sewn onto the main cloth, it has now been determined to be a selvedge, that is, a piece of cloth woven into

1

the main cloth so that it will not unravel. It is done in such a manner as to require no hem. The reason for adding the selvedge is not known for certain. However, historian and renowned English sindonologist Ian Wilson speculates that the selvedge may have been added at a later date perhaps to center the image on the cloth for viewing. He considers this the most logical explanation and points out that the selvedge was added at the same time as the fringe and gold covering, the overall purpose being to transform the cloth from a shroud to what seems to have been some sort of "portrait."

Human Images on the Shroud

On one side of the linen cloth are images of the front and back views of a man who appears to be laid out in an attitude of death. The two views — or double image — show that the Man of the Shroud (as we shall call him at this point) was laid out on his back on one end of the cloth with his head toward the center of the cloth. The cloth was then folded over his head to cover the front of his body from head to foot. The color of the images is a faint sepia (straw-color) contrasting with the off-white, ivory-color of the ancient cloth. The images most resemble a scorch as one might discover on a linen handkerchief that has been lightly burned on the surface by an iron. Those who have directly viewed the Shroud maintain that *the closer one gets to the Shroud of Turin, the more the mysterious images disappear to the naked eye.* The Shroud is best viewed from a distance of approximately six or more feet.

Bloodstains

Along with the images are bloodstains that are brownish-red or carmine in color. The bloodstains are heaviest at the wrists and feet and at a wound on the right side of the body, corresponding precisely to the wounds inflicted on Jesus at the time of His crucifixion. In classical Roman style, Jesus was nailed through His wrists. After He had hung on the cross for some time, a Roman soldier pierced His right side with a lance between the fifth and sixth ribs to ensure that He was, in fact, dead. Professor Gino Zanninotto, Italian crucifixion expert, points out that the Romans used nails for crucifixion only in Palestine in the first and second centuries. The images also reflect bloodstains covering the top of the head and the face. In addition many smaller bloodstains cover the front and back of the man, corresponding to the biblical description of the cap of thorns and the beating from a Roman whip (*flagrum*) inflicted on Jesus during His crucifixion. There are no signs of physical decomposition or bodily deterioration on the cloth. More will be said about the wounds and bloodstains in a later chapter.

Scorches, Watermarks and Patches

On the Shroud are marks of an incident that occurred on the night between the 3rd and the 4th of December 1532 when a fire damaged the cloth as it lay in a silver casket reliquary set into the wall of the Sainte-Chapelle at Chambery (eastern France). The fire, set perhaps by an over-turned candle, was so intense (estimated at 900-960 degrees Celsius, 1650-1760 degrees Fahrenheit) that the Shroud's silver casket had begun to melt and a drop of molten silver was found to have fallen on one edge of the Shroud's folds.

Fortunately, due to the quick intervention of the Duke of Savoy's counselor Philip Lambert and two Franciscan priests, the casket was carried to safety. While there was damage to the Shroud itself, the images were barely touched by the fierce fire. As a result of this fire, there are water-stains from the dousing (creating several lozenge-shapes) and scorch marks on the cloth. In 1534, Cardinal Louis de Gorrevod sent the cloth to the nearby Convent of Poor Clares where a team of nuns repaired the cloth. The linen was strengthened by the sewing on of a holland-cloth backing sheet. In 1868 this backing was changed by Princess Clotilde of Savoy to the crimson silk-lined backing the Shroud has today.[2] The chemical ramifications of this fire on the cloth will be discussed toward the end of this book.

Burn Holes

Finally, there are *four sets of triple holes* that appear to have been created prior to the fire of 1532, since these holes appear in a 1516 painting of the Shroud attributed to Albrecht Dürer and kept in the archives of the Church of Saint Gommare in Lierre, Belgium. Some scholars speculate that reconstruction of their original arrangement suggests that at one stage the cloth was folded in four and deliberately run through three times with something like a red-hot poker, perhaps as a test, a sort of "trial-by-fire," to which legend has it the Shroud was subjected on April 14, 1503.[3] However, Atlanta sindonologist Rev. Albert Dreisbach speculates that the holes were made, more likely, by pieces of incense falling on the folded cloth.

When seen under a magnifying glass, the image areas appear to be totally lacking in any substance such as pigments or paints and the entire image does not show the slightest semblance of any artist's style of any historical period.[4] There are no brush strokes, no directionality characteristic of any artistic style, and *the image is confined to the very top fibrils of the linen fibers with no penetration. It is a unique surface phenomenon.*

The Shroud as a Photographic Negative

One of the most fascinating aspects of the Shroud was the discovery in 1898 by a young amateur photographer in Italy, Secondo Pia, who was permitted to take two photographs of the Shroud during an exposition in Turin. Photography was a relatively young science at the time. Secondo took two photos in black-and-white on the evening of May 28, 1898. One he exposed for fourteen minutes and the other for twenty minutes on large glass photographic plates which he then took to his studio for development. To his utter shock and amazement as the images on the Shroud began to emerge Secondo noticed that they were developing as positives instead of negatives. *The images as they appeared on the cloth were, therefore, negatives that when photographed produced positives.* Conversely, *the blood stains on the Shroud appeared in the photos as negatives whereas they were actually positives on the Shroud.* Secondo was awestruck. He realized that he was probably the first person in the world to look upon an actual "photo" of Jesus. "What he saw caused his hands to shake so that the wet film started to slip from his grasp," John Walsh, author of the book *The Shroud*, writes. "The face with its closed eyes had acquired a reality that was nothing less than stupefying." The black-and-white heightened the contrast. Could an artist of the medieval or Renaissance period have "painted" an image as a perfect photographic negative at a time when photographs were as yet unknown? And even if an artist could have done this, why would he forge a painting in the negative that could not have been understood or appreciated by its viewers?

In 1931, Giuseppe Enrie, considered one of the finest professional Italian photographers of his day, was chosen by Cardinal Maurilio Fossati, the Archbishop of Turin, to take a series of photographs with special close-ups of the face and bloodstains. These photos revealed many details, including the possible presence of Roman coins over the eyes of the image (a subject to be reviewed in detail further on). Additional photos were taken in 1969 and 1973 by Giovanni Battista Judica Cordiglia, this time in color, some of them under ultraviolet and infrared light during the investigation of the commission appointed by Cardinal Michele Pellegrino. Further photographs were taken in 1978 by Vernon Miller using slides and transparencies. Radiography, macrophotography and thermographic techniques were likewise used during these photo shoots. As Wilson points out, "every technical advance in black-and-white photography has revealed the negative characteristics in greater clarity."[5]

As of yet, in spite of many theories, no one has been able to present a convincing argument or demonstration to show how the mysterious images were created. Wilson notes that the images have a curious "lack of physical outline." He states that:

> throughout the history of art, virtually until Turner and the Impressionists of the nineteenth century, artists relied to a greater or lesser degree on outlines to give shape to their work. The character of these and the manner of modeling any painting has always provided reliable dates from which the art historian can make a confident judgment of dating and origin. But in the case of the Shroud there is nothing on which to base any judgment, no other work with which to compare it.[6]

The Man of the Shroud — A Description of Jesus?

The Man of the Shroud appears to have been a powerfully built man of approximately thirty to forty-five years of age with long hair parted in the middle and falling to the shoulders. He has side locks, a mustache and a beard, and he is naked. In refutation of a medieval forgery theory, British genealogist Noel Currer-Briggs points out that "the fourteenth century was not alone in disapproving men with long hair. (Medieval) contemporary iconography depicted Jesus with fairly short hair."[7] Currer-Briggs even intimates that this very fact may have incited the medieval Inquisitors to attack the Knights Templar — the military/religious group that Ian Wilson suggests became custodians of the Shroud after it disappeared from Constantinople in 1204 during the infamous Fourth Crusade. The Romans themselves — until the time of the Emperor Hadrian, a century after the crucifixion — tended to be clean-shaven while the Jews traced their long hair and beards back to the time of Moses. Aaron, Moses' brother, for example, is specifically stated as having had a beard.

On the dorsal (posterior) image of the Shroud there is a long strand of hair — a *braid* approximately 8-10 inches from the base of the head to a point midway between the shoulder blades that appears to be a *pigtail* or *ponytail*, common among Jewish males in Palestine during Jesus' time. The man's beard seems to have twin points characteristic of the Nazarene men of that day. Shroud author Rev. Kenneth Stevenson from New York points out that the traditional hair style for an orthodox Jewish man of two thousand years ago is much the same for him today: a ponytail and side locks, precisely what we see on the Shroud.[8] One of the world's most distinguished ethnologists, former Harvard Professor Dr. Carleton S. Coon has associated the man with a very pure Semitic type found today among noble Arabs and Sephardic Jews.

There are broad hints of Jewishness in this hair styling. Wilson goes on to point out that the hair at the back of the head accords with what German biblical scholar H. Greeman has referred to as one of the most common fashions for Jewish men in antiquity. French scriptural authority Henri Daniel-Rops has supportively added the information that the Jews normally wore this pony tail "plaited and rolled up under their headgear" except on public holidays.

By most estimates of medical experts, the Man of the Shroud appears to have been 5'10.5" to 5'11" in height. Recent researchers, however, have tended to scale this down to 5'7" (1.7 m.). Some have considered that even 5'7" was very tall for the average man of two thousand years ago, but Wilson points out that the idea that people of antiquity were significantly shorter than ourselves is simply a widespread popular fallacy. A University of California investigation of the skeletons of ten adult males from a recently discovered first-century Jewish burial ground in Jerusalem included one even of the upper height estimate of the Man of the Shroud and there is no reason to believe that 5'7" (1.7 m.) would be any more exceptional in Jesus' time than today.[9] His weight was likely 165-180 lbs.

A research program was undertaken by two U.S. Air Force assistant professors, physicists Dr. John Jackson and Dr. Eric Jumper, leaders of the 1978 S.T.U.R.P. (Shroud of Turin Research Project) testing team. Using a full-size muslin replica of the Shroud, they marked out on this cloth all the salient body features and then among friends and associates recruited volunteers to fit the markings. Using individuals of appropriate height and weight, they not only found convincing physical correspondence but were able to reconstruct closely the hypothetical burial attitude of the body.

The Burial Attitude

The body in the Shroud had to have been set at a slight angle, the head raised by some pillow-type support, the arms drawn very stiffly over the pelvis — left hand over right — the right shoulder set lower than the left, the legs decisively flexed at the knee and the left foot partly over the right. As Wilson remarked, "If the Shroud is a forgery, the care with which even the post crucifixion lie of the body has been thought out is quite remarkable."[10] The body is clearly laid out in an attitude of death.

It would appear, then, that the Man of the Shroud was of Jewish origin and that the bloodstains and wounds studied by forensic pathologists in their careful examination of the

Shroud are remarkably coordinated with the testimony of the Gospels relative to the Roman crucifixion weapons and procedures regarding the passion, death and resurrection of the historical Jesus Christ. His burial is consistent with Jewish burial practices of the day as outlined in the Mishnah which contains interpretations of scriptural ordinances as compiled by the Rabbis in the first and second centuries.

A Prayer Box?

More recent investigations of the Shroud by Dr. Alan Whanger, Professor Emeritus of Duke University in North Carolina, utilizing modern scientific instrumentation such as the polarized image overlay technique, appear to reveal the presence of a *tephillin* — a Jewish phylactery or prayer box that contains a portion of Scripture — attached to the forehead and the right arm. Rev. Kenneth Stevenson discussed this possibility with Eleazor Erbach, an Orthodox Rabbi from Denver. Rabbi Erbach not only confirmed its size and shape but also suggested that the broken blood flow on the right arm might have been caused by the corresponding arm phylactery.[11]

In addition to the possible phylactery, previous investigations of the Shroud point to the presence of Roman coins over the eyes (identified by some as *leptons* or widow's mites minted during the administration of Pontius Pilate), pollen from the ancient Near East, calcium carbonate (limestone) dust from the cave-tombs of Jerusalem, mites from the ancient Near East as well as possible floral images around the head area. Such findings, to be discussed throughout this book, confirm the longevity and antiquity of this cloth. As several authors point out, *if the Shroud was the work of a forger, its creation would be more "miraculous" than if it were the actual burial cloth of Jesus.*

The Shroud as a Well-Preserved Textile

That the Shroud could have survived almost 2,000 years with little sign of deterioration should not be a surprise. There are many surviving Egyptian burial linens that are three times as old — preserved from 4000-6000 B.C. Jonathon D. Beard reported recently in *Popular Science* the finding of a 9,000-year-old piece of linen the size of a business card in an ancient village in southeast Turkey. What makes the Shroud unique, of course, is that no other known cloth of antiquity bears any images, much less the full-length image of a man meeting all the criteria of someone subjected to Roman crucifixion. Some consider the images to have been formed by some as yet unknown "natural phenomena." However, as Stevenson rightly points out, "If this type of body-on-cloth is natural, why are there so many burial garments that have no images of the person buried in them?"[12]

Sindonologist Robert Wilcox states that "even if (researchers) come up with some 'natural' process, the failure, so far, to find anything like the Shroud amongst the world's body cloths and artifacts leaves them with the further problem of why the process occurred only once in the history of the world, so far as is yet known."[13] The late Dr. John Heller, who was a research scientist at the New England Institute and author of the book *Report on the Shroud of Turin*, commented: "We do know, however, that there are thousands on thousands of pieces of funerary linens going back to millennia before Christ, and another huge number of linens of Coptic Christian burials. On none of these is there any image of any kind."[14]

Author Frank Tribbe points out that no other cloth of antiquity has been subjected to the "scientific investigating and ecclesiastical speculation" to which the Shroud has been subjected. The preservation of such cloths is generally due to the exclusion of air and to an arid climate, both of which are factors in the Shroud's history. In its long history, the Shroud was locked away in various chests, reliquaries and containers rarely seeing the light of day. At one point in its history it was almost hermetically sealed in a stone wall in the city of Edessa (in modern Turkey) for nearly five hundred years.

In addition, the first century Roman historian Pliny described the steps of processing yarn to include washing it in a "struthium" solution as a softener. Struthium is assumed to be soapweed and it was used to effectively preclude mildew, mold and decay. This retting process of linen in *saponaria* or soapweed could provide a clue to the Shroud's remarkable preservation, but scientifically no evidence of soapweed has been found on the Shroud.

The Cloths of Gayet

Interestingly, French archaeologist and Egyptologist M. Gayet spoke in his volume *Annals* of his excavations at the turn of the century near Antinoe, Egypt, where markings were found on linen cloths. Gayet wrote: "Among these documents (burial shrouds) the most important one is a face-veil, folded in four and carrying the impression of the face to which it was applied. These imprints formed something like dark spots where the prominences of the face were, and show up black. This image gives us the face of a dead man."[15]

Drawings that accompanied this text suggested that the face of the corpse had been covered by a veil, then the body wrapped in a shroud and bound mummy-style. Shroud researcher Robert K. Wilcox traced down this information when he visited Paris. He went to the Coptic section of the Egyptian collection in the Louvre and asked to see the Gayet group of Egyptian artifacts. The curator of the Coptic section told Wilcox that he was very familiar with all the items of that group of artifacts, but there was no such item as a face-veil with the image of a face on it. The next day they went to see the collection together and laboriously examined every cloth in the collection — three trunks with approximately seventy-five burial garments in each. There was no hint of a face or body image on any of them. Wilcox did notice that corpses wrapped in linen will leave stains of the body's decomposition on the cloth. If and when the cloth rots, it will discolor.

Later, Wilcox was reading the last chapter of a book written by the eminent sindonologist, Paul Vignon, in which Vignon describes several shrouds shown to him by the Egyptologist M. Gayet as having on them some vague brown stains, devoid of shape or gradation. Vignon considered that they must prove the vast difference between ordinary, unremarkable stains on burial cloths resulting from decomposition and the Shroud of Turin, which he considered "equivalent to a portrait" and lacking any signs of decomposition. With respect to images on the linen, the Shroud is utterly unique among ancient cloths.

Textile Tests on the Shroud: The Turin Commission

In June 1969 Cardinal Pellegrino (then Archbishop of Turin), with the approval of the Vatican and of King Umberto II of Savoy appointed a special commission of Italian scientists — among them the noted Egyptologist from the University of Turin and Superintendent of Egyptian Antiquities, Silvio Curto — to examine the Shroud. The Team, called the Turin Commission, was to conduct limited tests, advise the Cardinal about the storage and preservation of the Shroud and recommend a program of extensive scientific testing. The group was to perform nondestructive testing. They made examinations visually and with the microscope, by normal as well as with ultraviolet and infrared light. Having determined that the cloth was extraordinarily resistant to alterations from atmospheric changes, the Commission recommended more extensive examination and testing, including attempts to date the Shroud. They further suggested tests of select threads and small samples of the cloth as well as documentary video taping of the precious relic.

Later, in 1973, French scholar, Professor Gilbert Raes of the Ghent Institute of Textile Technology in Belgium, was permitted to join the team to carefully examine two small linen samples (one 13 x 40 millimeters, the other 10 x 40 millimeters) from the Shroud. Dr. Max Frei, a Swiss criminologist and botanist, also joined the team to study pollen samples on the Shroud. Dr. Raes reported that the Shroud was indeed woven of linen with a three-to-one herringbone twill with a Z-twist and that it is sewn with linen thread (all the warp, weft and sewing threads of the Shroud are of linen). He noted that the yarn was indicative of a good-quality workmanship and the weave density an average of a little over thirty-five threads per centimeter, corresponding favorably with the thirty thread per centimeter average of the finest Egyptian mummy fabrics. The normal weave in Palestinian, Roman and Egyptian loom-technology was a one-over-one. The three-to-one herringbone twill was a more refined weave. It would have been an expensive piece of cloth for the first century. However, we know from the Gospels that Joseph of Arimathea was a rich man and it was he who provided the Shroud used to bury Jesus (Mt 27:57-61).

During the radiocarbon analysis done at Oxford in 1988, cotton fibers were found on the Shroud. "The cotton," according to Peter H. South, director of the laboratory for textile analysis at Ambergate in Great Britain, "is a very fine dark yellow color, probably of Egyptian origin and very old. Unfortunately, how it found its way into the Shroud is impossible to say." Dr. Raes, using polarized light for microscopic viewing, had also identified traces of cotton fibers (fibrils) that he classified as of the *Gossypium herbaceum* type, a cotton that existed in the Middle East of the first century.[16] Professor Philip McNair of Birmingham University, England, supports these finds and points out that the occasional cotton fibers in the

Shroud were of the *Gossypium herbaceum* type that was cultivated in the Middle East during the first century, but was not known in Europe during the period when possible faking of the Shroud could have occurred. The cotton traces indicated that the Shroud was woven on a loom that had been used previously to weave cotton cloth. Paul Maloney, a research archaeologist and sindonologist from Pennsylvania, notes that cotton was actually a part of the linen thread.

Dr. Raes says that these findings support the contention that the Shroud linen was woven in the Middle East, since raw cotton was unknown in Europe until the ninth century when it was first planted in Spain by the Moors. Cotton was first woven in Venice and Milan in the fourteenth century and cotton cloth was not even seen in England until the fifteenth century. Cotton was grown in China and India in antiquity and was expertly woven in India several centuries before the Christian era. By the first century it was grown extensively in Mesopotamia and Egypt. Wilson notes that cotton is also known to have been introduced to the Middle East by the monarch Sennacherib during the seventh century B.C.

By the time of Christ it would certainly have been established in the environs of Palestine, and therefore offers no difficulty to the authenticity of the Shroud. Dr. Raes concluded that this piece of linen could have been manufactured in the first century. He could not say with certainty that it was. The late John Tyrer, a chartered textile technologist who worked in the field for twenty-five years as an associate of the Textile Institute of Manchester, England, discovered that while Middle East linens similar to the Shroud exist as far back as 3600 B.C., not much medieval linen has survived. He states that "it would be reasonable to conclude that linen textiles with Z-twist yarns and woven 3-1 reversing twill similar to the Turin Shroud could have been produced in the first-century Syria-Palestine."[17] The Mishnah makes it very clear that cotton may be added to linen without fear of a transgression of the prohibition known as the "mixing of kinds," but that the slightest amount of wool mixed with the linen would not have been tolerated. The Shroud, therefore, would have been a perfectly proper burial linen for a Jew in the first century. The Book of Leviticus 19:19 states: "Neither shall a garment mingled of linen and wool come upon thee." This was a prohibition against blending vegetable fiber (flax) with animal (wool).

The Linen and the Image

In 1978 the S.T.U.R.P. team with over 40 scientists conducted a thorough scientific investigation of the Shroud using the latest equipment. The group determined that the actual image was created by a phenomenon (as yet unknown) or a momentous event that *caused a rapid cellulose degradation (aging) of the linen fibers, that is, an accelerated dehydration and oxidation of the very top linen fibrils of the cellulose fibers of the Shroud, thereby creating a sepia or straw-yellow colored image similar to that of a scorch.* Whatever precipitated this rapid aging affected only the very top fibrils of the fibers of the linen. As noted previously, the images are a *surface phenomenon.* Most scientists compare it to a light scorch such as might be created if an iron touched a handkerchief for too long a period.

What caused this to happen? This is a central part of the mystery of the Shroud. No one has yet been able to provide a comprehensive explanation, and we will discuss various theories later in the book. Those who believe in the Resurrection of Jesus believe that something startling occurred at the moment of the Resurrection — some phenomenon as yet not understood by science that left its mark on the Shroud — a photo of the Resurrection for people of all eras to ponder. Many call the Shroud the "silent witness" for this reason and claim that the Shroud is a modern witness to the Resurrection.

Material Traces of Jesus' Life

It should not be all that surprising that Jesus would leave "material traces" of His life. On April 21, 1902, Yves Delage, Professor of Anatomy at the Paris Sorbonne and an agnostic gave a lecture to his rationalist colleagues of the French Academy of Sciences in which he claimed that the body images on the Shroud were so physiologically flawless and meaningful that he found it impossible to believe they could be the work of an artist. As Yves Delage stated in a letter to Charles Richet, editor of the *Revue Scientifique* in response to his skeptical colleagues at the Academy of Sciences:

> I willingly recognize that none of these given arguments offer the features of an irrefutable demonstration, but it must be recognized that their whole constitutes a bundle of imposing probabilities, some of which are very near being proven. A religious question has been needlessly injected into a problem which in itself is purely scientific, with the result that feelings have run high and reason has been led astray. If, instead of Christ, there were a question of some person like a Sargon, an Achilles or one of the Pharaohs, no one would have thought of making any objection. In dealing with this question, I have been faithful to the true spirit of science, intent only on the truth, not concerned in the least whether or not it might impinge on the interests of any religious group. I recognize Christ as an historical personage and I see no reason why anyone should be scandalized that there still exist material traces of His earthly life.[18]

The Presence of Natron on the Shroud

Dr. Garza-Valdéz of the Microbiology Department of the University of Texas at San Antonio (whose recent theory refuting the Carbon-14 test will be discussed later) reported in

June 1995 the presence of bacteria known as natronococcus on the Shroud. Micro-analyst Dr. Giovanni Riggi also identified a substance chemically resembling natron. These bacteria thrive only in the presence of sodium carbonate (natron) used in preserving the mummies in ancient Egypt and for bleaching in ancient Turkey and Palestine. *Their presence creates a presumption that the Shroud once had natron on it whose traces have disappeared over a long period of time.* This raises the questions of who in the fourteenth century would have put natron from Turkey, Palestine or Egypt on the Shroud or why an individual would have done this.

CHAPTER TWO

Pollen, Mites and Flowers — A Unique Cloth

"If the Shroud was a creation of the Middle Ages, then its forger must have ordered the mites (and pollen) to go with it."

Rev. Kenneth Stevenson

In our search for antiquity, the examination of the Shroud as a textile is only the beginning of the quest. More information has come to light in recent years that enables us to date the Shroud to ancient Palestine (contrary to the apparent finds of the Carbon-14 test, which will be examined at length toward the end of this book). Among the finds are the presence of pollen, mites and possible floral images on the Shroud.

Ancient Pollen on the Shroud?

The late Protestant Swiss botanist and criminologist Dr. Max Frei was permitted in 1973 and 1978 as part of the S.T.U.R.P. team to take sticky-tape samples of pollen grains directly from the Shroud. Pollen grains are of special interest because they have an exceptionally hard outer shell, the exine, which can last literally millions of years. Dr. Frei was highly respected in Europe, having founded the scientific department of the Zurich Police. He wrote his doctoral thesis on the flora of Sicily and continued this study of the Shroud's pollen until his death in 1983. The entire Frei Collection, formerly in the possession of the Association of Scientists and Scholars International for the Shroud of Turin, Inc. (A.S.S.I.S.T.), was transferred to the United States in 1988 and placed under the guardianship of Dr. Alan Whanger of Duke University in North Carolina where further studies have been done under the aegis of research archaeologist Paul C. Maloney.

Before his death in 1983, Dr. Frei had identified fifty-eight different types of pollen on the sticky tapes and further demonstrated that some of this grouping came from Jerusalem at the time of Jesus; some from Eastern Turkey and some from Europe, the final resting place of the Shroud. With regard to Turkey, Dr. Frei was certain that the Shroud had been in the area he describes as the Anatolian steppe, which he qualifies as a phytogeographical term for the region of the towns of Bitlis, Diyarbakir, Mardin, Urfa, Gaziantep and Malatya. Urfa is the modern Turkish name for the former Byzantine city of Edessa, believed to have been home to the Shroud until 944.[1]

At the time of his death, Frei was seeking to identify nineteen other pollens which would have brought the number to seventy-seven. Maloney placed this work in the hands of Aharon Horowitz, an illustrious Israeli palynologist, who noted that the pollens found on the Shroud can be compared to pollens found in Palestine but not in North Africa. Avinoam Danin, the chief expert in Israeli desert flora, agrees with him and adds that it is possible to demonstrate, on the basis of the pollens present on the Shroud, an itinerary across the Negev to the highlands of Lebanon.[2]

Some critics have proposed that pollen could have been airborne from the Middle East to Europe and made their way to the Shroud. However, Dr. Frei, responding to this claim stated:

> Groups A, B, and C of plants on the Shroud from Palestine and Anatolia are so numerous, compared to the

species from Europe, that a casual contamination or a pollen-transport from the Near East by storms in different seasons cannot be responsible for their presence... the predominance of these pollen must be the result of the Shroud's stay in such countries. Migrating birds or contamination with desert plants by pilgrims can be excluded because they had no possibility of direct contact with the Shroud. It should also be noted that the prevailing winds in the region move from Europe to the Middle East, not the reverse.[3]

The Presence of Mites on the Shroud

Dr. Frei concluded that many pollen matched species found "almost exclusively" in halophyte fossils from the Dead Sea. To Frei's mind, the weight of evidence mitigated against a medieval fraud. Stevenson further points out that this was Dr. Frei's field of expertise and his work has been confirmed by Turin microbiologist Dr. Giovanni Riggi Di Numana, who also found samples of mites or "minute animal forms extremely similar in their aspects and dimension to those from Egyptian burial fabrics."[4] During Dr. Riggi's analysis of samples vacuumed from between the Shroud and its backing cloth in 1978, he isolated and identified a mite peculiar to ancient burial linens, specifically Egyptian mummy wrappings.

As Stevenson points out: "If the Shroud was a creation of the Middle Ages, then its forger must have ordered the mites (and pollen) to go with it."[5] In addition, the work of Oswald Scheuermann and Dr. Alan Whanger (reviewed later in this chapter regarding floral patterns on the Shroud) further confirms the work of Dr. Frei since the flowers they identified are consistent with the pollen identified by Dr. Frei. Renowned archaeologist William Meacham further stated that "pollen... is empirical data... ipso facto evidence of exposure to the air in those regions."[6]

Some have voiced concern that the S.T.U.R.P. team, in

an independent investigation in 1978, found only one pollen on the Shroud. However, Dr. Max Frei utilized a hand application of sticky tape to the Shroud that ensured the transfer of particles that the non-pressure method of S.T.U.R.P. likely missed. Stevenson points out that the hand application of tape was much more likely to contact the pollen that almost certainly would have settled deeper into the fibers and crevices of the linen fabric. The purely surface roller method used by S.T.U.R.P. barely disturbed that cloth and did not penetrate to the level of the pollen.[7]

Linking History and Science

Ian Wilson's brilliant historical study that links the Shroud with the Image of Edessa (a theory discussed at length further on) confirms Dr. Frei's discovery of pollen from these areas. Wilson postulated that the Shroud was in Edessa in Eastern Turkey (a small city about 400 miles north of Jerusalem) from shortly after Jesus' death until 944 and then in Constantinople until 1204. He quotes Dr. Frei as saying:

> These plants are of great diagnostic value for our geographical studies as identical plants are missing in all other countries where the Shroud has been exposed to the open air. Consequently a forgery, produced somewhere in France during the Middle Ages, in a country lacking these typical halophytes, could not contain such characteristic pollen grains from the desert regions of Palestine.[8]

Stevenson rightly states: "It is doubtful that a medieval forger could have known, let alone produced, a cloth with just the right pollen spread."[9]

The pollen discovered by Dr. Frei represent these main groups:

1. Halophyte type desert plants, which are "very typical" of the Palestine area around the Dead Sea and the Negev.
2. Steppic plants which are characteristic of the area of the Anatolian Steppe defined by Dr. Frei as including Bitlis, Diyarbakir, Mardim, Urfa and Malatya. This is the dry zone where no natural pollen can grow on account of inadequate summer rainfall. Urfa, as previously noted, was ancient Edessa where historians have now placed the Shroud for nearly a millennium.
3. A small group of plants that are characteristic of the environs of Istanbul. This city in modern Turkey was the Constantinople of the Byzantine Empire founded by the Emperor Constantine in 325. Before that, Constantinople was called Byzantium — a city with a long and great history.
4. Northern European plants that are consistent with the Shroud's known history in France and Italy.[10] The Shroud was in Europe and specifically France from approximately 1205 and was moved to Turin in the sixteenth century.

Werner Bulst, S.J., in an article in *Shroud Spectrum International*, made the following observations:

> (Of) pollen from fifty-eight species of plants... less than one-third grow in France or Italy. (This) astonishing... small number of European species can be explained by the history of the Shroud in Europe, for, normally kept in a closed reliquary, the Shroud was protected from pollen contamination. Only on special occasions was it exposed in the open.... The spectrum of non-European species is highly astonishing. There is only one place where all of these plants, with the exception of three... grow in a very small radius: Jerusalem. This cannot be an accident. Pollen could have been carried to Europe on winds... but a transport of pollen from the Middle East is highly improbable.[11]

Bulst further states:

> Pollen grains can come upon the Shroud only when it is
> exposed in the open. It would have been a stupendous
> miracle if, precisely in the few days when the Shroud was
> being exposed, storms would have brought pollen over
> a distance of 2,500 kilometers and — even more miracu-
> lous — if those winds were carrying many more pollen
> from the East than from the European environment.
> Moreover, the pollen on the Shroud are from plants
> which bloom in different seasons of the year. Therefore
> the same improbable accident must have happened re-
> peatedly.[12]

Stevenson points out that "pollen analysis is acceptable
evidence in a court of law and therefore certainly empirical
data as to the Shroud's authenticity, antiquity and non-Euro-
pean origin and the value of the presence of ancient pollen
and mites on the Shroud should not be underestimated."[13]

Dreisbach advises that archaeologist and cave-tomb specialist James Strange of Florida, with assistance from Dr.
Giovanni Riggi, found pollen on the outside of the Shroud
differing from those of the inside. *The outside pollen were mineral coated, reflecting the likelihood that the outside of the cloth came
in contact with the limestone ledge of the grave.*

A Cloth Ordered by a Medieval or Renaissance Forger?

But what of the argument advanced by some that a medieval or Renaissance forger could have ordered or happened
upon a burial cloth, even an ancient burial cloth, from the
Near East already containing pollen and mites? Could not a
Crusader have brought back a cloth from Palestine to Europe
which then was utilized by a medieval or Renaissance artist to
create or fake the Shroud as some contend?

Kenneth Stevenson replies that:

> After all, it is possible, though not very likely, that a forger could have been wise enough to order a cloth from Palestine, even that he might have ordered an "old" cloth from Palestine. But to suppose he could have ordered a cloth woven in the Middle East and then specified that the cloth must be exposed to open air in the areas of both Turkey and Istanbul to ensure the proper pollen spread boggles the imagination. Anyway, the existence of pollen would not be discovered for at least another six hundred years. Moreover, the historical path of the Shroud (from Jerusalem to Edessa to Constantinople to Europe) would not be reconstructed for nearly eight hundred years.[14]

A Unique Ancient Cloth

The microscope was not invented for several hundred more years, logically raising the question of why a medieval or Renaissance artist would have gone through such great lengths to procure an ancient cloth containing the proper spread of microscopic pollen as well as mites that no one of this period (medieval or Renaissance) could possibly have known, understood or appreciated. The case then becomes overwhelming that the Shroud was not only an ancient cloth but *a unique ancient cloth* that followed a long historical path well before the medieval and Renaissance period.

Floral Images on the Shroud?

During his studies in 1983, Oswald Scheuermann made an observation that there seemed to be flowerlike patterns around the face of the Man of the Shroud. Two years later, Dr. Alan Whanger, while examining photographs of the

PLANT IMAGES TENTATIVELY IDENTIFIED ON THE SHROUD OF TURIN
by Dr. and Mrs. Alan D. Whanger as of August 1989

F=Flower	Y=Yes	?=Uncertain	JD=Judean Desert	EM=Eastern Mediterranean
B=Bush	N=No	S=Species	DS=Dead Sea Areas	(found predominantly in
T=Thorn				Israel, Lebanon, and Turkey;
				hence not likely Italy)

Zone I= Euro-Siberian; i.e., possibly France
Zone IV= Mediterranean; i.e., possibly Italy

Plant-Genus/Species*	Type of Plant	Found in Israel	Found in Jerusalem**	Pollen Found On Shroud By Dr. Max Frei	Flowering Time	Those Potentially Found in Europe Zone I	Zone IV
1. Alcea*** Chrysantha? c. 60S-9S	F	Y	Y? (also desert)	Y (althea S)	Apr-May	N	N
2. Anemone coronaria c.120S-1S	F	Y	Y	Y	Jan-Mar	N	Y
3. Anthemis palestina? 150S-23S	F	Y	Y	N	Mar-Jun	N	S?
4. Artimisia Judaica c. 400S-45S	B	Y	N (JD)	Y,S	Mar-Apr	N	N
5. Capparis ovata c. 350S-4S	F	Y (arid)	Y	Y	Apr-Aug	N	N
6. Chrysanthemum coronarium 5S-4S	F	Y	Y	N	Mar-May	N	Y
7. Cistus creticus c. 20S-2S	F	Y	Y	Y	Mar-Jun	Y	Y
8. Echinops gaillardotti? 100S-6S	T	Y	Y? (also JD, DS)	Y,S	Jun-Jul	N	N? (mostly)
9. Fagonia mollis 40S-7S	F,T	Y	N (JD, DS)	Y	Mar-Apr	N	N
10. Glaucium glandiflorium c. 20S-5S	F	Y	Y	Y	Mar-May	N	N
11. Gundelia tournefortii 1S-1S	T	Y	Y	Y	Mar-May	N	N
12. Haplophyllym tuberculatum c. 65S-5S	F,B	Y	N (JD, DS)	Y	Mar-Apr	N	N
13. Helianthemum versicarium c. 100S-12S	F	Y	Y (JD)	Y	Jan-May	N	N

Plant-Genus/Species*	Type of Plant	Found in Israel	Found in Jerusalem**	Pollen Found On Shroud By Dr. Max Frei	Flowering Time	Those Potentially Found in Europe Zone I	Zone IV
14. Hippocrepis multisiliquosa	F	Y	Y	N	Mar-May	N	N?
15. Hyoscyamus aureus c.2S-5S	F	Y	Y	Y	Mar-Jun	N	(EM?)
16. Hyoscyamus reticulatus c.20S-5S	F	Y	N (JD)	Y	Feb-Apr	N	N
17. Linum mucronatum c.200S-9S	F	Y	Y	Y	Mar-May	N	N
18. Oligomerus subulata 8S-1S	B	Y	N (JD,DS)	Y	Mar-May	N	N
19. Onosma syriacum or frutescens c.150S-4S	F	Y	Y? (also S in JD,DS)	Y,S	Mar-Jun	N	N
20. Paliurus spina-Christi 8S-1S	F,T	Y	Y	Y	Apr-Jun	N	N
21. Pistacia lentiscus 9S-5S	B	Y	Y	Y	Mar-Apr	N	Y
22. Prosopis farcta c.305-1S	F,B	Y	N (DS)	Y	Apr-Aug	N	N? (EM)
23. Pteranthus duchotomus (1S-1S)	F	Y	N (JD, DS)	Y	Jan-Apr	N	N
24. Reaumuria hirtella c.20S-3S	F	Y	Y	Y	Mar-Jul	N	N
25. Ridolfia segetum 1S-1S	F	Y	Y	Y	Apr-Jun	Y	Y
26. Roemeria hybrida 6S-2S	F	Y	Y	Y	Feb-Apr	N	Y
27. Scabiosa prolifera c. 100S-6S	F	Y	Y		Mar-May	N	Y
28. Zygophyllym dumosum c.100S-5S	F	Y	N (JD,DS)	Y	Mar-Apr	N	N
Totals:							
28		28	20	25	27 Mar-Apr	3Y	9Y, 5?

Shroud with a magnifying lens, suddenly saw out of the corner of his eye the image of a large chrysanthemum-like flower on the anatomic left side about fifteen centimeters lateral to and six centimeters above the midline top of the head.[15] Dr. Whanger and Oswald Scheuermann collaborated in further studies.

Dr. Whanger utilized many life-size second generation photos of parts of the Shroud as well as the full length images from the Giuseppe Enrie negatives of 1931. These were processed and enlarged by Gamma Photographic Laboratories of Chicago, Illinois. Some were processed with the specific request to maximize the detail in the off-body area. By standing some distance away from the photographs and looking at the off-body areas, definite patterns became apparent to Dr. Whanger. He secured the definitive set of volumes of *Flora Palaestina* by Michael Zohary[15] and reviewed drawings of the 1,900 plants depicted therein. Whanger worked with flowers, buds, stems, leaves and fruits that are reasonably clear. He did side-by-side comparisons of images — and polarized image overlay comparisons in a number of instances — to show reasonable compatibility of the drawings of the plants from *Flora Palaestina* with what is seen on the Shroud.

While there are vague or partial images of many flowers on the Shroud, Dr. Whanger and Oswald Scheuermann believe that they have tentatively identified twenty-eight plants whose images are sufficiently clear on the Shroud to make a good comparison and to be compatible with the drawings in *Flora Palaestina*. Of the twenty-eight plants identified on the Shroud, twenty-three are flowers, three are small bushes and two are thorns. All twenty-eight plants grow in Israel and twenty grow in Jerusalem itself (i.e., the Judean mountains). The other eight plants grew either in the Judean desert or the Dead Sea area or in both. Hence, these plants or flowers would have been available in Jerusalem's market in a fresh state.[17]

They noted that a rather high percentage of the flower

images identified *have corresponding pollen found on the Shroud by Dr. Max Frei.* Of the twenty-eight plants whose images they believe they have identified, Dr. Frei had already identified the pollen of twenty-five of them. In addition, they noted with great interest that twenty-seven of the twenty-eight plants bloom during March and April, which would correspond to the time of Passover and of the Crucifixion.

Dr. Whanger also states that the age of the flowers between the time they were picked and the time that the image was formed can be reasonably determined. He notes that the evidence indicates that the image of the body was formed (mysteriously) in a very brief time by some type of high energy process sometime between twenty-four and forty hours after death when decomposition (not seen on the Shroud image) would have begun to be apparent. Whanger believes that most of the flowers whose images are on the Shroud would be between twenty-four and thirty-six hours old after picking. He notes that the image formation of the flowers and other non-body objects may not be from the same mechanism that formed the body image.

Flower Images in Early Christian Art

Dr. Whanger notes that *there is ample evidence of the presence of flower images on the Shroud, as flowers congruent with the Shroud images were portrayed in numerous works of art.* One of the earliest portraits of Christ in the third century in the Roman catacombs shows a patterning around the head very similar to the flower-banked facial image in the Mandylion frame. (The Mandylion is believed to be the Shroud folded and mounted in a frame with only the face showing.) Another portrait of Christ from the early fourth century in a Roman catacomb has about 150 points of congruence with the Shroud's facial image and shows a number of flower images in the nimbus or halo. He notes that the Pantocrator Icon of St. Catherine's Monastery at Mount Sinai, probably produced about 550 at Edessa at the request of Byzantine Emperor Justinian I, is the most accurate of the many portraits he has studied which have been derived from the image on the Shroud and which has over 250 points of congruence with it. In the halo of this icon are many dozens of images of flowers highly congruent with those on the Shroud of Turin.

Even more striking are the very accurate copies of the images of the flowers on the Shroud on the gold *solidus* coins of Justinian II struck in 692-695. Flowers are accurately portrayed on the gold coins of Constantine VII in 950 after the Mandylion was brought with great ceremony to Constantinople. In the earlier years of the Shroud, floral images were quite vivid. Dr. Whanger points out that it is not clear when or how the images of the flowers became so indistinct or imperceptible.

Conclusion

A very brief newscast on CBS News in April 1997 indicates that an Israeli botanist had identified floral images on the Shroud representing flowers known to be in ancient Jerusalem and acknowledged that the Shroud was in Jerusalem at the time of Jesus. I contacted Dr. Alan Whanger by telephone and discussed this with him. He indicates that the Israeli botanist with whom he has been in contact for some time was Professor Avinoam Danin, Professor of Botany at Hebrew University and recognized as the leading botanist in Israel. Professor Danin indicated that *the flowers associated with the Shroud came from a 10 kilometer area between Jerusalem and Jericho and, to him, indicated that the Shroud was an ancient Israelite cloth.* This is a strong statement of support favoring the earlier finds of Whanger and Scheuermann.

Whanger further notes that this observable data of the floral images and the pollen from the Shroud, in addition to vast information from other sources, indicate that the 1988 Carbon-14 test dating the Shroud as being of medieval (i.e., thirteenth or fourteenth century) origin is anomalous and clearly erroneous, and that the Shroud originated in first-century Israel.[18] His conclusions are strongly supported by the data of Dr. Max Frei's pollen finds and Dr. Giovanni Riggi's determination of ancient mites on the cloth and Dr. Raes' conclusions regarding the consistency of the Shroud with ancient linen.

CHAPTER THREE

Ancient Roman Coins Over the Eyes?

"The result ... revealed objects resting on the eyes, objects which resembled small disks or 'buttons.'"

Physicists Dr. John Jackson and Dr. Eric Jumper

One of the most significant discoveries favoring the first century dating of the Shroud (and thereby helping to refute the Carbon-14 test dates) comes from the identification of ancient Roman coins — *leptons* minted by Pontius Pilate — over the eyes of the Man of the Shroud.

The VP-8 Image Analyzer

The story, as related by Ian Wilson,[1] begins on February 19, 1976 at the Sandia Scientific Laboratories in Albuquerque, New Mexico. Research physicists Dr. John Jackson and Dr. Eric Jumper were, at that time, Captains in the U.S. Air Force and Instructors in Albuquerque (later associated with the U.S. Air Force Academy in Colorado). Ever since he was a teenager, Dr. John Jackson had been interested in the Shroud as a hobby and wanted to gain a better understanding of how the image might have been formed. On that day, Drs. Jackson and Jumper visited the Sandia Scientific Laboratory and were introduced by William Mottern, an industrial radiographer, to a recently developed instrument known as the Interpretation Systems VP-8 Image Analyzer, a spin-off of the NASA Space

Program research. They were joined shortly thereafter by Kenneth Stevenson and Giles Charter.

Discovering a Three-Dimensional Image

This instrument was utilized to interpret light and dark as functions of distance in space. Essentially, the VP-8 Image Analyzer translated light and shade, as on a black-and-white photograph, into relief, viewable in dimension on a television monitor. As an example, two photographs taken at varying angles on a lunar surface could be fed into the VP-8 Image Analyzer and seen in their original relief on a TV screen, providing a three-dimensional view. Such relief would not normally be expected from a single photograph of a person, which would contain insufficient relief information.

The group decided to place a photo of the Shroud into the Analyzer, not expecting to see anything meaningful. But, as Ian Wilson relates:

It was… with some astonishment that, after the Shroud negative had been placed in the Analyzer, the two scientists found themselves looking at a convincing, properly three-dimensional image which could be consistently rotated without distortion, the only anomalies being creases and the 1532 fire marks.[2]

It appeared that the Shroud was encoded with relief information of the body it once enveloped. Subsequent experiments revealed that no paintings produced the same effect under the Analyzer. The three-dimensional information of the Shroud image discovered in 1976 was now added to the photographic negativity of the Shroud image (with actual positive blood) discovered by Secondo Pia in 1898 and enhanced by the photographs of Giuseppe Enrie in 1931 to deepen the mystery surrounding the formation of the images on the Shroud. Further progress was obtained by Giovanni Tamburelli, professor at the University of Turin, above all with respect to the three-dimensional aspects of the facial features of the Man of the Shroud.

Another Unique Discovery

The story of the coins begins two years later in July 1978 with an article in *The Numismatist* magazine. Drs. Jackson and Jumper along with Reverend Kenneth Stevenson made another startling discovery. The investigators stated in their article in *The Numismatist* that:

> The result of this process (VP-8 Image Analyzer)... revealed objects resting on the eyes, objects which resembled small disks or 'buttons.' ... In summary, ... the objects are circular, about the same size and flat.[3]

They noted that the object on the right eye was more noticeable. The thickness of the objects was approximately 1 to 5 millimeters and the average diameter was approximately 14 millimeters.

The researchers theorized that these objects could be coins and they mentioned this to Ian Wilson to determine what coins might be likely candidates. Wilson noted that several coins from the time of Pontius Pilate were possible on the score of their size — approximately 15 millimeters (5/8 inch, or about the size of a United States dime). But he favored a *lepton*, the traditional widow's mite of the Bible. The authors state:

> The result of his (Ian Wilson's) study produced the possibility of a Roman Bronze *lepton* of Pontius Pilate minted between 29-31 A.D. One of Wilson's observations was that it lacked the image of Caesar and was therefore likely to

be in the possession of Orthodox Jews. Rather amazingly, the size and shape of the *lepton* are perfect.

The researchers further noted the observation of what appeared to be a "backward question mark" on the object on the left eye that seemed to correspond to the striking Augur's Wand (*lituus*, or astrologer's staff) on a *lepton*.[4] Italian numismatic expert Mario Moroni also identified the *lepton*.

The Filas Report

In 1979, the late Rev. Francis Filas, a Jesuit priest and professor of theology at Loyola University in Chicago, photographed an enlargement of the face of the Shroud that he had been using on television programs. The enlargement was made from a second generation sepia print based on the original 1931 photographic plates of Giuseppe Enrie. Fr. Filas stated: "To my surprise, I happened to notice a sort of design directly over the right eye."[5] He brought the print to Michael Marx, a Greek classical numismatist in Chicago.

As Marx scanned the photograph with his magnifier, he called Fr. Filas' attention to four curving capital letters: **UCAI**. Together, they obtained Frederick W. Madden's *History of Jewish Coinage and of Money in the Old and New Testament* and consulted the catalog of all Pontius Pilate coins in the British Museum. The projected objects on the eyes matched in size and shape a coin of Pontius Pilate. Letter-like shapes that Filas (and later Dr. Robert M. Haralick of the Spatial Data Analysis Laboratory at Virginia's Polytechnic Institute and State University) read as **UCAI** occur in the correct position on the projected object on the *lepton* of Pilate.[6]

Using high magnification photography of the right eye on a large print of the Guiseppi Enrie negative revealed four letters: **UCAI**. The VP-8 Image Analyzer showed raised letters. Fr. Filas identified these as belonging to the *lepton* (or widow's

mite) of Pontius Pilate where the words TIBERIOU
CAISAROS were found. The **UCAI** was arranged in a coin-like
curve surrounding a shape resembling a shepherd's staff. The
tiny *lepton* or mite of Pilate (a coin consisting of 96.5 percent
copper and 3.5 percent tin) bears an astrologer's staff (*lituus*)
accompanied by the inscription TIBERIOU **KAI**SAROS. But
how does one explain the use of **UCAI** versus **UKAI**?

Fr. Filas surmised that the Shroud's **UCAI** might be the
central letters with a **C** substituted for the Greek **K**, a contention received with considerable skepticism until there came
to light two actual examples (now four) of Pontius Pilate *leptons* with precisely this misspelling.[7] The problem of the misspelling will be addressed shortly. Filas noted that the **UCAI**
was angled from 9:30 o'clock to 11:30 o'clock around the curve
of the astrologer's staff. The *lituus* was a constant motif in coins
minted by Pontius Pilate between 29-32 but never minted
again by any official in Palestine nor anywhere else in the
Roman world as an independent symbol. In addition, a
clipped area of the coin from 1:30 o'clock to 3:30 o'clock was
evident.[8] William Yarbrough, a numismatist in Atlanta, Geor-
gia, provided Fr. Filas with an actual Pilate coin. Later, a
confrere of Michael Marx, John Aiello, contributed another
Pilate coin that exhibited a more elegant style. Michael Avi-
Yonah's modern *Prologomenon* to the re-issuance of Madden's
*History of Jewish Coinage and of Money in the Old and New Testa-
ment*, made the point that Pilate minted his coins in the Roman years of Tiberius, 16-18 (corresponding to 30-32 A.D.).
Fr. Filas concluded that there existed a combination of size,
position, angular rotation, relative mutual proportion, accuracy of duplication (with the exception of a **C** on the Shroud
coin where a **K** existed on the Pontius Pilate coins that were
examined) and parity (i.e., turned in the proper direction)
that proved beyond reasonable doubt that these were real
coins and not just "weave anomalies" of the linen of the
Shroud. He goes on to say that the mathematical probability
suggests that to have four letters so appear in the correct po-

sitioning around the *lituus* would be in the range of one chance in eight million.[9]

The Julia Lepton Over the Left Eye

The image of the coin area over the left eye is less distinct, but, as Dr. Alan Whanger stated: "We are able to determine that another Filas coin, a '*Julia*' *lepton* struck only in 29 A.D. by Pontius Pilate (and named after Julia, the mother of Tiberius Caesar) matches this rather well, having 73 points of congruence in an area smaller than a finger print."[10] The *Julia lepton* was also identified (independently) by Dr. Baima Bollone (forensic medicine) and Dr. Nello Balossino (computer sciences) — both of the University of Turin.

Coins Over the Eyes: An Ancient Jewish Burial Custom?

Recent archaeological digs have unearthed skeletons around Jericho that date back to the time of Christ with coins placed on the head and in En Boqeq in the desert of Judah, a skeleton dating to the second century with coins in each of the eye sockets — evidence that Jews, on occasion, placed coins over the eyes of the deceased in the time of Jesus. Some critics, however, state that it was not necessary to place coins over Jesus' eyes. Professor James Cameron, a pathologist, points out that such closing of the eyelids would have been quite unnecessary in the case of an individual who had died upright, the weight of the super orbital muscles performing this function automatically. However, this opinion is not shared by U.S. pathologist Dr. Robert Bucklin, formerly of the Los Angeles Medical Examiner's Office.

Additionally, Cameron's statement assumes that the purpose of the coins was to keep the eyes closed. There were, however, other reasons for such a practice in antiquity. The

Greeks, for example, placed coins over the eyes as a tribute by the deceased to the mythical Charon, who had to ferry the dead across the River Styx. Early Christian graves revealed that coins were sometimes placed in the hand, pocket or mouth of early Christians who were buried. The Gates of Heaven had replaced the River Styx. It is quite probable that this Christian custom commenced from the tradition that coins were placed over the eyes of Jesus and that the practice, even among the Jews, has a purpose other than a physical one of keeping the eyes closed. In any case, placing coins over the eyes was a custom of antiquity, and the conclusions of the pathologist should take into consideration the facts that objects were, in fact, found over the eyes of the Man of the Shroud, and that such placement of coins has been noted by archaeologists on occasion in Jewish burials and is consistent with the customs of antiquity. (See endnote 10)

The Haralick Report

It became apparent that computer enhancement or some such sophisticated technique might be an important avenue to allow identification. Fr. Filas subsequently submitted the coin and Shroud image for comparative analysis at the Virginia Polytechnic Institute and State University's Spatial Data Analysis Laboratory. Dr. Robert Haralick, then at the Institute, offered cautious support to Filas' hypothesis while stressing the fundamental problem that science has no way of determining whether what appears as a coin inscription is anything but a random quirk of the Shroud's weave. In the abstract introducing his report, Dr. Haralick advises that:

> A number of digital enhancements were performed on imagery digitized from the 1931 Enrie photographs of the Shroud and a 1978 S.T.U.R.P. photograph taken by Vernon Miller. The enhancements provide supporting

evidence that the right eye area of the Shroud image contains remnants of patterns similar to those of a known Pontius Pilate coin dating from 29 A.D.[11]

After extensive study, Dr. Haralick concludes:

Thus, in the enlargement of the right eye image we find supporting evidence for a bright oval area: a shepherd's staff pattern as the main feature in the bright area; and bright segment patterns just to the side and top of the staff pattern, which in varying degrees match to the letters **OUCAIC**.[12]

Haralick goes on to caution the reader that:

This evidence cannot be said to be conclusive evidence that an image of the Pontius Pilate coin appears in the right eye of the Enrie Shroud Image. . . however, *the evidence is definitely supporting evidence because there is some degree of match between what one would expect to find if the Shroud did indeed contain a faint image of the Pilate coin and what we can in fact observe in the original and in the digitally produced images.*[13]

The Problem of the *C* Versus the *K*

The problem still remained that the letters on the Shroud coin read **UCAI**, whereas the Pontius Pilate coin in Fr. Filas' possession read **UKAI**. Logic said that if a coinmaker were to make an error, the substitution of a **C** for a **K** in a Roman province was the most logical error to make. The pronunciation of "Caesar" in Latin and "Kaisaros" in Greek would have been identical for the hard **K** sound. In addition, repeated admonitions in modern coin manuals and from numismatists indicate that the coins of Pontius Pilate are, as a class, of wretched technical quality, poorly pressed, off-center and showing misspellings.[14]

An Actual Maverick Coin

In 1981, Fr. Filas took the photograph of the Pilate coin he had received from William Yarbrough to Gamma Laboratories in Chicago and asked them to enlarge the coin to about twenty-five times life size in black-and-white. When Fr. Filas mounted the photo and stepped back to look at it, *he noticed a definite C where the K of Kaisaros should have been located.* He could not believe his eyes or believe that he had in his possession a coin with a maverick misspelling that had never been known to exist before this. The coin provided concrete proof that the misspelling had to exist in the past not only on the Shroud but also on an earlier example as well.[15] In 1982 a second misspelled coin was found. A coin dealer advised Fr. Filas that he had just sold a batch of Pilate *leptons* to the Rare Coin Department of the Marshall Field Department Store in Chicago. On November 12, 1981 Peter Meissner, Manager of Field's coin sales, showed Fr. Filas his Pilate coins. The third coin viewed under the magnifier seemed to read "**CAISAROS**" confirming the misspelling of **C** for **K**.[16]

The Polarized Image Overlay of Dr. Alan Whanger

Dr. Whanger made a breakthrough in Shroud studies in December 1981 when he came across what is called the polarized image overlay technique — a procedure for comparing various images. He utilized this technique to examine the areas over the eyes of the Man of the Shroud, and published his results in early April 1982. As he describes the technique:

> Subsequently, in 1981 we developed a method for exacting image comparison which we called the polarized image overlay technique in which the two images for comparison are projected one on top of the other on the same screen through polarizing filters at right angles to

each other. By observing these images through a third polarizing filter which is rotated, one can shift from one image to the other and compare the two images in great detail.[17]

In an article in 1985, Dr. Whanger tells us that, using the polarized image overlay technique with a photograph of Filas' coin and a computer enhanced photograph of the area over the right eye, produced by Log E/Interpretation Systems of Overland Park, Kansas, from the Enrie 1931 photograph:

> We found that there is a nearly perfect match between these two images. Using the same technique of image overlay, we were able to identify the rest of the eroded letters **RIOU CAICAROC**, with a reasonable degree of certainty and found congruencies between the coin and the Shroud image on several of these letters.[18]

He goes on to say that "our conclusion is that indeed there is an identifiable coin image over the right eye of the Shroud of Turin and it is so similar to a known coin that the two coins must have been struck from the same die."[19] Whanger also states that the use of the polarized image overlay technique "enabled us to confirm that indeed there is an image of a coin over the right eye and that the coin from which that image was formed was a die mate of a rare Pontius Pilate *lepton*, the only known one of its striking, in existence."[20] (Note: To date, six examples have been found.)

The Coronal Discharge

In 1982, Dr. Alan Whanger observed that the congruencies between the image on the Shroud and the actual coins (i.e., the die mate) were on the elevated points and irregularities on the coin's surface, following a pattern that one would expect from a coronal-type high energy discharge.[21]

Oswald Scheuermann, with whom Whanger collaborated, then picked up and pursued this line of investigation. Scheuermann has developed remarkable skill and experience in producing coronal type images both photographically and on linen. Dr. Whanger states:

> His (Scheuermann's) methods are similar to electro-photography or Kirlian photography. He has produced coronal images of, and off of, a wide variety of materials which have enabled us to have much better ideas of what various images might look like and this has made it much easier to identify and understand images and patterns seen on the Shroud, even though the exact mechanism of formation of the Shroud image remains a mystery.[22]

He further notes that coronal-type images tend to come off of pointed and irregular surfaces, as well as margins. Where the object is in touch with the surface (Shroud, linen, photographic plate), the image tends to be dense. Where the object is partially in contact with the surface, the outline is dense and partial, with a light central area.[23] The presence of such coronal discharges and the ability to duplicate them on linen seems to provide further proof (or certainly lend credence to the claim), that *there were in fact real coins over the eyes on the Shroud and not just quirks or anomalies of the linen weave of the Shroud.* It should be noted that optical specialist Kevin Moran of Charlotte, North Carolina, questions this conclusion of coronal discharges and more research is recommended.

A Medieval or Renaissance Artist?

Dr. Whanger observes that, since this unique coin, struck in 29 A.D., was not found until 1977, it is hardly plausible to claim that a medieval artist (or forger) would have included this tiny detail of a coin then unknown and that could not be discerned for at least another five hundred years when opti-

cal, photographic and computer imaging techniques would
first be able to demonstrate such fine points.[24] Fr. Filas supports the authenticity also by saying that:

> The conclusion points in one inescapable direction: forg-
> ery of the Shroud is utterly impossible. No forger in the
> Middle Ages or even earlier would have been able to fab-
> ricate tiny imprints over both eyes on the Shroud cloth
> in photographic negative — with no pigment — reflect-
> ing letters 1/32 inches high with a rare misspelling, in-
> cluding an astrologer's staff existing practically nowhere
> else in numismatic history in full size of 1/2 inch, from
> one Roman coin (*Pilate lepton*) issued certainly in Pales-
> tine in 29 A.D. — and a second Roman coin (*Julia lep-
> ton*) whose traces point again to Palestine and 29 A.D.[25]

Three questions begin to emerge that apply to so many
aspects of the study of the Shroud with regard to a medieval
or Renaissance forgery theory:

1. How would a medieval or Renaissance artist (or forger)
   have had access to refined information encoded in the
   Shroud, information only recently discovered by scientists, artists, historians, archaeologists and forensic pathologists?
2. Even if such an artist or forger had the information, *how*
   could that artist or forger have duplicated such information in microscopic detail well before the invention of
   the microscope and then done this in negative reverse
   photography, and three-dimensionality?
3. Finally, *why* would such an artist or forger have utilized
   this information or methodology at a point in history
   when the people of that time could not possibly have
   realized or appreciated the microscopic presence of a
   rare, misspelled coin, not to mention pollen, mites, limestone dust from the cave-tombs of Jerusalem or microscopic dirt on the heel, knee or tip of the nose of the victim?

Conclusion

As noted previously, there are some today who think the coins over the eyes may represent a weave anomaly or a quirk of the linen-weave, or even that the coins may be a figment of a vivid imagination. The evidence, however, seems overwhelming in favor of the presence of coins over the eyes. In this regard, Picknett and Prince in their book *Turin Shroud: In Whose Image?*, in an effort to prove that Leonardo da Vinci "faked" the Shroud, make the astounding statement that Fr. Francis Filas is an "enthusiastic researcher," and that "most other researchers ascribed this to Filas' imagination, and when S.T.U.R.P. made a special search for the coins, they could not find them."[26] Picknett and Prince simply gloss over in one sentence the evidence just presented to promote their Leonardo theory.

However, in their recent book *The Shroud and the Controversy*, S.T.U.R.P. researcher Kenneth Stevenson and his colleague Gary Habermas state, regarding objects over the eyes:

> there is definitely something in both locations, not merely anomalies in the weave patterns of the cloth as some Shroud opponents and even team members have suggested. All of the three-dimensional images that I (Stevenson) have examined give evidence of something round and solid on the eyes. The fact remains that something is there, and the most logical explanation still suggests that they are coins....[27]

We noted at the beginning of this chapter that the original report published by S.T.U.R.P. leaders Dr. John Jackson, Dr. Eric Jumper and Rev. Kenneth Stevenson in *The Numismatist* showed dense, circular disks or button-like objects that must still be explained and cannot be explained by the "weave anomaly theory." The application of mathematical probability as explained by Fr. Filas; the utilization of various methodologies including the NASA VP-8 Image Analyzer for three-dimensionality by physicists and S.T.U.R.P. leaders Jackson and Jumper; the use of macro-photography to enlarge the image; the computerized digital enhancement by Dr. Robert Haralick at the Virginia Polytechnic Institute and State University Spatial Data Analysis Laboratory; the coronal discharge and polarized image overlay for congruence as explained by Dr. Alan Whanger and Oswald Scheuermann — all point to objects over the eyes of the Man of the Shroud. This is hardly the work of "Filas' imagination," but rather overwhelmingly supports the presence of ancient Roman *lepton* coins. Such evidence, while not convenient for Picknett and Prince, strongly refutes the medieval/Renaissance forgery theory and the medieval dating of the Carbon-14 test to be addressed further on.

CHAPTER FOUR

The Signature of Roman Crucifixion: Matching the Words, the Weapons and the Wounds

"So many there be that stand gazing in horror; was ever a human form so mishandled, human beauty ever so defaced?"

Isaiah 52:14

Identifying the Man of the Shroud

The previous three chapters attempted to establish the antiquity of the Shroud, linking this unique linen cloth to first-century Palestine. It is a linen cloth containing ancient pollen, mites and floral images from the Dead Sea area around Jerusalem with a weave consistent with the loom technology of Palestine at the time of Jesus. The cloth followed *a unique historical path* as identified by its pollen spread (and other historical evidence to be discussed later in the book) that distinguishes it from other linen cloths of the period. Finally, the case for antiquity is further enhanced by the presence of Roman coins over the eyes of the Man of the Shroud. But until now, we have been cautious not to identify the images as those of Jesus. In establishing the case for antiquity the issue of the person depicted by the frontal and dorsal images on the Shroud has remained open, except to say that ethnologists believe he is of Semitic origin, having long hair, beard, mustache and a pony tail or braid characteristic of Semitic men of the early period.

47

The logical question arises as to *who* precisely is the individual whose images appear so vividly and mysteriously on the Shroud? Is this individual Jesus or could he be some other Jewish man of the period who might have been crucified? The evidence points to the identity of the Man of the Shroud as none other than Jesus Christ. As Cardinal Saldarini noted earlier, the image on the Shroud is that of Jesus and "no one else." The signature of the crucifixion gives us the clues needed to help make this correlation.

Matching Words, Weapons and Wounds

In studying the Shroud, the New Testament accounts of the passion, death and resurrection of Jesus provided by the four Evangelists in the Gospels correlate precisely with Roman crucifixion practices and weapons as known from history and archaeology. Additionally, contemporary forensic pathologists and surgeons have viewed the wounds apparent on the images of the Shroud and have demonstrated how this information correlates exactly with the statements from the New Testament and with the weapons and practices of Roman crucifixion. This unique match of the words of the New Testament, the Roman weapons and the wounds studied by the pathologists provides a "signature" or "fingerprint," if you will, that identifies the Man of the Shroud with the historical Jesus of Nazareth.

Ian Wilson advises: "It is important… that we consider carefully to what extent the crucifixion visible on the Shroud is compatible with that recorded of Jesus Christ; also to what extent the entire picture furnished by the Shroud and its image is compatible with what is known of everyday life in the New Testament."[1] Kenneth Stevenson tells us that "an artist or a forger could attempt a duplication. But if there are many similarities, including some an artist or forger would likely miss or be unable to reproduce, and if there are no differences, then the probability that Jesus was the man buried in the

Shroud increases dramatically."[2] Indeed, if this were the work of a forger, this accomplishment itself would be more miraculous than the contention that the Shroud is the actual burial cloth of Jesus, as Donald Lynn of S.T.U.R.P. noted in 1979.

Roman Crucifixion

Crucifixion was a particularly ignoble form of capital punishment and the Romans reserved it for non-Roman citizens, particularly captives of war, civil rebels, criminals and slaves in the Provinces. Both men and women were crucified. It was a common form of punishment throughout the Roman Empire for almost four hundred years, but it was not uniquely Roman. In fact, crucifixion was practiced long before the Romans by the Sythians, Persians, Phoenicians and Carthaginians, and thousands of Jews and Gentiles went to their deaths in this manner. Alexander the Great crucified over two thousand inhabitants in the city of Tyre.[3] During the siege and capture of Jerusalem by the Romans in 70 A.D., almost five hundred Jews a day were crucified. Crucifixion was ultimately banned by the Emperor Constantine in the year 313.

The Roman historian Tacitus wrote extensively in his *Annals* (15:44) about the different techniques of crucifixion. Various types of crosses were used, including the conventional cross (T-shaped) used in the Crucifixion of Jesus. However, the Romans also used Y-shaped and X-shaped crosses. Sometimes the victims were nailed to the crossbeam and sometimes they were tied with leather thongs. On occasion, a small seat (*sedile*) was provided for the buttocks. The feet might be perched on a small shelf or nailed to the cross separately with two nails or together with one nail.[4] St. Peter requested to be crucified upside down so as not to imitate the manner of Jesus' Crucifixion.

Some of the very weapons and methods utilized to crucify Jesus, as outlined in the New Testament texts and as reinforced by the finds of archaeology, and the combination of such unique weapons and methods when compared with the types of wounds appearing on the Shroud provide a "signature" that pathologists have studied in an effort to identify the Man of the Shroud. Let us start with what the New Testament writers tell us about crucifixion as applied to Jesus while providing commentary on some of the Roman weapons and practices utilized during this historical period.

The Historical Accounts

We begin with a careful examination of what each of the Gospel writers has to say about what actually happened to Jesus with regard to the Crucifixion. The author notes that the information may at times be graphic, especially with regard to details of medical pathology, but such information reflects the harsh reality of Jesus' sacrifice and is also critical to making the case for the identification of the Man of the Shroud with Jesus of Nazareth. The evidence will be reviewed as provided by medical pathologists and surgeons studying the wounds noted on the Shroud to determine how such information correlates with the Gospel accounts and the known Roman crucifixion methods and weapons. Many pathologists and surgeons have studied the Shroud, most notably Dr. Robert Bucklin, Dr. Pierre Barbet, Dr. Frederick Zugibe, Dr. Anthony Sava, Dr. Joseph Gambeschia, Dr. Hermann Moedder, Dr. David Willis and Dr. Yves Delage. Dr. Delage was the Professor of Anatomy at the Paris Sorbonne in 1903 who told his colleagues, as noted earlier, that the body image and wounds are physically so flawless and meaningful that he found it impossible to believe that the Shroud could be the work of an artist.

1. Jesus is Arrested in the Garden of Gethsemane

The Passion Narratives establish that Jesus was arrested by "men with swords and clubs" (Mt 26:47), and taken off to Caiaphas the High Priest (see also Mk 14:43; Lk 22:47-53 and Jn 18:1-11). The fact that the arresting mob bore swords and clubs would indicate that they were not very gentle with Jesus and most likely physically abused Him and treated Him harshly even in the Garden of Gethsemane where the arrest took place.

2. Jesus is Struck with Fists

In the presence of the chief priests and scribes of the Sanhedrin, Jesus was struck: "Then they spat in His face and struck Him with their fists; others said as they hit Him, 'Prophesy to us, Messiah! Who was it who struck you?'" (Mt 26:67-68). Mark tells us: "Then some began to spit on Him and, covering His face, they struck Him with their fists, saying, 'Prophesy!' And the Temple attendants took Him away, beating Him as they went" (Mk 14:65; see also Lk 22:63-65). The Gospel of John adds: "When He said these things one of the attendants who was standing by gave Jesus a slap in the face..." (Jn 18:22).

There are several references to Jesus being hit with fists and having blows rained on Him. Dr. Robert Bucklin, the former Los Angeles forensic pathologist and Deputy Coroner, now retired, carefully studied the full-length photos of the Shroud and analyzed the wounds and weapons that may have caused them. In the video tape *The Silent Witness* as well as in various medical journals, Dr. Bucklin outlines his findings.[5] He notes that there are several facial and head injuries. Among these are indications that Jesus was violently struck on the right cheek. There is swelling and partial closing of the right eye and a contusion below the right eye. The nose of Jesus appears elongated, and Bucklin indicates that there appears to be a separation of the nasal cartilage and possible fracture incurred by a blow or a fall. Also, the tip of the nose has an abrasion as if the victim has fallen or has been struck. There is a rivulet of blood and saliva on the right side of the mouth.

3. Jesus is Bound and Taken to Pilate

"After they had Him bound, they led Him away…" (Mt 27:2; see also Mk 15:1 and Lk 23:1). Luke adds that Jesus was then sent to Herod. Then "after Herod and his soldiers had treated Him with contempt and mocked Him, he had Him dressed in fine apparel and sent Him back to Pilate" (Lk 23:11). Jesus was not allowed to be put to death under Jewish law. He was brought by the Sanhedrin to Pilate to induce the Romans to utilize capital punishment against Jesus as a "rebel" because He claimed He was the "King of the Jews" (Jn 18:34) — thereby appearing to usurp the authority of the Roman Emperor.

4. Jesus is Questioned by Pilate and Scourged with Roman Whips

Pilate, after an appeal to the crowd for the release of Jesus, ultimately gave in to the crowd and ordered Jesus scourged and readied for crucifixion: "He (Pilate) had Jesus scourged and then handed Him over to be crucified" (Mt 27:26; see also Mk 15:15 and Jn 19:1). He was turned over to the Roman soldiers, four men led by a fifth (a centurion called the *Exactor mortis*) — a team specially trained in crucifixion procedures and techniques. The Romans utilized a whip that consisted of three leather thongs attached to a handle, each thong having two dumbbell-shaped pieces of bone or lead on the end. *The Dictionary of Greek and Roman Antiquity* identifies this as the Roman *flagrum* frequently mentioned in the accounts of the Christian martyrs and dreaded for its *plumbatae* — pellets of lead or bone attached to the end of the leather thongs.[6] Examples of the *flagrum* are illustrated occasionally on Roman coins. During the excavation of Herculaneum, the sister city of Pompeii, an actual specimen was discovered.[7] Each whip mark (estimated between 60-120 lashes) would leave six welts in the flesh. Such marks, each about 3.7 cm. long, frequently caused contusions or hematomas, that is, wellings of blood into the flesh tissues without necessarily breaking the skin.[8]

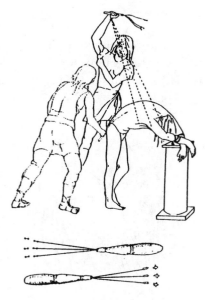

Jesus was apparently whipped by two men, one on each side (or by one man who changed sides), accounting for the different angles of the whip marks on His front and back. Pathologist Dr. Robert Bucklin indicates that the Shroud whip marks are spread from the tops of the shoulders to the lower reaches of the calves in a fanned-out pattern. From horizontal across the loins, they fan upward over the upper back, crisscross over the shoulders and fan downward on the thighs and calves. Bucklin points out that there are double puncture type wounds going lateral to downward, apparently inflicted by an implement with sharp edges with a flicking motion. Such a whipping left many marks on the front and back of the victim. Jewish practice limited the scourging of the victim to 39 lashes. Roman scourging, however, was unlimited, but it was incumbent on the soldiers whipping the victim not to kill him. In such a case, the scourger was made to substitute for the victim. The lashers, therefore, became artists at keeping the victim alive.

5. Jesus was Crowned (Capped) with Thorns

The governor's soldiers stripped Jesus and crowned Him with thorns: "Then they stripped Him and put a scarlet robe on Him, and after having twisted some thorns into a crown

they put this on His head" (Mt 27:27-29; also Mk 15:27 and Jn 19:1-2). Bucklin tells us that Jesus' forehead and scalp were pierced with many sharp objects with blood visible in the hair on top of Jesus' head, on the sides of His face and on His forehead. Blood is also visible on the hair at the back of His head. The bloodflow on the back of the neck shows

seven of twelve trickles directed to the left, three to the right and two perpendicular. The hair on the left is soaked with blood. This is consistent with the manner in which Jesus' head was tilted on the cross.

Such wounds are consistent with a capping of thorns. *Capping with thorns was a unique event in crucifixion history and no other victim, to our knowledge, was ever recorded as having been capped with thorns.* Herein is one part of the "signature" of Jesus' Crucifixion. Artists, medieval and otherwise, have traditionally depicted a *circlet* or *crown of thorns*, and not a *cap*, but the evidence on the Shroud indicates it was a cap pressed on the top of Jesus' head.

6. Jesus Carries a Cross

The Romans made Jesus carry a cross and then forced Simon the Cyrene to carry it for Him because of His weakened state. Dr. Frederick Zugibe, a pathologist who was the Chief Medical Examiner of Rockland County, New York, points out that Jesus must have been suffering great fatigue at this point from His agony in the garden, where He sweat blood, and from the night-long trial that included beating, flogging and abuse. The team of Roman soldiers could not let Him die before the appointed time, so they solicited the help of Simon the Cyrene. We read in the New Testament that "As they were going out, they came across a man from Cyrene, Simon by name, and enlisted him to carry His cross" (Mt 27:32; see also Mk 15:21 and Lk 23:26). The Gospel of John states: "So they took Jesus in charge. And carrying the cross Himself, He went out to what was called 'the Place of the Skull,' in Hebrew, *Golgotha*, where they crucified Him and with Him two others..." (Jn 19:17-18).

Normally, the Romans would leave the upright piece of the cross (*stipes*) in place on Golgotha and have the victim carry a heavy crossbeam (*patibulum*) weighing approximately 50-100 pounds across both shoulders. If there was more than one victim (such as the two thieves crucified with Jesus), the Romans would tie a rope connecting the ankles of the victims and the ends of the *patibula*, preventing the victims from running away or swinging the beam to hit a soldier. Any effort to do this would literally pull the victim's own legs from under him and cause him to fall to the ground.

The evidence on the Shroud, as Bucklin points out, shows that the man has large rub marks or "chafing marks" on both sides of the upper back area in the scapular region. These rub marks were formed after the scourging because the scourge marks are smeared in these areas. While they could have been formed from the rubbing motion of the back on the cross, they are more consistent with the carrying of the *patibulum* across the shoulders.

Professor Cameron points out that "in the shoulder regions these injuries appear to have been succeeded by some major source of abrasion, evident from the appearance of rubbing high on the left shoulder blade and lower down on the right."[9] Cameron interprets this as the carrying of some heavy weight on the back, inevitably recalling the crossbeam. From experiments with volunteers, Cameron observed that a right-handed person with a heavy beam tied to his outstretched arms tends naturally to carry this beam high on his left shoulder and lower down on his right. When he falls, he will most likely fall on his left knee.[10] This is consistent with the wound of the Shroud, showing serious damage to the left knee. *There are also microscopic dirt particles embedded in the Shroud linen on the left knee.*

7. Jesus Falls

Although the Gospels do not specifically state that Jesus fell three times on the way to Calvary, Christian tradition has strongly maintained this. It is not unreasonable to assume that, in His weakened state, He fell. Bucklin points out that the left leg of Jesus is tied to the lower part of the crossbeam being carried on His shoulders. His left kneecap is damaged in a fall. *Dirt on the knee, left eyebrow and left cheek, and damage to His right eyebrow and center of the forehead indicate a series of falls,* traditionally considered to be three. Additionally, there is dirt on the tip of the nose.

8. Jesus is Nailed to the Cross

We know from archaeological discoveries of Roman work-sites and the discovery of the bones of a crucifixion victim, Jehohanan, that the Romans used seven-inch roofing spikes. Roman nails were made of iron with a gradually tapering square shaft from the head to the point. About eighteen years ago, seven tons of homemade nails (almost a million nails) were unearthed in Scotland by Professor I.A. Richmond, Professor of Archaeology of the Roman Empire at Oxford, at the site of a Roman fortress at Inchtuthill, built in 83 A.D. These nails range from 1-40 centimeters long.[11] Although the Passion narratives do not specifically state that nails were used, we know they were used from a later Resurrection account in which Jesus invites the Apostle Thomas to place his hands in the place where the nails pierced Jesus' hands. We recall the words of the Prophet Isaiah: "They have pierced my hands and my feet; they have numbered all my bones" (Is 53:5).

In the Gospel of John, Jesus makes a post-Resurrection appearance to the Apostles in Thomas' absence. Later, the Apostles relate the appearance to Thomas who tells them: "Unless I see the marks that the nails made in His hands and put my finger into the holes they made, and put my hand into His side, I won't believe" (Jn 20:25). Eight days later, Jesus appeared again and permitted Thomas to put his fingers into the wounds of the hand and side (Jn 20:26). In Luke, Jesus told the Apostles to "look at my hands and my feet," asking them to witness the nail wounds (Lk 24:39). Earlier in John, before the Apostles tell Thomas that they have seen the Lord, Jesus appeared to the Apostles and "showed them His hands and His side" (Jn 20:20).

Nail through the Wrists versus the Palms

The nail wounds on the Shroud appear to be through the wrists and the feet. The nails through the wrists are contrary to the depiction of Christian art throughout the centuries, which shows the nails through the palms. Kenneth Stevenson points out that throughout the history of the Church, the punctures in Jesus' hands have been pictured in the palms. Art historian Philip McNair claims that in his entire experience with hundreds of examples of medieval art, the nail wounds are always located in the palms of Jesus.[12]

Dr. Pierre Barbet, a French surgeon and Shroud scholar who wrote the book *A Doctor at Calvary*, demonstrated that nails through the center of the palms would never hold a man on the cross. Such nails would easily tear through the flesh.[13] According to Dr. Barbet's extensive studies on this issue, *Jesus had to have been nailed through the wrists*, specifically through an area that Dr. Barbet calls the Space of Destot — a point in the wrist where eight bones meet.

The New Testament speaks of the "hand." However, in biblical Greek (*cheir*) and in Aramaic (*yad*) there is only one word used for both hand and wrist. Dr. Barbet tells us that the thumbs on the Shroud are hidden. One does not see an image of the thumbs on the Shroud. He notes that when a nail is driven through the wrists, the median nerve of the hand is damaged or severed, and this forces the thumbs into the palm. Looking at the Shroud photos, the thumbs do not show — a unique physiological phenomenon. A nail driven through the Space of Destot in the wrists would both support the body and cause the thumbs to be driven into the palms.

It should be noted that pathologist Dr. Frederick Zugibe does not completely agree with the Space of Destot theory, but does agree that the nails were high up in the palm toward the wrist or in the wrist but not in the Space of Destot (but rather on the opposite side of the wrist). Dr. Zugibe also challenges the severing of the median nerve as the reason for the hidden thumbs. He postulates that "the thumbs are missing from the Shroud image because the natural position of the thumb, both in death and in the living person, is in the front of and slightly to the side of the index finger... therefore it would be next to impossible to have thumb impressions because the thumbs would never have even touched the

Shroud."[14] Pathologists, while they may not agree on all the details, do agree that *the nails were high in the palm or in the wrist and not in the center of the palm as depicted in art; and that the thumb image is missing* — details not likely known in the relatively primitive pathology of the medieval period and contrary to any medieval artist's or forger's then contemporary artistic information.

Bucklin also states that the left wrist is punctured and there are *two divergent streams of blood on the forearm relating to the two angles of bloodflow from the changing position of the arms on the cross* as the victim lifted himself up to breathe and then dropped back down again. He also notes that there is a 35-degree angle formed from the rivulets of blood flowing from the hand, again showing the positions of the body on the Cross. There is injury to the feet as seen on the dorsal image. It appears that the left foot is lifted and elevated over the right. A single spike was likely driven through the second metatarsal space with the left foot placed over the right.

Evidence of Dirt

We noted earlier that evidence of dirt appears on the Shroud. Dr. Bucklin noted microscopic dirt on the knee, tip of the nose and under the right heel of the Man of the Shroud. During the 1978 investigation of the Shroud, Dr. Eric Jumper and optical engineer Sam Pellicori rigged up a microscope and aligned it with the heel of the Shroud. Careful examination under full magnification determined that there was in fact dirt on the heel.[15] It was a dramatic moment, yet one so logical. No one was crucified wearing shoes or sandals, so it is logical that dirt would be present. Dr. Joseph Kohlbeck of the Hercules Labs in Colorado identified it as *travertine argonite*, and Dr. Levi Setti of the Enrico Fermi Institute in Batavia, Illinois confirmed the find.

The Crucifixion of Jehohanan

Frank Tribbe, author of *Portrait of Jesus?*, recounts that in 1968, during construction excavation in Jerusalem, workers discovered an ancient Jewish cemetery in northern Jerusalem called Giv'at ha'Mivtar. They found a group of burials dated precisely to the Roman massacre that occurred during the Jewish revolt of 70 A.D. They were preserved in stone burial chests called ossuaries which contained only the bones of the deceased after the flesh had decayed. One of these, Jehohanan ben Ha'galgol (identified by the name written in Aramaic on his ossuary) had been crucified.

A 7-inch spike was still sideways through his heel bones, through a block of acacia wood, and had splinters of olive wood from the upright of the cross (*stipes*) still adhering to its tip. Nails had also been driven through his wrists where the radius bones were noticeably worn from the grating on the nail as Jehohanan pulled himself up so he could breathe. The tibia and fibula bones of his calves were crushed from the Roman practice of *crucifragium* — the procedure of breaking the leg bones to hasten death. Archaeologist Vasilius Tzaferis and Hebrew University pathologist Nicu Haas examined Jehohanan's bones and reported on them in the *Israel Exploration Journal* in 1970.[16]

Up until the time of the discovery of Jehohanan's grave, no actual victims of crucifixion had been found. Ian Wilson surmises that the reason for this was almost certainly because the telltale evidence, the presence of nails, were never found. The Romans believed that nails used in a crucifixion were highly efficacious in curing epilepsy, fever, swellings and stings: hence these rarely remained with the body of a crucifixion victim.[17] They were likely taken and kept as amulets by soldiers and interested bystanders.

9. The Sign Placed Over the Cross

When they reached Golgotha, they gave Jesus wine mixed with gall (a bitter herb) and crucified Him. They then placed a *titulus* (or sign) over His head saying: "This is Jesus, the King of the Jews" (Mt 27:37; also Mk 15:26). John says: "Now Pilate wrote out a notice and had it fixed to the cross. It read: 'Jesus of Nazareth, King of the Jews'" (Jn 19:19). It was written in Hebrew, Greek and Latin. Usually, the *titulus* was placed above the head, although in the case of Jehohanan, it was placed at the feet.

10. Jesus is Mocked and Dies

Jesus was mocked by passers-by and died at the ninth hour (Mt 27:39-56; see also Mk 15:29-39; Lk 23:44-46; and Jn 19:29-30). The ninth hour would be 3:00 P.M., or mid-afternoon.

11. The *Crucifragium* and Lancing of the Side

John adds two unique aspects of the Crucifixion not covered by the other Evangelists, and these indeed contribute strongly to the "signature" of Jesus' Crucifixion. He notes: "It was Preparation Day, and to prevent the bodies remaining on the Cross during the Sabbath — since the Sabbath was a day of special solemnity — the Jews asked Pilate to have the legs broken and the bodies taken away. Consequently, the soldiers came and broke the legs of the first man who had been crucified with Him and then of the other. When they came to Jesus, they found He was already dead, and so instead of breaking His legs, one of the soldiers pierced His side with a lance; and immediately there came out blood and water" (Jn 19:31-34). This particular day was quite important since it was the beginning of a double religious holiday: the Passover and the Sabbath. Sundown would occur shortly and the bodies could not remain on the crosses.

The Romans employed a practice called *crucifragium* which consisted of breaking the legs of the victim to prevent him from raising himself up to breathe, and thereby hastening death. This would induce a quick death and in this case the Jews were anxious to end the crucifixion before the onset of the Sabbath at sundown. Jewish law prohibited leaving the body on the cross after sundown, especially before the Sabbath. The discovery of the skeleton of Jehohanan shows that his legs were broken by the *crucifragium*.

Dr. Bucklin confirms that the legs of the Man of the Shroud *were not broken*, reinforcing the New Testament texts about Jesus. John here quotes Psalm 34:20 and Exodus 12:46 to show that Jesus' legs were not broken as foretold in the Scriptures saying: "This is the evidence of one who saw it — trustworthy evidence, and he knows he speaks the truth — and he gives it so that you may believe as well. Because all this happened to fulfill the words of Scripture: 'Not one bone of His will be broken'" (Jn 19:35-36).

In addition, the soldiers saw that Jesus was already dead and pierced His side with a *lancea* (a Roman lance) between  the fifth and sixth ribs on the right side of His body. Origen (3rd century) notes the thrust was administered in military custom *sub alas* (below the armpits). The wound, as identified by pathologists, was 1 3/4" high and 7/16" wide (4.4 x 1.5 centimeters). From excavated examples, the lance blade corresponds exactly to the elliptical wound on the side of the victim visible on the Shroud. The lance appears to have been standard issue for the soldiers (militia) of the garrison at Antonia and other fortresses guarding Jerusalem. William Meachem notes it does not match the typical points of the *hasta* (spear), *hasta veliaris* (short spear) or *pilum* (javelin) used by the infantry. In the New Testament we read that "they will look on the one whom they have pierced" (Jn 19:35-37). The New Testament texts of a "lancing" and the images of a lancing on the Shroud further corroborate the identity of the victim of the Shroud as Jesus of Nazareth.

The Blood and Water

John tells us that after Jesus was pierced with the lance, "immediately there came out blood and water" (19:34). This is an entirely unique event not understood by the Evangelists, but explained by modern medical pathology. Dr. Ugo Wedenissow, professor at the University of Milan offers this explanation: During His agony in the Garden of Gethsemane, as reported in the Gospel of St. Luke (22:43-44), Jesus was in the throes of such profound emotion that "his sweat became like drops of blood falling to the ground" (haematidrosis). That a vessel on the surface of the heart might well have burst as a result of such a trauma and over the next hours gradually leaked into the pericardium, that thin sack which surrounds the heart, is not unlikely. The pressure around the heart as it built up would eventually cause the heart to cease beating, thus explaining the premature death of Christ on the cross.[18] In the hours He hung there, Dr. Bucklin tells us, the plasma (serum) and blood corpuscles would have separated in the pericardial sack, with the plasma rising to the top. Piercing of this sack caused the blood first and then the serum to ooze out, giving the appearance to a medically untrained soldier or follower at the foot of the Cross that it was blood mixed with water. This blood and serum flowed from the lance wound on the victim's right side, and when he was laid down on the Shroud and carried to the tomb horizontally, the blood and serum flowed downward off the side and around the back across the kidneys. Pathologists state this is very evident on the

Shroud and again links the lancing, bloodflow and carrying of the body of Jesus with the images of the crucifixion wounds of the victim of the Shroud.

The Burial Attitude

It is worth noting that pathologists have studied the body's reconstructed burial attitude. As Wilson points out:

> It had, for instance, to have been set at a slight angle, the head raised by some pillow-type support, the arms drawn very stiffly over the pelvis, the right shoulder set lower than the left, the legs decisively flexed at the knee and the left foot partly over the right. If the Shroud is a forgery, the care with which even the post-crucifixion lie of the body had been thought out is quite remarkable.[19]

Conclusion: Identifying the Man of the Shroud with Jesus

The study of the testimony of the Gospels, when matched with Roman weapons and practices of crucifixion as well as with the findings of medical pathologists studying the Shroud, shows a strong correlation of these sources. The uniqueness of the markings on the Shroud, especially when taken in their totality, with the testimony of the Gospels provides the signature or the fingerprint of the Crucifixion that identifies the Man of the Shroud with Jesus. This is especially true of the capping of thorns to mock Jesus' "kingship," a unique event never recorded with any other crucifixion victim; the lancing of the right side to assure that Jesus was dead instead of the usual *crucifragium*; the nails through the wrists; the scourge marks all over his back; the marks of the crossbeam (*patibulum*) on the shoulders, and the swollen face from the beating of the Sanhedrin guards. In all cases, the words match the wounds which match the weapons.

Barrie Schwortz, a photographer from Santa Barbara's Brooks Institute of Photography, and one of the Jewish members of the S.T.U.R.P. Research team has said:

> The image on the Shroud matches the account of the crucifixion in the New Testament down to the nth degree. Evidence is mounting that the Gospels are quite accurate. This may cause consternation among my family and other Jewish people, but in my own mind, the Shroud is the piece of cloth which wrapped Jesus after He was crucified.[20]

Sindonologist Robert Wilcox stated that there are just too many coincidences in the agreements between Jesus' Crucifixion and that of the Man of the Shroud to be explained away easily. He notes that these similarities do not fit any other known victim of crucifixion except Jesus.[21] Wilson quotes a statement of the Jesuit historian Herbert Thurston in 1903, a man originally convinced of the Shroud's fraudulence, who was later obliged to admit:

> As to the identity of the body whose image is seen on the Shroud, no question is possible. The five wounds, the cruel flagellation, the punctures encircling the head, can still be clearly distinguished. If this is not the impression of the Christ, it was designed as the counterfeit of that impression. In no other person since the world began could these details be verified.[22]

Notes on the Blood

The blood on the Shroud has been identified by the late Dr. John H. Heller as being mammalian, primate and probably human. Dr. Alan D. Adler, a research chemist who worked with Dr. Heller at the New England Institute, even declared: "It is as certain that there is blood on the Shroud as it is that there is blood in your veins. The marks on the shroud are of exuded blood, belonging to a man who was tortured and crucified. It cannot be from the 14th century, but is much older and far more consistent with what we know of the crucifixion of Christ."[23] Professor Pier Luigi Baima Bollone reported in the *Journal Sindon* that by use of fluorescent antibodies he has demonstrated the presence of human globulins in the Shroud bloodstains, a fact confirmed by Adler and Heller.[24] Whereas the bodily images have a mist-like quality with no sharp lines, the bloodstains are richer and darker in color and have more precise lines. They also have a "halo effect" typically suggestive of the separation of blood and serum, which happens after the heart has stopped.

When Secondo Pia took his photographs in 1898, he noted that the bodily images were a photographic negative that when developed became a positive. Conversely, the blood, which was positive in reality, showed as a negative in his photos.[25] Further, examination of the Shroud indicates that *the blood stains were on the Shroud before the image was formed, and there is no image in the area of the bloodstains — the blood somehow impeding the image formation and protecting the Shroud from the image-making process.* As Dr. Heller stated it: "Surely this was a weird way to paint a picture."[26] If a forger had painted or created a picture and added human blood to make it realistic, he would likely have added the blood afterward and over part of this painting, not the reverse. In addition the blood stains penetrate the Shroud while the image appears only on the very surface fibrils of the fibers of the linen.

Veins and Arteries

Physicians Giuseppe Caselli (1939), Pierre Barbet (1950) and Sebastian Rodante (1982) carefully examined the bloodflows on the forehead with special reference to the location of the veins and arteries of the scalp. Frank Tribbe states that "they (were) able to conclude with absolute certainty that each discernible rivulet of blood shows distinctive character- istics of either venous flow or arterial flow in every case cor- rect for the location of the thorn-puncture from which the rivulet starts."[27] Arterial bloodflow is always to be distinguished by the spurts of blood that emerge from a wound due to heart pulses; conversely, thicker venous bloodflow is slow and steady and coagulates more quickly.

Knowledge about the circulation of human blood and the difference between arterial blood and venous blood was discovered only in 1593 by Andrea Cesalpino, as Dr. Rodante points out. This advanced anatomical data on the circulatory system of veins and arteries was not known in the medieval period alleged by the Carbon-14 test, and it is highly improb- able that a medieval or even Renaissance artist or forger could have utilized it so accurately on the Shroud.[28] The "prepon- derance of evidence" referred to by Atlanta sindonologist Rev. Albert Dreisbach again points to the antiquity and authentic- ity of the Shroud and to the identification of Jesus as the Man of the Shroud. The burden of proof now falls more on the skeptic to demonstrate otherwise.

DNA Blood-Testing and Camel Hair

The blood present on the Shroud has been studied in Europe by Dr. Pier Luigi Baima Bollone, professor of foren- sic medicine (Turin University), José Delfín Blanco, Spanish specialist in legal medicine and by hematologist Carlo Goldoni. They confirmed that the blood on the Shroud is human blood, indicating that "in light of its characteristics it would seem to appear as belonging to blood type AB."

Dr. Daniel Scavone of the University of Southern Indi- ana reports in an article of October 13, 1995 that in Septem- ber 1994 Dr. Victor Tryon, Director of DNA Technologies of the University of Texas Health Science Center-San Antonio

"... isolated three genes from Shroud blood remnants. He has obtained a segment of the Betaglobin gene from Chromosome 11 and the Amelogenin gene from both the X and Y chromosomes. Together with the blood analysis, the DNA research also identifies the occipital blood from the Shroud as that of an adult human male." Dr. Tryon noted in a CBS special *The Mysterious Man of the Shroud* (Executive Producer Terry A. Landau, April '97) that the blood was human, male and contained *degraded DNA* consistent with the supposition of ancient blood. Further, Scavone notes that embedded in a blood-glob from the occipital region of the head is a microscopic textile fragment (five-microns in diameter) appearing to be woven of camel hair. This possible but questionable identification could be important for authenticating the Shroud.

Many sindonologists, while optimistic, are cautious about these promising finds which are reported to be from Shroud fibers obtained by Dr. Giovanni Riggi Di Numana from fibers and blood specks vacuumed from the fourth sample cut from the Shroud in 1988 and provided to Dr. Tryon by Riggi in 1994. Italian writers Ida Molinari and Alberto Chiara in *Famiglia Cristiana* (Volume 4, 1996) report that the removal of the fibers was not authorized, and some dispute remains with the Papal Custodian, Cardinal Giovanni Saldarini. We urge further authorized testing of the blood of the Shroud to help clarify the accuracy of the testing.

The Question of Cloning

The question of whether it is possible to utilize the blood of Jesus from the Shroud to create a clone has recently been raised. Obviously, this is a serious question resulting from contemporary research on animal cloning and the vivid imagination of the popular mind. However, DNA scientists dismiss it as impossible with regard to the degenerated blood on the Shroud. According to Dr. Jennifer Smith, Chief of the DNA

Analysis Unit for the Federal Bureau of Investigation in Washington, D.C., for example, such a possibility exists "only in Fantasyland." (Reported in *The Tidings*, Southern California's Catholic Weekly, March 21, 1997, pp. 14-15, 23).

The Victim: A Crucified Medieval or Renaissance Man?

The anatomical correctness and perfection of the wounds as outlined by pathologists and surgeons (and other information such as the three-dimensionality of the image) *have demonstrated that an actual body — a victim of crucifixion — lay in the cloth.* The knowledge of medieval or even Renaissance anatomy was quite undeveloped, and it is highly improbable that any artist or forger of the period could have achieved such a level of anatomical accuracy. However, some have suggested that this problem was overcome by the fact that perhaps an actual medieval or Renaissance victim of crucifixion was utilized. The proponents of the Leonardo da Vinci theory hold strongly to this explanation. Such a proposition, while interesting on the surface, simply does not hold together.

Crucifixion was banned by the Emperor Constantine in the year 313 and was not seen again as a practice in the Western world. While this does not preclude an isolated act from having occurred, the proponents of the medieval or Renaissance crucifixion theory have never produced the slightest evidence regarding who such a victim might have been, or when, where, why and how he was crucified or further what artist, and how such an artist, might have come upon the body in such a timely fashion.

Further, if a victim was crucified in medieval or Renaissance Europe, such a victim would likely have been a criminal or heretic. For churchmen to have resorted to such a method of execution or torture in direct imitation of Jesus' execution would clearly have been sacrilegious to the medieval and Renaissance mind. Even during the famed Roman and Spanish Inquisitions, such a method was never utilized by the cruel proponents of torture in Europe. In addition, utilizing such a method is clearly countercultural and in violation of the period ethic, since the victim was naked. Painting or copying Jesus in the nude was unheard of in medieval/ Renaissance art. Additionally, the victim, if medieval, would have been crucified (or depicted as such) with nails through the palms (all art in the Middle Ages shows crucifixion through the palms) and with a crown rather than a cap of thorns. This, as all paintings of the Crucifixion during this period reveal, was the medieval/Renaissance mindset.

When we add the fact that not only were the victim's wounds correct anatomically and in perfect accord with the words of the Gospel, but that they clearly matched the Roman weapons utilized by the Crucifixion team in ancient Palestine, we achieve the "signature" of the Crucifixion that was addressed earlier identifying the victim with the historical Jesus and no other person in recorded history.

A medieval/Renaissance crucifixion theory duplicating Jesus' death would have been unthinkable to the mindset of the day. Such a theory in addition would have to provide some record as to a victim: who was crucified, when, where, why and how. The victim would have to have been a Semitic male. Proponents would need to demonstrate why or how the crucifixion team would have followed the Gospel words precisely while utilizing the specific Roman weapons used to crucify Jesus, and then promptly (since there are no signs of decomposition) turned over the body to an unknown medieval or Renaissance artist who remains unnamed.

This artist or forger would then have had to create the image in a three-dimensionality and in photographic negativity around the bloodstains which — contrary to any artistic style — would have had to precede the image on the cloth. Further, this artist, forger or copyist would have had to procure an ancient burial cloth from Palestine with the precise proper spread of pollen from Jerusalem through Edessa,

Constantinople and Europe over approximately 1,500 years (an historical path not known until recently), not to mention a dose of ancient mites, images of ancient flowers and limestone dust matching dust from the Jerusalem cave-tombs. This individual would have had to be sure to add Roman coins over the eyes with microscopic lettering (thus demonstrating an intricate knowledge of Jewish burial practices of the Second Temple period) for an audience that could neither have understood nor appreciated such information as pollen, mites and digitized images of coins. Then he would have had to be sure that his crucifixion victim had microscopic dirt on the tip of the nose, left knee and heel for an audience that knew nothing of microscopes — the dirt itself (*travertine argonite*) matching dirt from the Jerusalem area. And none of this begins to address how the incredible images were actually formed on the top surface fibrils of the fibers with no outlines, paints, dyes, brush strokes of any artist or penetration of the cloth.

When taken as a total picture, the idea of a medieval or Renaissance crucifixion or artistic rendering of such a crucifixion is simply refuted by the facts of the case and is more incredible to believe than the authenticity of the Shroud as the burial cloth of Jesus. The unique signature of Roman crucifixion matching the words of the Gospel, the weapons of the Roman team and the wounds as outlined on the Shroud *demonstrate beyond a reasonable doubt that the Man of the Shroud was none other than the crucified, historical Jesus of Nazareth.*

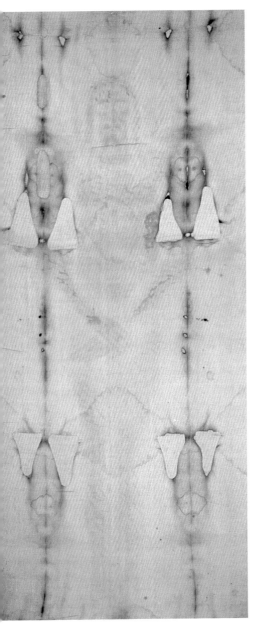

The face of the Man on the Shroud as it is seen from a distance of approximately six feet. It is an unreal image because the areas which in reality are the lightest appear to be the darkest and vice versa. Only the bloodstains appear dark red as they truly are. (© 1978, Vernon Miller)

The Shroud of Turin, detail. (© 1978, Vernon Miller)

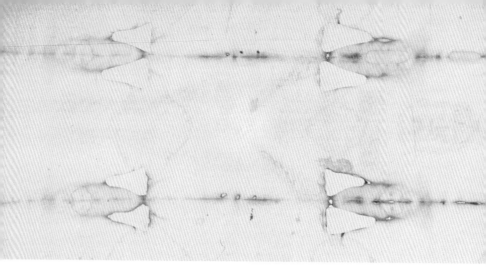

The Shroud is a piece of linen cloth 14'3" long and 3'7" wide. The double figure (front and back of the Man of the Shroud) is a "mirror image" of a young man who died by crucifixion. The cloth is off-white ivory in color which contrasts only slightly with the straw-colored sepia of the image which lies on the surface of the linen fibers. There is no trace of pigments, paints, dyes or stains on the Shroud.

Evident on the cloth are two dark stripes which enlarge to create eight symmetrical marks.

The first photograph taken by Secondo Pia in 1898 reveals the secret of the image on the Shroud. The mysterious figure was inexplicably impressed on the cloth as a photographic negative. In fact, the celebrated image becomes a positive where the dark and light portions of the image are seen as they are in reality. (Courtesy, Holy Shroud Guild, Esopus, NY)

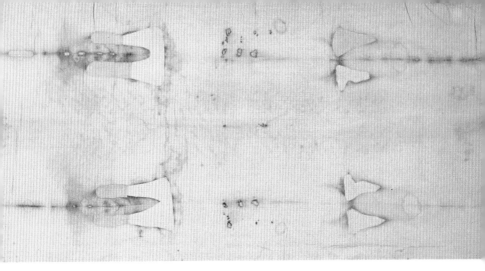

These are the burn marks produced by the fire in the chapel at Chambery on the night of December 3, 1532. The eight clear triangles show where the cloth was patched. The Shroud was kept in a silver-plated reliquary which began to melt in the fire causing serious damage along the folds of the cloth, now irreversibly carbonized. The water used to put out the fire soaked the cloth, forming the rhomboid-shaped watermarks visible along the edges, above the head, and at the level of the chest and knees of the figure on the Shroud. (© 1978, Vernon Miller)

The Shroud in a watercolor painting by G. B. Della Rovere from the early 1600's (*Pinacoteca Sabauda*). In reproducing the Shroud, the artist erroneously painted the right hand reposing on the left. Since the image on the Shroud is a "mirror image," the position of the hands and arms are inverted with respect to the actual subject. (Courtesy, Edizioni San Paolo, s.r.l.)

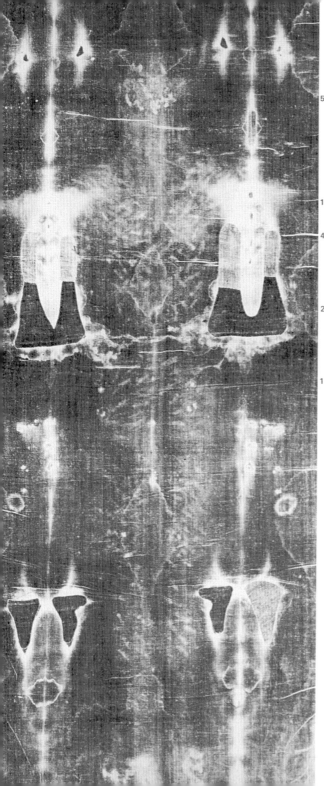
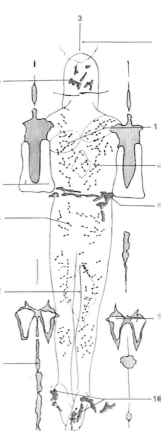

The Shroud shows the image of the victim of a brutal crucifixion, mysteriously imprinted on the cloth as a photographic negative and as if viewed in a mirror. The photographic positive (shown on these two pages) reveals the image as it should be seen.

1. Stains and burns due to the fire of 1532. 2. Watermarks produced in putting out the fire. 3. Dual image, front and back, of the body of a strong man. 4. Wounds caused by flagellation. 5. Blood on the forehead, top and sides of the head from the cap of thorns. 6. Wound from the nail which pierced the left wrist. 7. Blood which flowed down both arms as the figure hung on the cross with

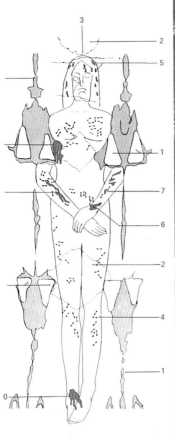

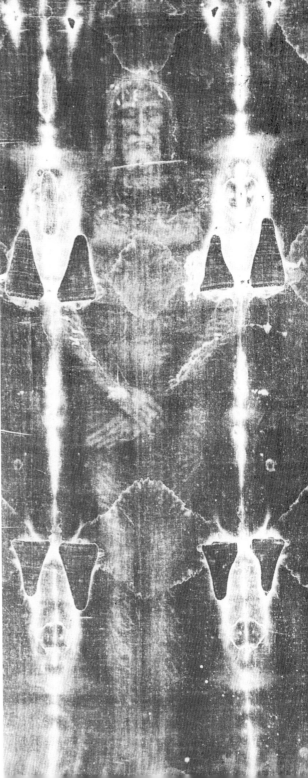

his arms outstretched. 8. Bloodstains caused by the spear which pierced the heart, allowing blood and water to flow out and around the body. Unfortunately these stains were destroyed in part by the fire of 1532. 9. Large bloodstain at the waistline on the back of the body where the blood from the heart collected. 10. Blood from the nailing of the feet: the left leg is slightly bent and the feet are placed one on top of the other. The legs seem longer on the frontal image (at the right) because the sheet was not equally taut below and above the body. 11. Bruises due to the carrying of the crossbeam (*patibulum*). (© 1978, Vernon Miller)

Close-up showing the weave of the Shroud and some particulate matter in the area of the nose. The nose in fuller view appears elongated and there seems to be a separation of the nasal cartilage and possible fracture. Also the tip of the nose has an abrasion as if the victim had fallen or been struck. (© 1978, Vernon Miller)

Macro view of the burn area. The cloth of the Shroud was severely damaged by the fire of 1532. An initial attempt at repair was done by the Claretian nuns in 1534 and additional attempts to reinforce the fabric were undertaken by Blessed Sebastian Valfrè in 1694. (© 1978, Vernon Miller)

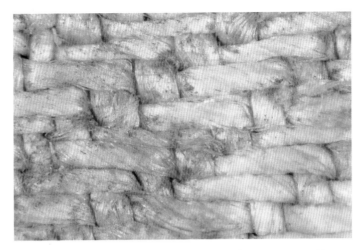

Lance area blood. Pathologists state that the blood and serum are very evident on the Shroud, thus linking the lancing, blood flow and images of the crucifixion wounds of the victim of the Shroud with those of Jesus. (© 1978, Vernon Miller)

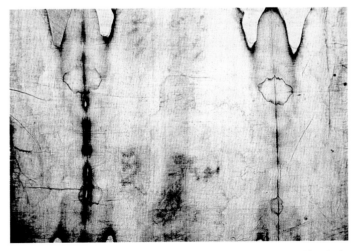

Foot detail, black and white negative. The feet were nailed to the cross with a single nail, one foot superimposed on the other. In His post-resurrection appearance, Jesus made it a point to invite His disciples to look at His hands and feet and to examine His wounds. (© 1978, Vernon Miller)

In the first few centuries Christ was represented without a beard, often as a shepherd, not unlike an Apollo. From the middle of the fourth century on, however, the Shroud sets the standard for the artistic depiction of Christ. From the face on the Shroud, artists began showing Christ with large asymmetric eyes, long forked beard, hair parted in the middle, ears covered, long mustache and prominent nose. (© 1978, Vernon Miller)

A sixth-century Icon of Jesus from Sinai's St. Catherine's Monastery painted by artists from Constantinople and given to the Monastery no later than 590 AD by the Emperor Justinian I. (Used by permission of Dr. Alan Whanger)

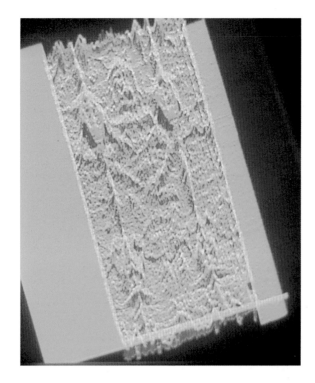

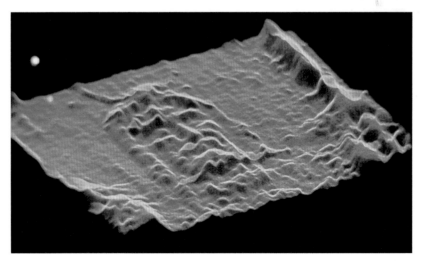

Three-dimensional elaboration of the Shroud, full frontal view and detail of the face. The image was created by the Interpretation Systems VP-8 Image Analyzer which translates light and shade, as on a black and white photograph, into relief, viewable in three dimensions on a television monitor. (© 1978, Vernon Miller)

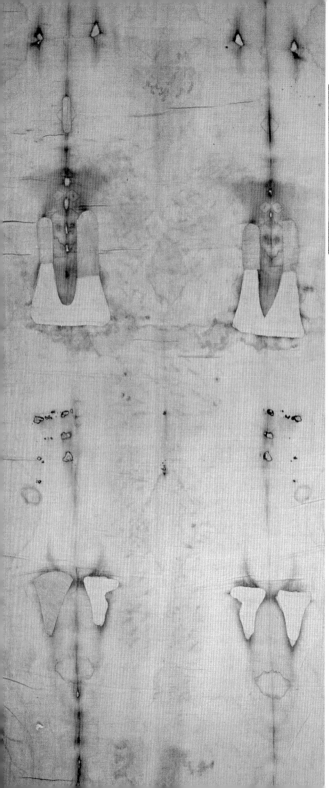

The Man of the Shroud shows evident signs of a terrible flagellation. The blows which He sustained (a hundred or so) are distributed with precision from both sides. The horrible flagellation was administered using three cords attached to a wooden handle. At the end of each cord there were pieces of lead which produced contusions and/or bits of bone which caused severe lacerations as seen in these photos. (© 1978, Vernon Miller)

The forehead and top of the head of the Man of the Shroud are marked by rivulets of blood provoked by sharp pointed thorns. It was not a usual method of torture. The only documented "crowning with thorns" is that of Jesus. The pattern of the wounds would indicate the use of a mass of thorny branches (the Palestinian "Crown of Thorns" bush?), bound together and placed on the head of the condemned in a gesture of extreme contempt and then driven into his head by beating on the thorns repeatedly and ferociously. (Courtesy, Holy Shroud Guild, Esopus, NY)

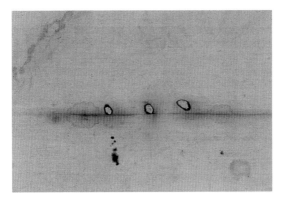

There are four sets of triple holes that appear to have been created prior to the fire of 1532, most likely caused by pieces of incense falling on the folded cloth. (© 1978, Vernon Miller)

At the wrist of the Man of the Shroud a rivulet of blood descends in two streams from a large puncture wound. A large nail driven through the Space of Destot is capable of sustaining the weight of a body, and injuring the median nerve causing the thumbs to be drawn into the palms of the hand. On the Shroud the thumbs are not visible. (© 1978, Vernon Miller)

Flemish artist Anton Van Dyck saw the Shroud in Genoa and painted the Crucifixion with the nails in the wrists, instead of the palms of the hands, as had almost always been the case in traditional iconography. (Courtesy, Edizioni San Paolo, s.r.l.)

The feet were also nailed to the cross. One, covered with blood, was pinned to the wood with the other on top of it. The color photo shows the blood stains of the feet on the Shroud; the detail in black and white is explained by the sketch to its left. 1. The hole created by the nail and the bloody sole of the foot. 2-3. Blood which during the burial collected around the heel. 4. Symmetrical reverse stains which were transferred to the cloth when it was folded over. (© 1978, Vernon Miller)

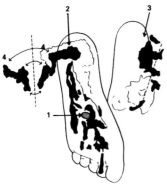

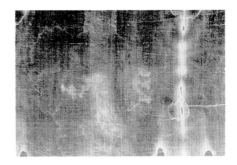

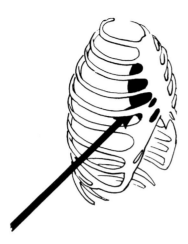

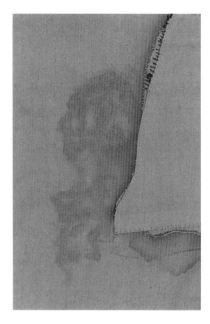

The Man of the Shroud suffered a profound wound in His side which produced a copious flow of blood from which it may be deduced that He probably died of heart failure. The wound caused by a lance which pierced His side between the fifth and sixth ribs punctured the pericardium first and then the heart. In the tomb, the blood from the wound along with the serum collected at the side and back of the body at the level of the waist. Scientific research on the blood on the Shroud indicates that it is the blood of a human male Type AB, with traces of aloes and myrrh. (© 1978, Vernon Miller)

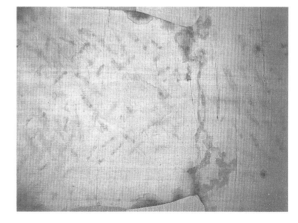

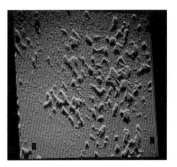

Three-dimensional photographs of the Shroud have enabled scientists to distinguish on the eyelids of the Man of the Shroud traces of two tiny coins, placed there perhaps to keep the eyelids closed. The coin shown in the photo is a *lepton* (a coin minted by Pontius Pilate between 29-31 AD) with what appears to be a backward question mark that corresponds to the Augur's Wand (*lituus*) which characterized that coin. Around the perimeter of the computer enhanced image of the coin over the right eye, portions of the Roman letters UCAI identifying Tiberius Caesar may be seen. (© 1978, Vernon Miller) and (Courtesy of Dr. Alan Whanger)

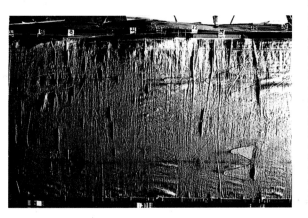

Raking-Light Test and Fold Marks. The doubling-in-four required three folds which created eight equal surfaces and seven fold marks. The raking-light test performed by physicist Dr. John Jackson as outlined in the publication *Shroud Spectrum* confirmed the presence of fold marks on the Shroud consistent with the fold marks on the Image of Edessa created by the Tetradiplon, further helping to confirm Ian Wilson's identification of the Image of Edessa with the Shroud of Turin. (© 1978, Vernon Miller)

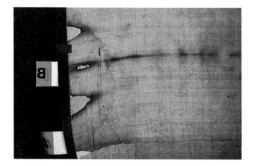

Using ultraviolet polarized light for microscopic viewing of the fabric of the Shroud, Dr. Gilbert Raes of the Ghent Institute of Textile Technology in Belgium, identified traces of cotton fibers (fibrils) that he classified as of the *Gossypium herbaceum* type, a cotton that existed in the Middle East of the first century. (© 1978, Vernon Miller)

On April 11, 1997 a fire heavily damaged the Cathedral of St. John Baptist in Turin — home of the Shroud since 1578. Firefighters rescued the Shroud without damage to the fabric. It took almost 200 firefighters to extinguish the blaze caused by a short circuit. The fire of 1532 was caused by a candle and did some damage to the Shroud. (courtesy, *Famiglia Cristiana*, April 23, 1997)

CHAPTER FIVE

The Shroud and
Ancient Jewish Burial Practices

The Shroud represents "a bundle of imposing probabilities."
Yves Delage to the French Academy of Sciences — 1903

We turn now to the Jewish burial practices of the Second Temple Period (the period from approximately 100 B.C. to 100 A.D. encompassing the period of Jesus' earthly life) to compare what the Gospels tell us of the death and burial of Jesus with the known burial practices of the period. The Gospel of John (19:40) tells us that Jesus was buried "following the Jewish burial custom." The late sindonologist Fr. Edward A. Wuenschel, C.Ss.R., author of *The Holy Shroud*, reminded us that the Shroud "is surely an archaeological object of the most profound significance bearing directly upon the principal phases of the Passion and upon the manner of Christ's burial."[1] Much can be learned from sources such as:

The accounts of the Gospels;
The information from Josephus and Philo, ancient historians;
The Mishnah (post-biblical and rabbinical literature written down in the first and second centuries from the oral traditions of the Rabbis);
The Tractate *Mourning* — a Talmudic document;
The Medieval Jewish Code of Law;
The findings of archaeology; and
Early Roman law.

Corroborating and Non-Contradictory Evidence

With the extensive excavations in 1967 of the Jewish necropolis (cemetery) at Jericho and the discovery of many tombs around Jerusalem like the large necropolis on the Mount of Olives near the church built on the site where the Gospels say Jesus wept over the city (*Dominus Flevit*) and the cemetery of the Essenes at the desert community of Qumran, much information has been collected clarifying early Jewish burial practices. This enables us to put together a composite picture of Jewish burial customs. Examining the Shroud and the procedures used to bury Jesus in light of this new information provides still further corroborating evidence of the Shroud's antiquity and authenticity.

Ancient Jewish Beliefs Regarding Death, Burial and Resurrection

Let us first provide some background on the evolution of ancient Jewish theological thought, especially during the Second Temple Period regarding death, burial and the idea of resurrection.

Primary Burial

When an individual died, the family was required to bury him as quickly as possible because of the climatic conditions favoring the onset of decay. Primary burial involved burial in either a wooden coffin in the ground or in a shroud in a cave-tomb cut from the soft limestone rocks. In the area of Jerusalem, most people were buried in the cave-tombs carved out of the soft limestone outside and near the walls of the city. Cemeteries were required to be outside the city walls. Coffins made of wood were more rare, probably caused by a desire to avoid anything that would prolong the process of decomposition of the body as well as the scarcity of wood in the area.[2]

The body was usually enveloped in a shroud (a large linen sheet called a *sindon* in the New Testament) and laid on a stone shelf in the cave-tomb. A mourning period for the family of from seven to thirty days ensued (depending upon the rapidness of decay). In the cave-tomb, the body would be allowed to decay until only the bones remained, usually a period of one year. The Jews of this period believed that sins of individuals are in the flesh, and expiation was achieved through decay of that flesh. When only the bones remained, the body was then considered pure and the bones ready for placement in ossuaries (smaller stone jars used for collecting and preserving bones).

The burial of Jesus was consistent with the primary burial procedures of the Jews. The New Testament relates that Joseph of Arimathea (a distinguished member of the Sanhedrin — the Jewish religious ruling body) buried Jesus in a cave-tomb cut from the rock nearby the crucifixion site on Golgotha (Calvary) and enveloped Him in a shroud. "Joseph took the body, wrapped it in a clean linen shroud and placed it in his new tomb which he had hewn in the rock. Then he rolled a large stone across the entrance of the tomb and went away" (Mt 27:59-60). Rt. Rev. John A.T. Robinson notes: "The corpse of Jesus enfolded in a simple linen cloth passing lengthwise over the head and covering the whole body back and front is not, I submit, what any forger with medieval or modern presuppositions would have thought of; but it makes complete sense of the texts and conforms with the other ancient evidence."[3] It was not customary in the ancient or medieval world for an artist to paint on linen, and painting Jesus naked was unheard of. The Shroud represents a true Jewish burial in a linen shroud.

The Second Burial (*Ossilegium*)

After a period of about one year, the family was responsible for carefully collecting the bones of the deceased and placing them in an ossuary — usually a stone jar — and normally inscribed. The purpose of this was to keep the bones together in preparation for the physical resurrection. The Hassidim (the righteous of early Maccabean times) and the Pharisees — strong in the time of Jesus — believed in a physical resurrection. The Sadducees denied such a resurrection. But during the time of Jesus, belief in a physical resurrection was strong among the Jews.

The Afterlife and Resurrection in Ancient Jewish Thought

Much of the information on Jewish religious thought about death and burial is contained in the Tractate *Mourning* (*Semahot* — literally "Rejoicings"). This third century Talmudic Tractate contains regulations relating to death, burial and mourning. In this Tractate, the ideas of the fate of the dead are clear. It involves a descent into a nether world (Sheol) called at times "dust" (Ps 22:30 or Is 26:19) or described as a "pit" (Is 14:15 and Pr 28:17). It is conceived as a dark place (Job 10:21-22) where one descends, never to return. There, one is counted among the "shadows," the "weak ones" never to rise again (Is 26:14). The dead are described as being cut off from the living and even from God (Pss 88:10-12 and 115:17).

L.Y. Rahmani of the Israel Department of Antiquities and Museums in Jerusalem tells us that "the concept of the nether world as conceived in Jewish thought... called for some provision of the fundamental necessities for those going down into a place of darkness, and some sort of existence is implied."[4] This idea of a vague, shadowy existence gave way gradually to a more defined concept of an afterlife and belief in a physical resurrection. The biblical reference for such a resurrection is first encountered in Daniel 12:2 written as late as the second century B.C. after the start of Antiochus IV Epiphanes' persecution.[5]

He notes that from the Maccabean times forward, we encounter this eschatological thinking (with Dn 12:2 and 2 M 7:14 — a period of great disasters and great expectations). In 2 Maccabees 7:14 we read of seven brethren and their mother enduring every torture commanded by the wicked king, proudly declaring their belief that "the King of the universe will raise us up to an everlasting renewal of life, because we have died for His laws." By the time of Jesus, belief in a physical resurrection, especially among the Pharisees, was well established in Jerusalem. Rahmani tells us that "belief in a personal and physical resurrection eventually evolved into a fundamental principle of Jewish faith."[6] It is against this background that we look at the Resurrection of Jesus. The followers of Jesus would have buried Him carefully according to Jewish custom.

The Cave Tombs

Hundreds of cave tombs have been unearthed in recent archaeological digs in Palestine (especially around Jerusalem) relating to the Herodian and Roman periods (middle of the first century B.C. through the first century A.D.). Jewish law required that people be buried outside the town limits. From archaeological sources, we have learned much about these cave tombs, especially from the work of noted archaeologist Dr. Eugenia Nitowski, formerly a Carmelite nun (Sr. Damien of the Cross) who is perhaps the foremost authority on the Jewish (Jerusalem) cave tombs, and from other recently published articles in archaeological journals.[7]

In a descriptive article in the *Biblical Archaeology Review*, Rachel Hachlili also describes excavated tombs similar to the one in which Jesus was laid.[8] Hachlili describes these tombs as hewn from rock (a soft chalky limestone identified as *calcium carbonate*) cut into the hillsides forming a man-made cave or chamber. The floor was square, about eight feet on a side. Usually, a pit about five feet square was dug into the floor of the room as a place for mourners to stand. This created ledges or benches along the sides of the tomb where the deceased would be laid down temporarily. Here they would be placed on a large linen sheet or shroud (*sindon*). The height of the caves from the benches to the ceiling was only three to four feet and the pit in the center increased this height to about six feet, allowing a person to stand upright inside the tomb. In addition, burial recesses, or *loculi* (*kochim* in Hebrew) were hewn into the walls above the benches on three sides of the

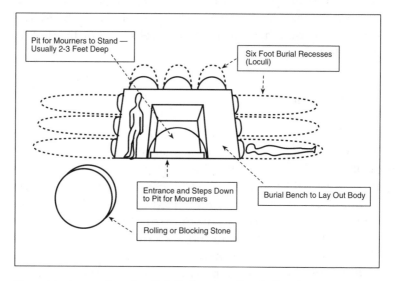

The rock tombs were hewn in soft chalky limestone. The pit allowed mourners to stand. Ledges, or benches accommodated the body laid out in a shroud (sindon) and prepared for burial. The body was then placed in a recess, or loculus, and a blocking stone rolled across to seal the entrance. Several bodies could be placed in the average tomb.

- Prepared by Kim Iannone, based on descriptions of Rachael Hachlili and Dr. Eugenia Nitowski.

tomb chamber. These *loculi* were semicircular in shape and longer than the height of a man approximately six feet, or long enough in fact to place in it a body, a coffin or an ossuary.

The entry was narrow and closed off by a circular blocking stone that was rolled into place and sealed with mortar and small stones. In the Resurrection narratives, the stone sealing Jesus' tomb was moved away (Jn 20:1). There were perhaps a few steps leading from the high entry way to the center pit. Usually each *loculus* or burial recess within the chamber was also sealed off by blocking stones, bricks or small stones held together by mortar or mud.[9] Dr. Eugenia Nitowski noticed a white, chalky substance (*calcium carbonate*) on her clothing while in the tombs and chemical analysis sent back to the United States revealed this to be limestone dust, also found on the Shroud which picked up traces of the soft limestone when Jesus was laid on the ledge of the tomb on the *sindon*, or burial linen.

We noted earlier that pollen was discovered on the outside of the Shroud where it came in contact with the stone ledge, and became embedded in the linen fibers.

The Main Burial Linen: The *Sindon*

After the death of Jesus, the New Testament tells us that Joseph of Arimathea went to Pilate to ask for the body before the commencement of the Sabbath which began at sunset with the sighting of the first three stars. Time was pressing because the bodies of the dead were not to be handled during the Sabbath. The ancient historian Josephus in his *Jewish Wars* tells us that "the Jews are so careful about funeral rites that even those who are crucified because they were found guilty are taken down and buried before sunset."[10] (This included even suicides and the bodies of enemies.) Pilate was astonished that Jesus had expired so quickly, Roman crucifixion being designed to make victims suffer for a longer period. Jesus, however, had suffered the Agony in the Garden where He sweat blood, as well as severe scourging and capping with thorns. He had been nailed (rather than tied) to the Cross and was greatly weakened by severe abuse preceding the actual crucifixion. Pilate gave permission for the removal from the Cross. With regard to the linens and the use of linens in the burial, we note the testimony of three Gospel writers (the Synoptics):

Matthew 27:59: "Joseph took the body and *wrapped* it in a clean linen *shroud* and placed it in his new tomb which he had hewn in the rock."

Mark 15:46: "Pilate was amazed that He was already dead... and after learning it from the centurion he bestowed the corpse on Joseph. So Joseph bought a linen *shroud* and took Jesus down, *wrapped* Him in the linen *shroud,* and placed Him in a tomb that had been hewn out of rock."

Luke 23:53: He (Joseph) came to Pilate and asked for Jesus' body, and after taking it down, he *wrapped* it in a linen *shroud* and placed it in a tomb hewn out of rock in which no one had yet been laid."

The New Testament word for "shroud" is the Greek *sindon.* The authors utilize this word when referring to the main cloth in which Jesus was buried. *Sindon* is defined in the Greek lexicons as *a large linen sheet* which we know the Shroud to be. The Synoptic writers go on to utilize the Greek term *entulissa,* which is defined as *"folded over the body,"* generally translated as *"wrapped"* in the sense of being *"enveloped."*[11] The picture portrayed here is that of a large linen sheet stretched out on the ledge of the cave-tomb. Jesus was placed at one end on His back with His head toward the center. The sheet was then drawn over the front of His body.

The Burial Strips: *Othonia*

Another term is introduced by the New Testament writers, namely *othonia*, defined as "binding cloths or strips of linen." We read in John 19:40: "They took Jesus' body and bound it in linen cloths (*othoniois*) with the spices, as is the custom among the Jews in preparing for burial." Luke 24:12 also uses the term: "But Peter got up and ran to the tomb, and when he stooped down he saw only the linen cloths (*othonia*)."

The late Shroud author Werner Bulst, S.J., pointed out that *othonia* as used in John 19:40 refers to a narrow cloth, a strip (such as is used for bandaging a wound). This is equivalent to the bindings (*keriai*) with which Lazarus was bound (Jn 11:44). Likewise the verb *deo* found in John 11:44 and 19:40 always meant *to bind* in the strict sense and never "to wrap up in or envelop" indicating that these were bandage strips differing from the larger cloth.[12] These binding strips were used to bind the hands and feet to permit easy carrying of the body, especially through the narrow entrance to the cave-tombs and to secure the position of the body (with hands folded across the loins). Rigor mortis likely began on the Cross and was broken to bind the hands and feet for carrying. Bulst points out that on the body image of the Shroud there is a gap above the wrists:

> Strangely, a little above the wrist, there is a gap of about a hand's breadth with no trace of the blood that trickled and caked along the forearm muscle of the Crucified. The blood transfers on the forearms are otherwise unusually clear and sharply outlined. The missing imprint above the wrists on either forearm would be readily explained if a linen strip had been bound about them here and knotted to keep the arms in the position as they are seen on the Cloth. Without some such bond, this position of the arms would be impossible.[13]

Bulst goes on to relate that the feet appear to have been similarly bound above the ankles. "The imprints of these extremities (on the Shroud) are noticeably dim both on the frontal and dorsal view."[14] This would imply that something (linen strips) interfered with the image-formation process.

The Chin Band: *Sudarion*

To complicate matters, New Testament writers used a third term — *sudarion* — referring to a chin band. The word can also mean a "sweat or face cloth." However, as Wuenschel points out, in the New Testament period the Jews did not veil the face of the dead in the final burial in the manner generally assumed. Not one of the many instances of Jewish burials described in the Bible, the Apocrypha or the rabbinical writings contain any hint of such a practice. (Weunschel is referring here specifically to a sweat or face cloth in addition to the Shroud and not a chin-band or separate face-cloth as we shall discuss further on.) In fact, he mentions Tabitha, who was raised from the dead by Peter (Ac 9:36-43). When Peter restored her to life, the New Testament says that from the moment when she was restored, she opened her eyes and saw Peter, implying that there was no cloth over her face to impede her vision. (However, this writer wants to point out that Tabitha was not in a state of final burial and it is possible, as we will note, that there was a face cloth over her face before entombment which Peter removed as he was in the process of restoring Tabitha to life.)

For a long time, biblical scholars were confused by the use of these three terms: *sindon, othonia* and *sudarion*. However, the following scenario is now more generally accepted by New Testament scholars: Jesus was buried "as is the custom among the Jews in preparing for burial" (Jn 19:40). We know from archaeology and early documents of the Mishnah that

Jews were not buried in the Egyptian mummy-like fashion or embalmed, but were buried usually with a shroud (*sindon*) defined as a large linen cloth *enveloping* (not wrapping mummy-style) the body. The general procedure was to place a chin-band (*sudarion*) around the chin and tie it over the top of the head to keep the mouth closed and slow down the process of decomposition. Rahmani, referring to the Tractate *Mourning* (*Semahot*) says that "when death had taken place, the eyes of the deceased were closed, as were all orifices: the mouth was bound up, so as not to stay agape."[15] We also know that strips of linen were tied about the wrists and ankles to keep the body in place when being carried to the tomb and for securing the burial position of the body with arms across the loins. These linen strips were called *othonia.*[16]

Recent investigations of the Shroud confirm that there does appear to be a chin-band around the face of Jesus and the break in blood flow down the arms seems to confirm that the wrists were bound with linen strips, linking science with the Gospels and ancient Jewish burial customs. With regard to the chin-band, Wuenschel referred to Paul Vignon in stating that "the presence of the chin-band offers a very reasonable explanation of the blank space which interrupts the imprint at the top of the head on the Shroud of Turin."[17] Robinson tells us that "the vertical dark strips on either side of the face between the cheeks and the locks, otherwise so odd, could similarly be caused by the band holding back the intervening hair."[18] This also provides a logical explanation of why one does not notice the ears of Jesus on the Shroud image. It should be noted that Dr. Allen Mills (*Interdisciplinary Science Review*, Dec. 1995, pp. 319-326) thinks this gap may be due to a "weave anomaly." This author disagrees with Dr. Mills since this theory would not sufficiently explain the size or precise similarity of the gap on both sides of the face.

The Story of the Resurrection of Lazarus

The story of the resurrection of Lazarus appears only in John, chapter 11, but it throws much light on ancient Jewish burial practices, specifically the use of the chin-band (*sudarion*) and the binding of hands and feet (*othonia*). John tells us that "after saying this, (Jesus) called out in a loud voice, 'Lazarus! Come out!' The dead man came out with his hands and feet bound with thongs (*keriais*, or grave cloths) and a cloth (*sudario*) around his face (*peridedeto*). Jesus said to them, 'Unbind him and let him go!'" *Peridedeto* is translated as "bound about/to bind around about" as with a chin band. *Keriai* were a kind of binder of twisted rushes, somewhat like a thong with which bedsteads were strung, which were used to hold the hands and feet in place for burial.[19]

Recreating the Burial of Jesus

From this information, we can recreate with high probability the burial procedure used with Jesus. Jesus was pronounced dead and removed from the Cross by His followers who needed to bury Him in haste before sundown. Philo, the early Jewish philosopher, quoting Deuteronomy 21:23, states: "Let not the sun go down upon the crucified but let them be buried in the earth before sundown."[20] The followers needed to comply with two rigorous laws: the Sabbath rest and the penal law of Deuteronomy 21:23. Jesus had been crucified just after noon (Pilate passed sentence according to John 19:14 at the sixth hour, i.e., around noon, and Jesus died around the ninth hour, or 3:00 P.M.). There was great haste in the burial since time was running out. The Sabbath began with the appearance of the first three visible stars. Joseph of Arimathea had to go to Pilate located at the Fortress of Antonia, the Roman garrison nearby, to request release of the body. Werner Bulst says that "since there was a question here of a legal act of some importance, more than likely a 'document of release' had to be prepared, especially since the Sanhedrin had asked permission, a short while before, to remove the bodies of the crucified (Jn 19:31)."[21] Noted New Testament scholar Raymond Brown tells us that the Roman custom or law dealing with the burial of crucified criminals as outlined in the *Digest of Justinian* gives the view of Ulpian and of Julius Paulus from the period ca. 200 A.D.: "The bodies of those who suffer capital punishment are not to be refused to their relatives (Ulpian) or to any who seek them for burial (Paulus)."[22] Jewish law permitted this.

Jesus was then removed from the Cross and His hands and feet were bound about with strips of linen (*othonia*), the left hand over the right and both over the loins, so that Jesus could be carried (perhaps on a litter or by hand) the short distance from Golgotha (Calvary) to the cave-tomb carved from limestone and owned by Joseph of Arimathea. The late Monsignor Giulio Ricci, former President of the Roman Center for the Study of the Passion of Christ and the Holy Shroud, in his 1978 book entitled *The Way of the Cross in the Light of the Holy Shroud* (pp. 63-64) pointed out a most interesting detail noted on the Shroud, namely the presence of fingerprints on the left heel made from one of the bearers of the body of Jesus. Ricci states that:

> these prints (on the heel) were caused by the blood that would have flowed out of the hole in the feet, which had just been freed from the nails, due to the edema occurring either before death through circulatory insufficiency or after death through hypostasis (Dr. Giordano). The blood ran down and concentrated in the area of the heels, where it left some unusual marks which allow perfect reconstruction of the hand to be made, with the fingers bent and tensed, showing the effort needed to carry the weight. *The little finger, and the ring and middle*

fingers of the left hand (of the individual bearing Jesus' body), in contact with the heel, were surrounded by the blood running from the hole in the left foot. The same thing happened with the right hand on the right heel, though the imprint is less clear.

Ricci believed this was evidence that the bearers of the body carried the body to the tomb feet first. It is also possible that Jesus' body was placed on a litter, as noted previously, and carried the short distance to the tomb.

The chin-band (*sudarion*) was placed around His chin and tied on top of His head to keep the mouth closed, as Jewish law required that orifices (mouth and jaw) be closed to delay decomposition. The eyes were closed and a face-cloth (*sudarium*) (as we shall discuss further on) was likely placed over His face as He was being carried to the tomb. The body was then laid upon one end of the Shroud (*Sindon*) which was on the stone ledge of the cave-tomb, and the body of Jesus gently and lovingly laid out on the cloth. Ian Wilson notes that Reverend Sox deemed the Shroud authentic because the arms appear placed "modestly across the loins rather than at the side of the body."[23] Wilson goes on to say that in Judea, a number of skeletons excavated in the Essene cemetery at Qumran on the shores of the Dead Sea (ca. 200 B.C. to 70 A.D.) were laid out flat, facing upward, elbows bent slightly and hands crossed across the pelvis, exactly the attitude visible on the Shroud.[24] The Essenes were a pious group in this period who differentiated themselves from the Pharisees and Sadducees and lived a highly disciplined life apart in the Desert of Qumran just off the Dead Sea in anticipation of the coming Messiah. They lived a quiet, contemplative, monk-like existence away from the worldliness of the hustle and bustle of Jerusalem and the Temple area.

The followers then likely placed Roman coins (*leptons*) over His eyes, a custom sometimes employed in Jewish burial. Spices (aloes and myrrh) were placed inside the Shroud. John

19:39-41 states: "Then Nicodemus came, too — the one who had first come to Jesus at night — bringing a mixture of myrrh and aloes, weighing about a hundred pounds. So they took the body of Jesus and bound it in linen cloths with the spices, as is the custom among the Jews in preparing for burial." Pier Luigi Baima Bollone, professor of Legal Medicine at the University of Turin, identified traces of aloe and myrrh on the Shroud, principally in the bloodstained areas. Wuenschel clarifies that these two spices were in the form of a dry powder. In the ancient world, aloe and myrrh were common articles of commerce. (Myrrh is a gum resin exuding from the trees of the genus commiphora or balsamodendron myrrh and quickly becomes dry and solid as its volatile oil evaporates. Aloe is an herb obtained by evaporating the juice of the leaves of several spices of aloe, a genus of the liliacaeae.) The aloe and myrrh is distinguished from the perfumed oil or unguent composed of spices mixed with oil (Lk 23:56) which the women prepared for the morning after the Sabbath.[25] Wuenschel relates (quoting Paul Vignon):

> The fact that the spices were in powdered form has a special significance with regard to the Shroud of Turin, for certain features of the imprints show that there was powder on the linen sheet at the time when it enveloped the body.[26]

The purpose of the spices was generally to delay the process of decomposition to permit a mourning period, and to serve as a perfume to combat the odor of decay until the women could return the morning after the Sabbath to properly cleanse and prepare the body. Dr. Whanger, as pointed out previously, notes that he has found evidence that fresh flowers were also placed within the Shroud along with the aloes and myrrh. With Jesus laying on one end of the Shroud, the remainder of the Shroud would then have been laid over the top of His body, completing the temporary burial. The wheel-shaped rock would then have been rolled in front of the tomb. The women noted the location of the tomb and planned to return after the Sabbath to complete the burial.

No Evidence of Corruption or Decay

There is no evidence on the Shroud of decomposition or corruption because Jesus was only in the tomb approximately twenty-four to thirty-six hours prior to His Resurrection. The New Testament proclaims that Jesus' body did not experience corruption. In Acts 2:22-32 we read that Peter addressed the crowd and, quoting King David concerning the Messiah, tells the crowd that God would not "allow [His] Holy One to suffer death's decay (Ps 16:8-11)." As Kenneth Stevenson noted, many of the ancient burial cloths in existence today, while not having any type of image, do contain marks of decomposition of bodies. The Shroud, however, exhibits no signs of bodily decomposition or corruption.[27]

Was the Body Washed?

Because of the haste of burial, the Shroud indicates that the body of Jesus was not washed or anointed with oil as is required by Jewish law. The blood and perspiration of the agonizing crucifixion remained. The burial was "provisional and not definitive" as Bulst points out, since the women intended to return on the morning after the Sabbath to complete the washing and anointing. Bulst notes that both Mark 14:8 and Matthew 26:12 report the words spoken by Jesus a few days before the Passion when Mary of Bethany anointed Him. According to this account, Mary had anticipated the anointing of His body for burial: "She has done a beautiful thing for me… When she put this oil on my body she did it to prepare me for burial."[28] Luke 23:55 tells us that the women "saw the tomb and how His body was laid" and went back to get the spices ready. Mark 16:2 tells us that on Easter morning (the morning after the Sabbath) the women came very early to complete the task of anointing the body of Jesus.

The ordinary prescription of Jewish law was that the body be washed. Jesus' followers, however, had very little time to perform a proper burial — evidence from the Shroud indicates that the body was prepared for burial within an hour and a half to two hours after the flow of blood had stopped — so approximately a hundred pounds of spices (aloes and myrrh) along with fresh flowers were placed with the body on Good Friday to preserve it until the Sabbath was over. Bonnie La Voie noted that the Code of Jewish Law had a special provision for those who were victims of a bloody and violent death:

> One who fell and died instantly, if his body was bruised and blood flowed from the wound, and there is apprehension that the blood of the soul was absorbed in his clothes, he should not be cleansed, but they should inter him in his garments and boots, but above his garments they should wrap a sheet which is called *sovev*.[29]

However, this would not seem to explain why, as the Gospels say, the women had planned to be back early in the morning after the Sabbath to properly wash and prepare the body. Dreisbach notes that the Jews believed the soul left after three days. The women were likely also going to the tomb to lament and place more fresh flowers there.

Easter Morning: A Startling Find

When Peter and John entered the tomb on that Easter morning after Mary Magdalene discovered the tomb empty, John tells us "Simon Peter… saw the linen cloths lying there, and also the cloth that had been over His head; this was not with the linen cloths but was rolled up and lying in a place by itself" (Jn 20:6-8). The fact that the face cloth or chin-band (*sudarion*) was in a place by itself seems to preclude grave robbers who would certainly not have taken the time to neatly roll it up and set it aside, and to remove the chin-band and bindings of the hands and feet in order to carry away the body. What purpose would this have served? Bulst writes:

> From his (John's) accounting of the finding of the cloths on Easter morning, it is fairly obvious that something in the arrangement of both the sweat cloth (chin-band) and binding strips assures him that the body could not possibly have been stolen, but that Christ had risen from the dead. The simplest clue to this startling information would have been to find these cloths each in its proper place: the binding strips looped together and knotted exactly as they had bound the hands and feet, the face cloth not together with the binding strips but lying in its own place by itself still holding the oval conformation of where it bound up the chin and still together lengthwise, and perhaps knotted at the time. In a state of glory, the risen body has no need of first untying knots.[30]

Later testimonies in the New Testament regarding the appearances of Jesus to the disciples at Emmaus and His ability to move through the walls when appearing to the Apostles indicate that the witnesses at the tomb were referring to a dematerialized, glorified body of the Risen Jesus. Rev. Kenneth Stevenson agrees that something about the cloths stunned John who, the Gospel relates, saw and believed that Jesus had risen. *Perhaps it was the position of the cloths reflecting the glorified body as described above, or perhaps Peter and John viewed the actual images left on the Shroud.*

Is the Cloth of Oviedo the Face-Cloth of the Burial?

Since the eighth century, there is, in the Cathedral in Oviedo, Spain, the *Sagrado Rostro* or Holy Face, a face-cloth (83 x 53 cm.) also known as the Cloth of Oviedo (*Sudarium Christi d'Oviedo*). Located in Jerusalem until 614, it was moved to North Africa and then Spain to protect it from the advancing Moslems. The first historical information we have about it after the year 614 goes back to 1075 when Alphonsus VI of Leon recognized it as one of the relics in the *Arca Santa* or Holy Ark, a wooden reliquary which had housed the *sudarium* in Carthage, North Africa, and Monsagro and Toledo, Spain. Franca Pastore Trossello, a forensic scientist from the University of Turin, conducted a comparative study of the fabrics of the Shroud and the Cloth of Oviedo and found them to be of the same weave and texture. Dr. Alan Whanger studied the cloth and is convinced that it touched the face of Jesus. Dr. Max Frei matched at least four pollen on the Cloth of Oviedo with four pollen from the Shroud. Whanger found at least seventy matches between a polarized image overlay of the blood stains of the Shroud and those found on the Cloth of Oviedo. Further computerized comparative studies by Nello Balossino of the University of Turin, indicated that the traces of blood present on the two pieces of cloth matched perfectly.

In a recent telephone interview, Dr. Whanger advised me that the Cloth of Oviedo contains blood stains, but no image. Further, it was a Jewish custom to place a cloth over the face prior to enshroudment. In a recent article, Mark Guscin provides a detailed description of the Cloth of Oviedo which substantially supports the fact that this linen once touched the face of Jesus.[31]

The Two *Sudaria* of Christ

In this author's opinion, the Gospel of John, the Cloth of Oviedo and Jewish burial practices strongly support the fact that there were *two sudaria*. One was a face or sweat cloth which, as Guscin points out, was placed over the face of Jesus while still on the Cross, and which covered and blotted His face when He was removed from the Cross and carried to the tomb (then folded and laid to the side before the *sindon* or shroud was laid over Him); and one was a chin-band required by Jewish law (*The Jewish Encyclopedia*, Vol. 3, pp. 434-436, 1925 Edition: "the mouth was shut and kept in position by a band") to close the mouth of the deceased. (See also the Tractate *Mourning* which says that "when death had taken place... the mouth was bound up so as not to stay agape.") The Gospel of John uses the term *sudarium* in these two ways. In the story of Lazarus (Jn 11:1-44) *sudarium* refers to a chin-band around Lazarus' head: "a cloth *(sudario)* round *(peridedeto)* his face." In the Passion Narrative *sudarium* refers to "the cloth *(sudarion)* that had been over His head; this was not with the linen cloths but rolled up in a place by itself" (Jn 20:7). This was likely the Cloth of Oviedo, bearing blood (AB type as on the Shroud), sweat, saliva and serum stains, but no image.

In concluding this chapter, I would like to respond to an article carried by the Associated Press — Jerusalem on Sunday, April 13, 1997 entitled "Some Scholars Say Shroud is a Forgery." The writer quotes Joe Zias, an anthropologist at Jerusalem's Rockefeller Museum. Zias and his colleague Amos Kloner, an archaeologist at the Israeli Antiquities Authority and Bar Ilan University, note five objections to the Shroud's authenticity.

1. The archaeologists point to an alleged discrepancy of 6 inches between the Shroud's imprints on the front and back. While I have not verified this discrepancy or its measurement in inches, such a discrepancy, if indeed it is a proper inter-

pretation of the cloth, does not come as a surprise. It is quite natural and logical and supports the presence of a real human body in the Shroud. If one were to lay a body on a piece of linen and note the distance between the top of the head and the point where the heel touches the cloth and then lay a piece of linen on top of the body and note the distance from the top of the head to where the cloth meets the tip of the toes, the toes would naturally be farther forward than the heels, accounting for a discrepancy. In addition, as noted by St. Louis sindonologist Fr. Joseph Marino, there is some draping of the cloth in the front.

2. Zias and Kloner note that no textiles from the first century have been found in the Mediterranean region because the climate is too humid. However, as will be noted in detail in our next two chapters on the history of the Shroud, the cloth spent over 900 years in the hot, dry climate of Edessa (a city in ancient Syria — modern Urfa in Turkey) about 400 miles northeast of Jerusalem and then spent approximately 250 years in Constantinople. During the centuries it has been in Europe (France and Italy), it has been sealed in an airtight silver reliquary and kept dry except for rare and brief expositions and would not be a victim to the Mediterranean humidity.

3. Zias notes that the "shadowy image of the shroud suggests that nails were driven through the palms." He goes on to say that "It has been known for centuries that you have to nail high on the arms" to keep the body upright on the cross, and that nailing the palms would not have sufficed." However, as we noted earlier, Shroud experts, following the lead of French surgeon Dr. Pierre Barbet and American pathologists Dr. Frederick Zugibe and Dr. Robert Bucklin, among others, have noted that the Shroud — in contradiction of all medieval and Renaissance art — shows that the nail holes are in the wrists, not the palms, the wrists being fully capable of supporting the body.

Further, the evidence of the crucifixion of Jehohanan —
crucified in the Second Temple Period as we noted in the
previous chapter — shows that a nail was placed just above the
wrist at the intersection of the arm bones (radius and ulna)
with the wrist, with evidence of the nail grating on the radius
bone. In fact, N. Haas of the Department of Anatomy at Hebrew University - Hadassah Medical School noted in his article
"Anthropological Observations on the Skeletal Remains from
Giv'at ha-Mivtar" in the *Israel Exploration Journal* (Volume 20,
Numbers 1-2, Jerusalem, 1970, pp. 38-59) that the iron nails
in the arm of Jehohanan "had been fixed in the distal region
of the forearms" (p. 57). Distal is defined in *Webster's Un-
abridged Dictionary* as follows: "In biology, farthest removed
from the... point of attachment or origin" (in other words,
low on the forearm close to the wrist and farthest from the
shoulder or elbow). He goes on further to state that the skeletal remains of Jehohanan show "penetration of the nail in
the interosseous space between the radius and the ulna
(bones). The abrupted proximal edge of this scratch is evidence of the first direct contact of the nail with the radial
bone" (p. 58). The nail wounds of the Shroud were not in the
palms or high up on the arm, as Zias suggests was the practice, but in the area where the wrists and arm bones join, showing that the Romans would nail through the wrist or very low
forearm — both areas capable of supporting the body.

4. Both Zias and Kloner point to the Carbon-14 tests as
indicating the Shroud's origin during the 14th century. However, as will be noted in detail in Chapter 9, the credibility of
this test as applied to linen cloth has now been seriously questioned, principally by the findings of Dr. Garza-Valdéz and Dr.
Stephen J. Mattingly, microbiologists at the University of Texas
in San Antonio, regarding the bio-plastic coating on the fibers
created by fungus/bacteria. Additionally, the studies of Russian physicist Dr. Dmitri Kouznetsov regarding bio-fraction-
ation and his creation of a fire-model duplicating the impact

of the great fire of 1532 on the carbon content of the Shroud
have changed the views of the accuracy of the Carbon-14 test
as applied to the linen of the Shroud — findings to be discussed in detail in a later chapter.

5. Finally, Zias indicated that the Jewish custom in the
first century required the head to be left uncovered when a
body was wrapped in a burial shroud. I was somewhat taken
aback by this statement as I can find no verification of this
practice in the Mishnah or Talmudic treatises, and I am pres-
ently attempting to correspond with Zias and Kloner on this
point.

Several years ago I had occasion to immerse myself in the
library of the Jewish Theological Seminary for two days in New
York and to study a book entitled *The Tractate 'Mourning'*
*(*Semahot*)* — *Regulations Relating to Death, Burial and Mourn-*
ing translated from Hebrew by Dov Zlotnick of the Jewish
Theological Seminary of America (New Haven and London,
Yale University Press, 1966) and representing Jewish burial
customs of the period of Jesus. L.Y. Rahmani of the Israel
Department of Antiquities and Museums in an article in the
Biblical Archaeologist[32] entitled "Ancient Jerusalem's Funerary
Customs and Tombs" mentions that the Tractate *Mourning* is
a 3rd century A.D. Talmudic Tractate "relating to customs a
hundred or two hundred years old." This would place such
customs at the time of Jesus. Rahmani, in his four-part article,
speaks of "winding sheets" or shrouds and never mentions that
the head was left uncovered. Dov Zlotnick mentions shrouds
on several occasions, and in a footnote to Chapter 7, p. 137,
states that "the early practice was to bare the faces of the rich,
whereas those of the poor, black with hunger, were left covered. In order to avoid shaming the poor, *it was then decreed*
that the faces of all corpses must remain covered (B. MK, 27a)" (Ital-
ics are mine). A.P. Bender, in his classic article in the *Jewish*
Quarterly Review entitled "Beliefs, Rites and Customs of the
Jews, Connected with Death, Burial and Mourning" mentions

several times the custom of placing the shroud over the body after death and never mentions that the burial cloth did not cover the head.[33]

Of note also is the fact that the Gospel of John (20:7) speaks of the "cloth that had been over His head" when referring to the body of Jesus. Earlier, John speaks of the resurrection of Lazarus: "The dead man came out with his hands and feet bound with thongs and a cloth around his face" (11:44). These references would certainly support the claim that it was the Jewish burial practice of the time to cover the head.

As noted earlier, a colleague of Zias and Kloner, Professor Avinoam Danin, Professor of Botany at Hebrew University and recognized as the leading botanist in Israel, has very recently acknowledged that *flowers and floral images associated with the Shroud came from a 10 kilometer area between Jerusalem and Jericho and, to him, indicated that the Shroud was an ancient Israelite cloth.* This strongly supports the previous work of Dr. Alan Whanger, Professor Emeritus of Duke University, North Carolina, regarding floral images on the Shroud, and the work of Swiss criminologist Dr. Max Frei on the presence of 58 varieties of pollen, some from ancient Jerusalem, on the Shroud.

CHAPTER SIX

Tracing the Historical Journey: The First Thousand Years

*"If, instead of Christ, there were a question of some person
like a Sargon, an Achilles, or one of the Pharaohs,
no one would have thought of making any objection."*

Yves Delage — French Academy of Science

As science delved into the mysteries of the Shroud, historians began poring over ancient and modern manuscripts hoping to shed light on the presence of the Shroud in literary or liturgical texts over the past 2,000 years. Historians have, indeed, located a number of texts that have enabled us to recreate a plausible history of the Shroud. While some of the historical information is circumstantial, the sum total of information provides a strong link between the modern Shroud of Turin and the ancient Shroud from the Tomb of Jesus.

The Silence of the New Testament

The most logical place to begin is in the New Testament itself. It appears puzzling that the Gospel writers, while speaking in some detail of the grave cloths, do not mention the images on the Shroud. One would think that the Apostles would go about showing everyone the images they had found on the burial cloth. However, there were good reasons for the followers of Jesus to keep the existence of the Shroud quiet. Most likely, Peter, as the leader, took control of the Shroud and guarded it carefully. Of necessity, the Apostles could not openly display the grave cloths of their Risen Lord. First, as a record of Christ's passion, it was something very precious to the early Church. Out of fear that it might be mishandled or even destroyed, it would not have been exposed to the eyes of the curious.

Second, Jewish religious regulations strictly forbade the handling of burial cloths, especially bloody ones of victims of violent death. Many Jews would not have understood or accepted the preservation of this bloody burial cloth by Jesus' followers.

Third, the Jews throughout the Old and New Testament period considered graven images (drawings, paintings, statues depicting God) as blasphemous. This is especially true in that the Shroud contained images of a naked man. If the Apostles had used, in a public manner, the images of a naked Jesus depicted on a bloody burial cloth, this act would have been considered as blasphemous and would have further jeopardized the very lives of the early disciples. Jesus was, after all, considered a criminal and crucified by the Romans.

Finally, the persecution of the early Church would have made the Shroud a target for confiscation by Roman soldiers and Jewish zealots. Peter and the Apostles, therefore, could not effectively utilize the Shroud as a proselytizing tool to convert their fellow Jews in or around Jerusalem. We surmise from the evidence that the Apostles made the decision to have the Shroud brought to a safe haven away from the dangers that the early Church faced in Palestine, especially around Jerusalem. This would account for the silence of the New Testament.

Apocryphal Texts

Having noted the reasons for the silence of the New Testament concerning the existence of the Shroud in the possession of the Apostles, we should add that some apocryphal writings, however, do make reference to the funeral cloths of Jesus. St. Jerome, for example, quotes a passage from the *Gospel of the Hebrews* (second century) and cites what is probably the most ancient non-biblical reference we have to the Shroud: "Now the Lord, after having given the Shroud to the servant of the priest, appeared to James." Others read: "After having given the Shroud to Simon Peter..." and this interpretation would seem to agree with what St. Paul says: "He appeared to Cephas and then to the Twelve. Finally, he appeared to James."

The *Mysteries of the Acts of the Savior*, also of the second century, reports that the Lord Himself, appearing to Joseph of Arimathea, showed him the Shroud (*Sindone*) and the face cloth (*sudario*).

Texts from the Egyptian Church (third and fourth centuries) mention that cadavers are wrapped in a shroud with aromatic spices, "as Joseph of Arimathea and Nicodemus had done with the body of the Lord, as the Shroud shows."[1]

While the persecutions raged around them during the first three centuries, the Christian community jealously guarded the relics of the martyrs and it is logical to think that the greatest veneration and care would have been reserved for the funeral Shroud of Christ. But where could the nascent Church safely send the Shroud?

The Journey to Edessa

J.B. Segal wrote a classic book entitled *Edessa: The Blessed City*.[2] He describes this great metropolis and its colorful history as a jewel in the Byzantine Empire. Byzantium, later called

Constantinople and now Istanbul, was the capital of the ancient Byzantine Empire covering most of what is now modern Turkey. Ancient Edessa (modern Urfa) was a city about 400 miles north of Jerusalem. At that time, Edessa was within the Roman Province of Osrhoene and on the outskirts of the Roman Empire. As such, it was close to the borders of the Parthian (Persian) Empire to the East — basically modern Iraq and Iran. Edessa was a cosmopolitan city that became the seat of an early Christian community similar to the one in Antioch, between Edessa and Jerusalem. Many early Jews-turned-Christian fled from the persecution in Palestine and settled in other cities such as Antioch and Edessa, especially after the Romans laid siege to Jerusalem in 70 A.D.

What rationale may have prompted Peter and the Apostles to send the Shroud for safe-keeping to Edessa? Interestingly, science confirms the presence of the Shroud in Edessa, as noted in Chapter Two. Dr. Max Frei found pollen from both the Dead Sea area of Jerusalem and from the area of Edessa, Constantinople and Europe. This find was independent, but supports the historians in saying that Edessa was the home of the Shroud for many centuries. What, therefore, is the historical rationale for believing that the Shroud moved to Edessa? Ancient Edessa was located in the Syria of New Testament times. There was considerable interaction between the Syrians and the inhabitants of Palestine.

Matthew 4:24-25 tells us that "News of Him (Jesus) went out through all Syria, and they brought Him all who were sick with various diseases and were suffering torments — the demon-possessed, epileptics, paralytics — and He healed them." Josephus, the early Jewish historian, talks of close contact between Jerusalem and the Jewish inhabitants of northern Mesopotamia.[3] Mesopotamia (literally the delta between two rivers, the Tigris and the Euphrates) was near Edessa.

We know from early sources that there were trade routes between Edessa, Antioch, Jerusalem and Egypt. Ananias, the courier for King Abgar in Edessa, visited the Praetor of Egypt on King Abgar's behalf. These caravan routes linked these great cities and travelers would have heard the stories of Jesus and inquired on their journeys. Therefore, Edessa was not an unlikely place to send the Shroud for safe haven. And, indeed, the strength of the evidence from early literary sources indicates that Edessa did become the home of the Shroud for many centuries (from approximately 40 to 944 A.D.).

Legend of King Abgar

The fact that Edessa was a logical and credible place to bring the Shroud does not necessarily mean that it was, in fact, brought there. However, support for Edessa as the home of the Shroud comes from the persistent legends about Abgar that appear in the early Christian literature. King Abgar V Ouchama (the Dark) was King of Edessa from about 13-50 A.D. during Jesus' life on earth while He ministered in Palestine. King Abgar had heard about the activities of Jesus curing the sick and he himself was suffering from leprosy. The legend relates that Abgar sent a letter to Jesus and sent Ananias, his emissary, to Jesus to encourage Him to come to Edessa. The legend, which has several variations, maintains that Jesus sent word back to King Abgar that, after His death, He would send someone to Edessa to cure Abgar. After Jesus' passion, death and resurrection, Thaddaeus (called Addai in Syrian), a disciple, was sent by Thomas the Apostle to cure the King of leprosy and to establish the Church in Edessa.

Eusebius the Historian

The legends first appear in the writings of an early and famed historian of the Church, Eusebius of Caesarea. In his *Ecclesiastical History* written about 320-325,[4] Eusebius uses a Syrian text from the Edessa archives and speaks of the letter

Abgar sent to Jesus. He tells us that Abgar was wasting away with an incurable disease and he heard about Jesus and His miracles. He then sent a letter carrier, Ananias, to Jesus asking for delivery from his disease. Eusebius mentions that Thomas sent Thaddaeus to Edessa who healed Abgar of his leprosy and founded the Church in Edessa.

Egeria, a pilgrim to Edessa in 384, mentions that the bishop of the city, in showing her the places of interest in Edessa, took her to the gate which Ananias entered bearing the letter of Jesus. No mention is made, however, of any image of the Lord. Possibly it had been hidden away on account of the persecutions of the first three centuries and memory of it had faded with time.

Cambridge classical historian Steven Runciman in his noted article on "The Image of Edessa" (now believed to be identical with the Shroud of Turin) tells us that: "Historians should not be so much victims to their skepticism as to dismiss a legend as false unless they can suggest how it was that the false legend arose. It is easy to show that the story of Abgar and Jesus as we now have it is untrue, and that the letter contains certain phrases copied from the Gospels and are framed according to the dictates of later theology. But that does not necessarily invalidate the tradition on which the story was based."[5] This is particularly true since the legend persisted for almost a thousand years and is contained in several documents. It is apparent that some type of communication existed between Jesus and King Abgar and that some sort of "portrait" was involved. This is the kernel of the story that will be pursued.

The Core of the Abgar Legend

Eusebius does not mention any portrait, but several authors suggest that Eusebius deliberately suppressed any such mention in his text since he was opposed to images as idolatrous. An image is, however, mentioned by later authors and it became known as the Image of Edessa. We have in Eusebius the beginnings of the Abgar Legend, a persistent legend of the early Church that Abgar knew and communicated with Jesus; that the Apostle Thomas, after Jesus' death, sent Thaddaeus to Abgar to cure him, and initiate the Church in Edessa; and that a "portrait" of Jesus was brought to Edessa that came, over time, to be considered as divinely-wrought.

Edessa — The Likely Place

Given the persecution of the early Church in Jerusalem and the likelihood that the Shroud needed to find safe haven outside Palestine; given the link between Jerusalem and Syria and the early Christian community in Edessa; given the persistence of the Abgar Legend suggesting that a "portrait" did exist in Edessa for centuries called the Image of Edessa, or *acheiropoietas* (image not made by human hands); given the scientific findings of Dr. Max Frei that pollen on the Shroud came from the area around Edessa during this early period; and given Ian Wilson's correlation (to be discussed further on) between the Image of Edessa rediscovered in Edessa in 524-544 and the artistic revolution that followed this rediscovery, the case is strong that the Shroud did indeed move to Edessa and was in fact one and the same with the Image of Edessa and the Mandylion of later Byzantine literature.

The Doctrine of Addai

Somewhere in the latter part of the fourth century (350-400) another Syrian text appears called the *Doctrine of Addai*. Addai is the Syrian name for the disciple Thaddaeus. The Abgar Legend reappears, but now we find mention of a portrait that Ananias "painted" of Jesus along with mention of a letter which Abgar had written to Jesus. In this document, Jesus gives a verbal response to Abgar. The document relates that "Ananias... took and painted the portrait of Jesus with choice pigments."[6] It is the first mention of the "portrait" in Edessa and reiterates that Thomas sent Thaddaeus to Edessa to cure him.

Acts of the Holy Apostle Thaddaeus

In the early sixth century, a document called the *Acts of the Holy Apostle Thaddaeus* again recalls the Legend of Abgar. This document is quite important since it repeats the Abgar Legend and expands on it by introducing another major clue in the early literature: namely, the *Tetradiplon*. The text reads:

> And Ananias, having gone and given the letter, was carefully looking at Christ, but was unable to fix Him in his mind. And He (Jesus) knew as knowing the heart and asked to wash Himself, and a towel (Greek: *tetradiplon*) was given to Him and when He had washed Himself, He wiped His face with it. And His image having been imprinted upon the linen, He gave it to Ananias, saying "Give this, and take back this message to him that sent thee (Abgar): Peace be to thee and to thy city."[7]

The basic rudiments of the Legend are repeated. But now a mysterious image on cloth (linen) is introduced, an image of Jesus and it is called a *tetradiplon*. The image is elevated from a "painting" to a "mysterious image on linen cloth" imprinted by Jesus when wiping His face with a towel (*tetradiplon*). It appears that in the earliest legends, the Shroud may have been considered initially as a "painting" by those who could not understand the images, but came to be recognized as an image of Jesus not-made-by-human-hands and began to be elevated to a "mysterious image" and later to a divinely wrought image. But attention is called now to this new word *tetradiplon* that carries a vital clue to the later identification of the Image of Edessa and the Shroud.

The Tetradiplon

The word "towel" used in the text intrigues Shroud historians because the literal translation of the Greek word used (*tetradiplon*) means doubled-in-four. *Tetradiplon* is an unusual Greek work lending credibility to the contention that this was a full-length linen cloth folded to show only the face (otherwise called the Image of Edessa) in a horizontal, or landscape form (width greater than height), rather than the normal vertical or portrait form (height greater than width) utilized by artists when painting a face. Such a horizontal versus vertical image-on-cloth lends credence to the image being a burial cloth. An artist would likely have worked on a vertical plane and not likely on linen cloth. The term "Mandylion" (little towel) was, it appears, used later on as a reference to this smaller, folded cloth-image. According to Professor Lampe of Cambridge University and editor of the *Lexicon of Patristic Greek*, the word *tetradiplon* is found only twice in Greek Byzantine literature — both times in reference to this linen cloth. The second example is from the tenth century *Monthly Lection* written in the year 945. In this text we read that after Jesus had washed, "there was given to Him a piece of cloth folded four times (*rhakos tetradiplon*) and after washing, He imprinted on it His undefiled and divine face."

Ian Wilson describes the process to mean doubled, then redoubled, then doubled again, i.e., doubling three times that has the effect of "doubling-in-four," producing 8 sections. As he points out, when folded in this manner the result is unmistakable. "The face alone appears, disembodied on a landscape aspect background in a manner of the most striking similarity to the early artist's copies of the Image of Edessa."[8] This also helps explain why some authors refer only to the face of

Jesus on cloth and others to His full body image. Most saw only the face of the folded Shroud (Image of Edessa or Mandylion) and were not ordinarily permitted to see the cloth stretched out. This would make sense in that a 14' cloth would be far more manageable if folded.

The Tetradiplon (or) Doubled-in-Four

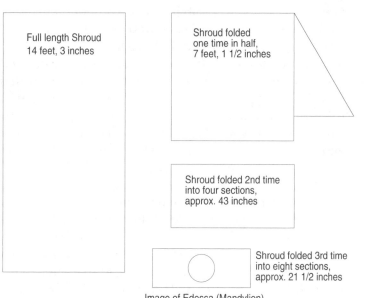

Full length Shroud
14 feet, 3 inches

Shroud folded
one time in half,
7 feet, 1 1/2 inches

Shroud folded 2nd time
into four sections,
approx. 43 inches

Shroud folded 3rd time
into eight sections,
approx. 21 1/2 inches

Image of Edessa (Mandylion)
Face of the Shroud of Turin

Above figure prepared by John C. Iannone from descriptions of the tetradiplon.

Tetradiplon is a unique Byzantine word found only two times — both in reference to the Image of Edessa. It means doubled-in-four. The cloth was folded three times creating eight sections and seven fold marks. This would leave only the facial image of Jesus appearing disembodied. The facial image appears on a horizontal or landscape surface (wider rather than higher). If this were only a portrait of the head created by an artist, the artist would likely have worked on a vertical or portrait surface where height exceeds width.

The Image of Edessa (archeiropoeitos or image-not-made-by-human-hands) was described by writers of the Court of Constantine Porphyrogenitus in 945 AD as brought to Constantinople in a "casket" or "container." It was fastened to a board and embellished with gold. Later records pointed out by Noel Currer-Briggs show the Shroud stretched taut, with a fringe and often with a curious trellis pattern. The trelliswork was later identified with the Holy Grail (Shroud container).

The Raking-Light Test of Dr. John Jackson

A fascinating link between the Shroud and the *tetradiplon* comes from the scientific tests performed in 1978 in Turin by the S.T.U.R.P. team. One of these tests performed by Dr. John Jackson, a physicist then stationed at the Air Force Academy in Colorado and now founder along with his wife Rebecca of the Turin Shroud Center of Colorado, was called the "raking-light" test and utilized high magnification. To his surprise, the raking-light test and the use of high magnification verified fold marks on the Shroud corresponding exactly to what would have appeared if the Shroud was "doubled-in-four" when it was hidden away in the walls of Edessa. This enhances the credibility that the Image of Edessa and the Shroud of Turin are one and the same cloth.[9]

The Image, Lost and Found

The Image of Edessa, which Ian Wilson came to identify as the Shroud, had been sealed up for protection in the walls around the city of Edessa to save it from the persecution launched by the grandson of King Abgar. We learn this from later Byzantine authors. It remained sealed for several centuries until somewhere between 525-544, when it was rediscovered. The rediscovery happened allegedly during an attack on Edessa by the Persian King Chosroes. Steven Runciman tells us that during the attack in 544, the Persians built a fortification to scale the walls of Edessa. The Edessans, in turn, dug a tunnel to attempt to set fire to the wooden fortifications of the Persians from below the ground and, while tunneling, found the Image of Edessa.[10] Wilson quotes Procopius of Caesarea, the historian of the period who, in his work *On the Persian Wars*, tells us:

> In 540 King Chosroes I of Persia had declared war on the (Roman) Empire; and in 544 he advanced in full force

into Mesopotamia and laid siege to Edessa. The walls of Edessa were tall and strong, but the Persians built a huge tower to overtop them; whence from their great number they could swamp the garrison. But before the tower was completed, the defenders burrowed underneath it, made a chamber and filled it with highly flammable material and set it ablaze....[11]

Wilson believes the rediscovery may have been a bit earlier possibly around 525, and he links the rediscovery with the famous flood of Edessa. In 525 the river flooded and severely damaged the walls of Edessa. During the repair of the walls, Wilson believes the Icon (the Image of Edessa) was rediscovered. He tells us: "The Bishop Eulalius went prayerfully to the spot, made a thorough search and found this sacred image intact."[12] While the historians disagree on the exact date of the rediscovery, they do agree that a rediscovery took place between 525-544. Wilson notes that the Emperor Justinian I dispatched engineers to Edessa in 525 to divert the river to prevent future floods. The Emperor also commissioned the construction of a beautiful shrine for the Icon, the Cathedral of Hagia Sophia in Edessa, which became home to the Image of Edessa until 944.

The Changing Image of Jesus

Wilson describes at length the impact of this rediscovery on the art of the period. Prior to the rediscovery, the common images of Jesus were of *a young, beardless, Apollo-like man with short hair pictured usually in profile. Jesus was most often depicted as a Shepherd and Teacher. The themes were mostly of the risen glorified Christ.* Wilson tells us that after the rediscovery of the Image of Edessa, Christian art takes a radical turn. Jesus' images in art appear remarkably similar to that of the Shroud of Turin, with Jesus as *a bearded man with long hair, pictured fron-*

tally. He notes particularly the front of the Image as a full facial Image. The rediscovery and its impact on Eastern and Western art will be discussed in Chapter Eight. Wilson is credited with making the brilliant link between the Image of Edessa, the Mandylion and the Shroud of Turin as being one and the same.

Ecclesiastical History of Evagrius

In 590, Evagrius Scholasticus became Bishop of Edessa. He wrote an *Ecclesiastical History* wherein he recalls the Legend of Abgar and states that Edessa was protected by an Icon, a divinely wrought portrait: "They bring the divinely wrought image which hands did not form, but which Christ our Lord sent to Abgar on his desiring to see Him...."[13] The Image, now recognized as a "divinely wrought portrait," was kept in the Cathedral of Hagia Sophia in Edessa and remained there until the year 944. Over the next few centuries prior to the movement of the Image to Constantinople, we find a number of other isolated texts that provide further clues to the Shroud's existence and presence in Edessa. For example, between 635-651, Braulio, Bishop of Saragossa (Spain) in his Epistle 42 says: "It is possible that many things happened then which have not been written down, just as we read of the linen cloths and the Shroud in which the body of Christ was wrapped, that they were found, yet we do not hear that they were preserved; still I do not suppose that the Apostles neglected to save these...."[14] During the 8th and 9th centuries, the Image of Edessa was often cited as an authoritative example in defense of the use of sacred images in church against the iconoclasts by such notables as Andrew of Crete, St. John Damascene, Pope Gregory II, Patriarchs Germanus I and Nicephorus, John of Jerusalem, James of Antioch and Basil of Jerusalem.

The *Himation* of St. John Damascene

In 730, St. John Damascene, a Syrian Christian, in his work *On Holy Images* says: "A tradition has come down to us that Abgar, King of Edessa, was drawn vehemently to divine love by hearing of our Lord, and that he sent envoys to ask for His likeness. If this were refused, they were ordered to have a likeness painted. Then He, who is All-knowing and All-powerful, is said to have taken a strip of cloth and left His likeness upon the cloth, which it retains to this day."[15] We call attention to the strip of cloth (*himation* in Greek). The Greek scholar Henry George Liddell in his *Greek-English Lexicon* defines a *himation* as "a piece of dress; in usage always as an outer garment, formed by an oblong piece of cloth." Further on, he relates it to a "Roman toga" and grave cloths. His definition suggests a large piece of linen (*sindon*) like the Shroud.[16] In 769, in his *Good Friday Sermon*, Pope Stephen III says:

> He stretched His whole body on a cloth, white as snow, on which the glorious image of the Lord's face and the length of His whole body was so divinely transformed that it was sufficient for those who could not see the Lord bodily in the flesh to see the transfiguration made on the cloth.[17]

Wilson, who brought this quote to light from Ernst von Dobschütz' monumental work *Christusbilder*, goes on to say that the "Byzantines... devised a super-Mass for special private showings, in which the figure of Christ was made to rise in a series of stages from the casket, each stage being regarded as a symbolic part of Jesus' earthly life... at the first hour of the day as a child, at the third hour as a boy, at the sixth hour as an adolescent, and at the ninth hour in his full manhood, in which form the Son of God went to his Passion when he bore for our sins the suffering of the Cross."

Implied here is a full-length cloth with a full-length image. In 800, the Latin Abgar Legend translated by Ernst von Dobschütz in *Christusbilder* quotes Jesus as saying: "But if you wish to see my face in the flesh, behold I send to you a linen, on which you will discover not only the features of my face, but a divinely copied configuration of my entire body." Also, "He... spread out His entire body on a linen cloth that was white as snow. On this cloth... the majestic form of His whole body was divinely transferred."[18] Again, reference is made to a full-length image presumably on a full-length cloth made of linen. The facial image of the Image of Edessa was likely opened up to reveal the entire body image on a linen cloth.

The Second Council of Nicea (787), ruling in favor of the veneration of icons, mentioned the Image of Edessa, "the one 'not made by human hands' that was sent to Abgar." The Council went on to say that "one can and one must be free to use images of our Lord and God, in mosaics, paintings, etc." and that "the icon must be an image that bears a very close resemblance to its prototype," presumably the Image of Edessa.

The Image Moves to Constantinople

Constantinople was the seat of the Byzantine Empire and the Greek Church for over 1,000 years until the Ottoman Turks captured it and renamed it Istanbul in the middle of the fifteenth century. Constantinople had been built by the Roman Emperor Constantine the Great around 325 and became the eastern seat of the Roman Empire, an impressive city envied by the Western world. The Emperor ruled from the Bucholeon Palace. Many of the relics of the Crucifixion were kept there, including such things as the cap of thorns and pieces of the Holy Cross. But for centuries, the Emperors wanted to bring the Image of Edessa from the city of Edessa to Constantinople. Dr. Max Frei relates that he found pollen from the area around Istanbul on the Shroud and this corroborates information we learn from Byzantine texts about the movement to Constantinople of the Image of Edessa and its identification with the Shroud.

On August 15, 944, the Byzantine army moved the Image of Edessa with great fanfare from Edessa to Constantinople. A manuscript called the *Narration on the Image of Edessa* describes in some detail how an "image not made by man (*acheiropoietas*) of Christ our God was transferred to Constantinople." It has "an impression of God's assumed human form by a moist secretion without coloring or painter's art. An impression of the face was made in the linen cloth." (The colors of the Shroud have often been described in this fashion.)

Out of Sight, Out of Mind

The image was brought to Constantinople with great fanfare and set-up in the Pharos Chapel.[19] Attention is drawn to the notation made by writers of the time in Constantinople that the Image had disappeared for a long time from men's minds. The image had been walled up for approximately 475 years. One Shroud student, Herbert Hall, made the astute observation of the fact that the earlier authors spoke of a cloth made by Jesus during His ministry on earth, and did not refer specifically to His passion and death. However, along with the disappearance from men's memories was the loss of association of the Image with the full-length burial cloth since only the facial image was showing when the cloth was sealed up in the walls of Edessa. This likely accounts for the fact that the earlier writers of the fourth and fifth centuries such as Eusebius and Evagrius, not being familiar with the actual full-length cloth with marks of the passion and death, heard of the Image and assumed it was an Image created by Jesus during His ministry. With time, as the full length of the cloth was revealed and signs of the passion were rediscovered, the real nature of the Image of Edessa as the full-length burial Shroud was reestablished.

The Great Bucholeon Palace

The Bucholeon Palace, also called the Great Palace, was a magnificent place, virtually a small city, within Constantinople begun by the Emperor Constantine the Great when he moved the center of the Roman Empire from Rome to Constantinople in the period shortly after 325. The Byzantine Emperors ruled the Eastern Empire from the Great Palace, a sumptuous complex on the water overlooking the Straits called the Golden Horn. The fourth century historian and biographer of Constantine, Eusebius, in his *Ecclesiastical History*, Book IV, 17 enumerates seven structures of the Bucholeon Palace which Constantine the Great built. The Palace was later enlarged by Justinian in 527-565 and was further built up by Justin II between 565-578 when he added the Christotriclinos. In 750, Constantine V Copronymos added the Pharos Chapel, which was completed by Michael III around 865.

The Pharos Chapel

The Pharos Chapel was a sumptuous chapel located within the Bucholeon Palace where the tenth century writers tell us the Image of Edessa was kept after being brought from Edessa to Constantinople in 944. The term "Pharos" in ancient Greek referred to "a large piece of cloth... wide cloak or mantle without sleeves... used as a shroud or pall."[20] Henry George Liddell, in his famous *Greek-English Lexicon* of 1887 points out that the word is used this way in Homer's *Iliad*. The naming of the Chapel after the burial cloth of Jesus would seem to indicate knowledge by the Emperor's people of the full length of the Shroud. The Image of Edessa was a facial image on a cloth doubled-in-four, which, when fully opened was the full length Shroud revealing the entire bodily images of Jesus. The Byzantine Greeks were steeped in the traditions of classical Greece and would have been familiar with Homer's use of this term.

However, it must be pointed out that Shroud author Dr. Daniel C. Scavone, History Professor at the University of Southern Indiana, maintains that the Pharos Chapel was named after the famous lighthouse in the waters off the Palace (see *Shroud News*, No. 61, October 1990). Scavone indicates that Pharos in that period (tenth century) also meant "lighthouse" and the term "*ho pharos*" applied to the lighthouse in Constantinople has been assumed to derive from "*he Pharos*," the famous lighthouse of Alexandria. He notes that twentieth century Byzantine historians Ebersolt and Janin have agreed, based on medieval Byzantine sources, that the Pharos was on the very terrace upon whose seaward extension sits the lighthouse known as the Pharos. Professor Scavone's case is supported by the fact that the Chapel was constructed between 750 and 865 when the Shroud (Image of Edessa) is known to have been in Edessa (until 944).

While Dr. Scavone presents a plausible case for Pharos as lighthouse versus Pharos as burial cloth, it is still difficult to understand why such an important and sumptuous Chapel containing alleged relics of the Crucifixion would be named after a lighthouse. This is puzzling, even allowing that the lighthouse played an important role in the historical and economic life of the city and served as a beacon for ships and as a source for fire-lights relaying messages between the Asiatic provinces as Scavone points out. It is also difficult to accept as purely a coincidence that a Greek people familiar with Homer's use of this term would, by pure coincidence, name the chapel after a lighthouse and then locate the burial cloth within. One would need to investigate whether there are other precedents in Constantinople for great chapels or churches being named after secular landmarks. For now, we will leave it to further research to determine the relationship between Pharos as lighthouse or as representing the fact that the Image of Edessa was placed in this Chapel.

Tetradiplon — a Second Reference

On the occasion of the first anniversary of the arrival of the Shroud in Constantinople, a liturgical homily was delivered called the *Monthly Lection* found in the *Festival of Sources.* In it the authors relate: "After Jesus had washed, there was given to Him a piece of cloth folded four times (*rhakos tetradiplon*). And after washing, He imprinted on it His undefiled and divine face."[21] Here, the authors refer only to the facial image. However, reference is made again to the unusual Greek term *tetradiplon* noted earlier as doubled-in-four and to the fold-marks found on the Shroud, supporting the contention that the Image of Edessa (a divinely wrought facial image on linen cloth) was the folded Shroud of Turin and mounted in such a manner as to manage the 14-foot cloth.

Atlanta sindonologist Rev. Albert Dreisbach pointed out to me that Gregory the Archdeacon of the Hagia Sophia, the magnificent Cathedral in Constantinople, in a sermon of August 16, 944 (MS. Vatican Graec. 511 folio 149 Verso translated by Professor Gino Zanninotto), referred to the "blood and water from the side wound of the cloth" clearly suggesting that a full-length Shroud was known and was not just a facial image. The Byzantine authors clearly understood that this Image of Edessa was in fact a full-length Shroud containing images of the Crucifixion.[22] During that same period, the Emperor Romanus Lacapenus and his two sons along with Constantine (the new Emperor) had a private showing of the new relic by candlelight. Constantine says: "As for the cause of the image, it is rather a moist secretion without colors or the art of a painting." Those who have directly studied the cloth point out that this matches their impressions. The image appears to disappear as one gets closer to the cloth.

The Mandylion

Reference has been made several times to the term "Mandylion," which means "little towel," and appears frequently in the Byzantine texts. Wilson has identified the Mandylion with the folded Image of Edessa and with the full-length Shroud of Turin and indicates that all three are one and the same. The term "Mandylion" appears first in the biography of the ascetic Paul of Mt. Latros around 990. "Paul, without ever leaving Mt. Latros was granted a miraculous vision of the 'Icon of Christ' not-made-by-hands which is commonly called the 'Holy Mandylion.'"[23] Ian Wilson provides the reasoning that links the Image of Edessa with the Mandylion and with the Shroud. He provides a list:

> The Mandylion is referred to as the *acheiropoietas,* or "image not made by human hands."
> It appears on a linen cloth.
> Those who view it think it was formed by a moist secretion.
> It is dim and difficult to perceive.
> It contains bloodstains.
> Its color is off-white or ivory.
> It is mounted and framed on a board embellished with gold (Note: the paintings show a trellis-like case). The shape of the Mandylion is a horizontal rectangle of the face versus the normal artist's upright vertical rectangle normal for a portrait.
> The encasement is like a slipcover or jacket embroidered with a trellis or net pattern in gold thread... fringe tacked to a board. We know that the Shroud image was folded and tightly packed against a board. It is referred to as a *tetradiplon* (doubled-in-four).[24]

Chart Tracing the Evolution of the King Abgar Legend in Byzantine Texts

SOURCE	LEGEND
Eusebius of Caesarea *Ecclesiastical History* (320-325)	Letter of Abgar to Jesus in Edessa archives asking Jesus to come to Edessa to cure Abgar of leprosy. The Apostle Thomas sends Jude Thaddeus (Addai).
Doctrine of Addai (Thaddeus, ca. 375-400)	Mentions portrait that Ananias painted of Jesus "...with choice pigments."
Acts of the Holy Apostle Thaddaeus (ca. 510-540)	Jesus wipes His face on a towel and imprints His image. It becomes known, not as a painting, but as an image imprinted on cloth, specifically a towel doubled-in-four, or *tetradiplon*.
Evagrius Scholasticus *Ecclesiastical History* (ca. 590)	Edessa is protected by a "divinely wrought portrait" or *acheiropoietos* which Jesus sent to Abgar.
St. John Damascene *On Holy Images* (ca. 730)	Jesus leaves His image on a strip of cloth (*himation*) defined as an oblong or grave cloth.
Narration on the Image of Edessa (ca. 944)	Cloth described as an *acheiropoietos*, "an impression of God's assumed Human Form," a "moist secretion without coloring or painter's art... made on linen cloth."

Conclusion

In the first thousand years, the historical and liturgical texts refer to the Image of Edessa and to the Mandylion with descriptions of both facial and full-length images of Jesus Christ on linen cloth. The texts speak of a cloth "doubled-in-four" or *tetradiplon* with fold marks matching those of the Shroud and indicate that the Image of Edessa and the Mandylion both refer to the top or facial image of the full-length cloth hidden under the trellised frame. The authors speak of a cloth "not made by human hands" (*acheiropoietas*) being placed in the Pharos Chapel, which recalls the Homeric Greek word for a burial cloth. Such references show us clearly that this ancient cloth was well known to the people of the Byzantine Empire. The historical texts, when combined with Dr. Max Frei's identification of pollen on the Shroud matching those of Edessa and Constantinople and requiring exposure of the Shroud for a long length of time in these areas, lend corroborating scientific evidence of the Shroud's historical journey from Jerusalem (33-50) to Edessa (50-944) to Constantinople (944-1204). Such texts further support the theory that the Image of Edessa, Mandylion and Shroud of Turin are one and the same. Simultaneously, they provide evidence of the Shroud's existence well before the medieval dates provided by the Carbon-14 testing of 1988. As Professor Daniel Scavone stated in an article of October 13, 1995:

> No unbroken certification of ownership or provenance exists that would prove the authenticity of the Turin Shroud as Jesus' burial cloth — or even as contemporaneous with Jesus. Still, the documents taken together comprise a fine thread of continuity through a labyrinthine history. This thread is broken at times, but research has shortened the lacunae and the ends of the thread leading backward to the first century and forward to 1355 may all someday be reattached.

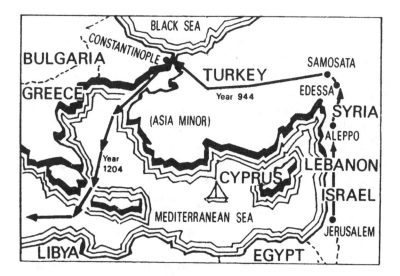

CHAPTER SEVEN

The Journey Continues:
The Second Thousand Years

*There exists "a cloth on which the image not only of my face
but of my whole body has been divinely transformed."*

Roman Codex 1130

The Emergence of Lamentation Scenes

By the year 944, the Image of Edessa, which we now identify as the Shroud, was transported to Constantinople and located in the beautiful Chapel of the Pharos — a long sought
prize for the Byzantine Emperor and the Eastern Church. But
knowledge of the Shroud's existence and whereabouts began
to spread to the West. In the eleventh century, we note the
appearance of Lamentation Scenes (called *Threnos*). The late
art historian Kurt Weitzmann told us that in both the East and
West, scenes emerge in art in which the body of Christ is lying in front of the Cross as the central figure.[1] Ian Wilson notes
that, common to all these lamentation scenes is a long white
cloth "obviously intended to envelop the body over the head,
a cloth we would unhesitatingly identify as a Shroud."[2] History
Professor Daniel Scavone points out the new artistic theme of
Jesus dead with hands folded as on the Shroud of Turin, lying upon a large white burial sheet.[3]

Western References

In 1080 Alexis I Comnenus of Constantinople sought the aid of the Emperor Henry IV and Robert of Flanders, in defending the relics which were kept in that city, especially "the cloth found in the sepulcher after the resurrection." And in Roman Codex No. 5696 of 1130 we read of "a cloth on which the image not only of my face but of my whole body has been divinely transformed."[4] In 1142, Orderic Vitalis, an English monk, wrote in his *Ecclesiastical History* that "Abgar, Toparch of Edessa, reigned there, to whom the Lord Jesus sent a sacred letter and the precious napkin with which He had wiped the sweat from His face and on which the image of our Savior Himself is miraculously preserved, which shows the lineaments and proportions of the divine body to the beholders."[5] The phrase "lineaments and proportions of the divine body" implies a full-length cloth with image. In 1147 King Louis VII of France venerated the Shroud in Constantinople and in 1157, Nicholas Soemundarson, an Icelandic Abbot, listing the relics of Constantinople, talks of both "linen bands with the sweat cloth" (*sveitakuk*) and a *maetull*, which scholars identified as the Mandylion (or little towel).[6]

Visit of King Amalric I to Constantinople

The noted medieval historian William of Tyre relates an incident in which King Amalric I of Jerusalem during the period of the Crusades paid a visit to the Emperor Manuel I Comnenus of Constantinople in 1171. At that time, the Eastern half of the Byzantine Empire was under threat from the Moslems who already occupied the Holy Land and Jerusalem since 638. The Western Church initiated the Crusades to drive "the infidels" from the Holy Land, and Amalric, a French nobleman, was named King of Jerusalem during this early period. The Byzantine Emperor saw the political advantage of remaining close to the Crusaders for protection of the Empire's eastern borders from the Saracen invaders, and offered the hand of his daughter in marriage to King Amalric, who then visited the Emperor in Constantinople. The writers of the period tell us that the King and his entourage were received with great pomp and circumstance.

King Amalric was accompanied by Philip de Milly (Grand Master of the Knights Templar) and others. More will be said shortly about the significance of the Knights Templar and the impact of this visit on future events relating to the Shroud. The King and his entourage stayed at the sumptuous Bucholeon Palace and visited the Pharos Chapel. The Emperor, in a rare move, ordered all relics of saints to be exposed as well as the "most precious evidence of the Passion of our Lord, namely the Cross, Nails, Lance, Sponge, Reed, Crown of Thorns, *Sindon* (that is, the cloth in which He was wrapped) and the Sandals."[7]

This is the first time, to our knowledge, that dignitaries of the West were introduced directly to the Shroud and the many treasures of the Eastern Church. It is possible, and even probable in this author's opinion, that this visit triggered the sequence of events among Western plotters that led eventually to the diversion of the Fourth Crusade to Constantinople — a temporary occupation of Constantinople which permitted Western Crusaders to barbarously attack and plunder the treasures of the Eastern Church and remove the Shroud to the West. Philip de Milly may have been instrumental in this plot since he accompanied King Amalric. The Knights Templar may have been involved in the attack on Constantinople and appear deeply implicated in the movement of the Shroud after the fall of Constantinople.

The Quest for the Holy Grail

Genealogist and Shroud/Grail historian Noel Currer-Briggs makes the intriguing case that the introduction of Western dignitaries to the relics of the East during the visit of King Amalric I marks the beginning of the Holy Grail legends. Currer-Briggs speculates that William of Tyre, the historian documenting the visit, told Walter Map at the Lateran Council in 1179, who in turn brought the story back to France. In 1180, Chretien de Troyes wrote his famous *Perceval: The Story of the Holy Grail* (*Conte del Graal*) at the request of Philip of Alsace, Count of Flanders and relative of King Amalric I. This is the first mention of the Grail in Western literature. Currer-Briggs points out that *the original Grail stories considered the Grail to be a receptacle for the Shroud. Somehow, the Grail contained the precious blood of Jesus.* As the story evolved and changed over the years, this receptacle became identified as a chalice containing the precious blood. But the earliest legends show that it was not a chalice, but rather the Shroud that contained the blood, the Grail being the receptacle for the Cloth.[8]

There appears to be a telltale link between the early Holy Grail legends and the appearance of the Shroud in Athens and Europe. In 1204, Helinand, Abbot of Froidmont, a Cistercian Abbey north of Paris, wrote of "the stories of the most holy vessel called the Grail into which the precious blood of the Savior was received on the day He was crucified to save mankind from hell..."[9] Currer-Briggs tells us that the Abbot used the word *gradalis* for Grail (a shallow dish) and *scutella lata* (dish, saucer, flat or broad bowl) referring to the receptacle in which the Shroud, containing the blood of Jesus, was placed for storage and veneration.

The Sacristan of the Pharos Chapel

In 1201, Nicholas Mesarites, the Sacristan and Keeper of the Relics for the Pharos Chapel wrote: "Here He rises again, and the *sindon* with the burial linens is the clear proof... they are of linen... still smelling fragrant of perfumes, defying corruption because they wrapped the mysterious naked dead body from head to feet."[10] Here again is a full-length cloth, and attention is drawn to the fact that the body was naked.

The Fourth Crusade and the Fall of Constantinople

One of the most ignominious episodes in Christian history, East or West, involves the attack on Constantinople by the Fourth Crusade in 1204. Constantinople was the jewel of the Eastern world, and home of the Eastern Byzantine Church. The Great Schism divided the Eastern Church from the Western Church and Rome. The Byzantine Emperors had collected over the centuries many relics, allegedly authentic, including the Shroud, and brought them to this great city. Constantinople was replete with churches, including the famed Hagia Sophia and the Bucholeon Palace which contained the Pharos Chapel, and the Palace of the Blachernae. The Western Church, after the visit by King Amalric I in 1171 with Philip de Milly, Grand Master of the Knights Templar, became acutely aware of the many treasures contained in Constantinople and, being perhaps jealous of its wealth and might, looked for an opportunity to plunder Constantinople's great resources, including the relics. This opportunity came in 1204.[11]

France and Venice — A Treacherous Alliance is Formed

Several chroniclers of the period, including Robert de Clary and Geoffrey de Villehardouin from the West and Nicetas Cholates of the East, related the tragic events of this period. The Fourth Crusade was organized in Europe under the guidance of Pope Innocent III and Philip II, King of France, to go to the Holy Land. Their mission was to defend the Western pilgrims and drive back the Moslems from Jerusalem. The reward, as Villehardouin relates it, was an indulgence: "All those who take the Cross and remain for one year in the service of God in the army shall obtain remission of any sins they have committed, provided they have confessed them. The hearts of the people were greatly moved by the generous terms of this indulgence and many on that account were moved to take the Cross."[12]

The Crusade leaders worked closely with the Venetians and reached a treaty in 1202 with Enrico Dandolo, the Doge of Venice, to build a fleet of vessels — warships and troop transports — capable of carrying the army, including knights and their horses, to Palestine. It was a monumental task. The Doge told the French emissaries: "We will build transports to carry 4,500 horses and 9,000 squires and other ships to accommodate 4,500 knights and 20,000 foot sergeants."[13] Also included were nine months of rations and fodder for all the horses. Shortly thereafter, the army chose its leader, the Marquis Boniface de Montferrat. Throughout France people prepared for this "pilgrimage." The Venetians did their job and created a great fleet. Villardhouin tells us that the "fleet they had got ready was so fine and well equipped that no man in the whole of Christendom has even seen one to surpass it. It comprised so great a number of warships, galleys and transports that it could easily have accommodated three times as many men as were in the whole of the army."[14]

The Fourth Crusade Diverts to Constantinople

For political reasons, the Crusade temporarily diverted to Constantinople. Emperor Isaac in Constantinople had been treacherously overthrown by his brother Alexis. Isaac escaped and went to Venice to meet with Boniface de Montferrat, the leader of the new army. Isaac made a deal that if he was restored to power in Constantinople, he would make available to Boniface and his army the vast resources of the Byzantine army to help in the Crusade to free Jerusalem. Apart from the East's desire to gain assistance in protecting its easternmost borders from the Moslems, and the West's desire to gain troops and resources to fight the "infidels" in the Holy Land, there was an underlying motive to help heal the rift created by the Great Schism between the Eastern and Western Churches. The Crusaders left for Constantinople in what was to be a temporary diversion to restore Isaac. But more sinister motives may have been involved on the part of the leaders. The Crusaders laid siege to Constantinople and ultimately forced Alexis to flee, restoring Isaac to the throne. However, Constantinople was to pay a terrible price for this temporary military occupation.

The 'Trojan Horse' of the Western Crusade had entered the gates of Constantinople! Many of these Crusaders were simple peasants from France and other parts of Europe and this crude army was overwhelmed by the riches and treasures of Constantinople, unmatched except perhaps by Rome. Villehardouin tells us that "many of our men, I may say, went to visit Constantinople to gaze at its many splendid palaces and tall churches, and view all the marvelous wealth of a city richer than any other since the beginning of time. As for the relics, they were beyond all description, for there were at that time as many in Constantinople as in all the rest of the world."[15]

Perhaps overcome with greed and desirous of possessing the precious relics of this city, especially the True Cross and the Holy Shroud, the leaders of the Fourth Crusade (Boniface de Montferrat, Otto de la Roche and Henri of Flanders) made the decision to attack and plunder Constantinople. Perhaps they were motivated with winning favor with Western Kings by bringing back such treasures. The story of this vicious attack is outlined by the chroniclers. The Crusaders set fire to Constantinople and, beside the great loss of life, destroyed forever many of the priceless treasures of Christendom, including many of the churches of Constantinople and their priceless works of art. Geoffrey de Villehardouin tell us that:

> The rest of the army, scattered throughout the City, also gained much booty; so much, indeed, that no one could estimate its amount or its value. It included gold and silver, table services and precious stone, satin and silk, mantles of squirrel fur, ermine and miniver and every choicest thing to be found on the earth... so much booty had never been gained in any city since the creation of the world.[16]

The leaders of the Crusade carefully secured the two great palaces. Marquis Boniface took the Bucholeon Palace with the Pharos Chapel and Henri of Flanders took the Palace of the Blachernae. The Shroud was in the Bucholeon Palace (Pharos Chapel).

The Shroud Disappears

Robert de Clary, who was part of the Fourth Crusade, wrote in his chronicle *The Conquest of Constantinople*:

> And among others there was another of the churches which was called My Lady Saint Mary Blachernae where was kept the *syndoine* in which our Lord had been wrapped, which stood up straight every Friday so that the *figure* of our Lord could be plainly seen. No one, either Greek or French even knew what became of the *syndoine* after the capture of the city.[17]

The *syndoine* was likely the *sindon* or Shroud. Dr. Peter Dembowski advised that in Old French, "figure" can be properly translated as "form or outline" of the body of our Lord.[18] The Shroud, normally housed in the Pharos Chapel, was taken by procession on Fridays to be displayed in the Church of Saint Mary Blachernae. Robert de Clary tells us that "the Marquis took possession of the Palace of Bucholeon and the Church of Saint Sophia (Hagia Sophia) and the houses of the patriarch. And the other high men, like the Counts, took possession of the richest palaces and richest abbeys to be found there."[19] He goes on to say that in this great palace with over five hundred halls made of gold mosaics there were some thirty chapels, great and small, and one of them was called the Pharos Chapel.

Within the chapel were two pieces of the True Cross, the iron lance that pierced Jesus' side, two nails, a phial with some of His blood, the tunic which He wore on His way to Calvary, the blessed Crown of Thorns and much more. Clary further related that there was still another relic hanging in a vessel — a cloth. Of the cloth, he says that "our Lord enveloped His face with it so that His features were imprinted on it."[20] Since the true *Sudarium* had no image and was likely in Oviedo, Spain, this was probably a copy on cloth of the face. The *syndoine* disappeared during this Crusade and was likely in the possession of the Marquis Boniface de Montferrat, leader of the Fourth Crusade and the individual who took personal command over the Pharos Chapel. But where did the Shroud go?

Interim Movement to Athens?

It appears that for a very short time, Boniface entrusted the Shroud to Otto de la Roche, his second-in-command. After the assault, Otto de la Roche was rewarded with the rule of Athens and Thessalonica. It is likely that he took the Shroud with him, based on information we read in a Letter to Pope Innocent III written by Theodore Ducas Angelos on August 1, 1205. Referring to the sack of Constantinople, Theodore states that:

> The Venetians partitioned the treasure of gold, silver and ivory, while the French did the same with the relics of the saints and most sacred of all, the linen in which our Lord Jesus Christ was wrapped after His death and before the Resurrection. We know that the sacred objects are preserved by their predators in Venice and France and in other places, the sacred linen in Athens.[21]

The Shroud was apparently kept in the Monastery at Daphni near the Parthenon. Three years later in 1207 Nicholas d'Orrante, Abbot of Casole and Papal Legate in Athens, listed the relics of the Passion that were "in the treasury of the great palace before the City (Constantinople) was taken by the French knights entering as robbers."[22] Speaking of the funerary cloths, he adds: "which we later saw with our own eyes" in Athens.

Somewhere between 1207 and 1357 the whereabouts of the Shroud becomes a mystery. We will jump ahead and consider its reappearance in 1357 and then attempt to solve the riddle of the Shroud's whereabouts for the prior 150 years.

Geoffrey II de Charny

In the year 1357, a French knight, Geoffrey II de Charny, displayed a cloth believed to be the Shroud at an exposition in a small church in Lirey, France, twelve miles from Troyes. This is the first documented public appearance of the Shroud in the West since the fall of Constantinople in 1204 and its brief respite in Athens. The Church of Lirey had been founded three years earlier by his father, Geoffrey I de Charny and his wife Jeanne de Vergy. Geoffrey I, who earned the title Porte

Oriflamme, was a famous decorated knight who died in battle three years later fighting alongside King John the Good. In the year of the exposition we find the famous Pilgrim's Medallion of Lirey, a medal minted specifically for the occasion of the exhibition showing shields with the arms of Geoffrey I de Charny and Jeanne de Vergy. His son, Geoffrey II with his (Geoffrey II's) daughter, Marguerite de Charny — having obtained permission from Pierre de Thury, Cardinal of Sainte-Suzanne and Papal Delegate to King Charles VI of France, but without having obtained permission from the local bishop — displayed the cloth at Lirey to the crowds.

Memorandum of Bishop d'Arcis

In the year 1389, Bishop d'Arcis wrote a letter to Pope Clement VII claiming that the cloth displayed by Geoffrey II de Charny during the tenure of Bishop Henry of Poitiers, his predecessor, was cunningly painted and that the artist had confessed. This purported Memorandum has been used by some to discredit the cloth of Geoffrey II de Charny as having been the Shroud. Scholars who have reviewed the Memorandum point out that the "artist" was never named, and that Bishop Henry of Poitiers did not object during the time of the exposition. French sindonologist Brother Bruno Bonnet-Eymard has convincingly demonstrated that the Memorandum was in fact proven to be an anonymous, unsigned, undated and unsealed paper copy, not at all consistent with official decrees by the Bishop. He also points out that the artist was never named, and that Pope Clement VII silenced the Bishop, even threatening him with excommunication. The Pope supported Geoffrey's exposition. Currer-Briggs notes the Shroud may have been confused with a painted copy known as the Besançon shroud.[23] Geoffrey II de Charny really believed the cloth he was exhibiting was more than just a painting. He presented the cloth with all the ritual and ceremony of a true relic.

Marguerite de Charny

Marguerite was the daughter of Geoffrey II and inherited the Shroud after his death. In 1443, the Canons of Lirey began to insist that the Shroud be returned to them. Marguerite ignored their demands and sought a more fitting home for it. In the year 1453 she signed a contract with the Duke of Savoy and passed title of the Shroud to the House of Savoy. In return, she received some land estates that would ensure her decent survival in old age. Duke Louis of Savoy represented the House of Savoy, which became the ruling family of Italy in the 19th century. As Frank Tribbe points out, Marguerite saw in the Duke and his wife a pious couple and a rising dynasty, wealthy and powerful enough to give security to the Shroud. The cloth remained with the Savoys until 1983 when King Umberto of Italy died and willed the Shroud to the Roman Catholic Church. Pope John Paul II left the Shroud in the Cathedral of Saint John the Baptist in Turin, Italy, where it remains today.

The Knights Templar and the Missing 150 Years

The Shroud, as was pointed out, disappeared from Constantinople in 1204 during the Fourth Crusade, and, notwithstanding a brief reference to its presence in Athens between 1204-1207, it basically remained in silence until its emergence in 1357 (150 years later) in Europe (Lirey, France) with Geoffrey II de Charny. What happened to the Shroud during this period?

The most prominent theory is that the Shroud was in the possession of the Knights Templar. But who were these mysterious Knights and what role might they have played in confiscating or protecting the Shroud from 1204 to 1357? The Templars were a military religious order founded in the Holy

Land in 1119 by Hugues de Payens during the Crusades. They were truly "warrior monks," religious Knights who believed in the medieval Christian ideal of death in battle. Saint Bernard of Clairvaux, a famous Cistercian monk who founded many Cistercian monasteries throughout Europe during this period, had a strong affiliation with the Knights Templar and even drafted their Rule or Constitutions. St. Bernard summed up the Templar's ideal when he said:

> Rejoice, brave warrior, if you live and conquer in the Lord but rejoice still more and give thanks if you die and go to join the Lord. This life can be fruitful and victory is glorious yet a holy death for righteousness is worth more. Certainly "blessed are they who die *in* the Lord" but how much more so are those who die *for* Him.[24]

The Order was formed initially to protect the pilgrims in the Holy Land from attacks by the Moslems. The Knights Templar were European noblemen who vowed poverty, chastity and obedience and who lived a monastic-style life in Preceptories — fortresses with a monastic flavor that were at the same time barracks. But they were monks whose mission was to be Knights fighting in the Holy Land. Seward Desmond tells us that "just as mendicant friars lived a conventual life preaching the Gospel, the brother Knights lived a conventual life defending it.... Monasticism had made a sacrament of battle."[25] In the early 1100's, there were three such Orders founded: the Hospitallers, the Teutonic Knights and the Knights Templar.

At that time, the land of the Crusades was called Outremer, the West's first colony. It encompassed the Holy Land with the Kingdom of Jerusalem as its center. Outremer was shaped somewhat like an hourglass, extending for nearly five hundred miles from the Gulf of Aqaba on the Red Sea to Edessa in modern Turkey.

The Crusades and the Templars

In 1095, Pope Urban II in Rome first called upon the faithful of Europe to recover Jerusalem from the Saracen armies who had occupied Jerusalem since 638. Shortly thereafter, the first attacks by the Crusaders occurred in 1099. Hugues de Payens was Lord of the Castle of Martigny in Burgundy, France, and may have been a relative of St. Bernard of Clairvaux. Hugues went to Outremer in 1115 and became a protector of pilgrims on the dangerous road from Jaffa to Jerusalem. He persuaded seven Knights from northern France to help him, and they all took a solemn oath before him to protect pilgrims and observe poverty, chastity and obedience. King Baldwin of Jerusalem was impressed and gave them a wing in the royal palace thought to be the Temple of Solomon.[26]

The Templars, as warrior Knights, were close to the Cistercian monks who were produced by the same wave of asceticism in Europe. In fact, Bernard of Clairvaux prepared a simple Rule for the Templars. Bernard of Clairvaux thought of them as "military Cistercians." The Templars even wore *a type of habit, white with a plain red cross* (a point we will return to later). Over the next two hundred years, the Templar Order became exceedingly wealthy and powerful throughout Europe. The Order set up a system of Preceptories — military fortresses throughout Europe — that were used for administering estates donated to the Templars; as well as for training or recruiting depots, arsenals for storing weapons, and as homes for elderly brethren.[27] The Templars became professional bankers and financiers, collecting vast sums of money for the Holy Land efforts. They acquired many European estates and in 1113 Pope Paschal II took them under his special protection. They were an independent army, answerable only to the Pope and the envy of local Church dignitaries and political leaders. Bishops and Kings did not always appreciate the fact that the Knights Templar had this special connection with the Papacy and political powers could not always control the Templar activities — a factor that many believe led to the plot to destroy the Order.

The Shroud and the Templars

Against this background, the theory emerges that during the period when the Shroud disappeared in 1207 to its reappearance in Europe in 1357, the Knights Templar had possession and protected the Shroud in conjunction with several powerful French families. While the evidence is circumstantial, it is quite strong and creates a credible link between Constantinople in 1204 and Europe in 1357.

Philip de Milly, Grand Master of the Knights Templar, accompanied King Amalric I of Jerusalem on the visit with Emperor Manuel I Comnenus in Constantinople in 1171, in preparation for the King's marriage to the Emperor's daughter. The alliance gained financial and military support for the Crusaders from the Byzantine Army. In return, the Crusaders would ensure protection of the Eastern borders of the Byzantine territories from the Moslem invaders. Overall, the alliance could help heal the rift between the Eastern and Western Churches. The visit was significant because it represented the first time that the Emperors in Constantinople allowed Western dignitaries to view the vast collection of precious relics and other riches of the Pharos Chapel, Bucholeon Palace and other treasures of Constantinople. The Knights Templar were now privy to the whereabouts of the Shroud, and, this author believes, were envious to possess the sacred cloth.

Some thirty-three years later in 1204, Tribbe tells us that the Templars were "prominent, if not dominant, in the Fourth Crusade, participating in the looting of Constantinople."[28] He goes on to say that in the weeks preceding the breaching of the city's walls they had been unwelcome guests roaming the city and they would have been very aware of the Shroud seen by Robert de Clary on display and would not have forgotten the stories told by their Grand Master Philip de Milly earlier about his visit to this precious Chapel of the Pharos. While this author does not find evidence of the Templars being prominent or dominant in the Fourth Crusade, the Templars may have had some involvement. Certainly they were aware of the treasure of the Shroud, and would likely have known of its removal to Athens. It is here, as we shall see, that the Shroud was likely transferred to them.

Boniface and Mary Margaret

During the assault, the leader of the Fourth Crusade, Marquis Boniface de Montferrat, took personal charge of the attack on the Bucholeon Palace and Pharos Chapel. The Shroud mysteriously disappeared, only to show up shortly thereafter in the trust of his right-hand man Otto de la Roche in Athens. Ian Wilson tells us that during the attack, Boniface de Montferrat took charge of the Imperial Palace and here met the just widowed Mary Margaret, a Hungarian Empress who, as a child of ten, had been married to Emperor Isaac II Angelus of Constantinople.[29] Boniface married Mary Margaret and shortly thereafter moved to Thessalonica in Greece. Perhaps here Otto de la Roche gave the Shroud back to Boniface.

Mary Margaret founded a Church of the Acheiropoietos (image not made by human hands) known today as the *Eski Coma Cami*, or Ancient Friday Church. This seems more than coincidental, although several churches bore this name. Also, one of the finest of all known *epitaphioi* (embroidered cloths relating to the Passion and Death) originated in Thessalonica. In 1207 Boniface died and Mary Margaret married Nicholas de Saint-Omer. They had a son William who became a Knight Templar. Wilson speculates that the Shroud was deposited with the Knights Templar in return for their making a loan to Baldwin II.

The Knights with Red Crosses

Noel Currer-Briggs points out that in the famous Holy Grail legend *Perlesvaus,* written between 1206-1212, possibly by a Templar, "the hermits who guard the Grail are also Knights who wear red crosses on their surcoats like the Knights of the Order of Templars."[30] The German legend of the Grail, *Parzival,* written between 1205-1208 by Wolfram Von Eschenbach mentions that the "formidable fighting men dwell at Munsalvaesche with the Grail."[31] While the identity of Munsalvaesche (which literally means "safe mountain") has been a matter of speculation, the "formidable fighting men" supports the theory that the Knights Templar, warrior monks who wore red crosses on their surcoats, were in possession of the Shroud, and further strengthens the relationship between the Holy Grail and the Shroud.

The Trial of the Templars

The Templars became a very powerful and secretive Order. King Philip IV of France was particularly resentful of the Knights and also envious of their great wealth which the King needed. On October 13, 1307 he ordered a well-executed raid on the Templar leaders in France, putting them on trial on various, often fabricated, charges. One charge in particular relates to our story, namely idol worship. The King's men accused the Templars of "idol worship carried on in secret receptions and chapter meetings of the Order."[32] Trials were held by the King supported by Pope Clement V. We can specu-

late that Philip IV was keenly aware of the fact that the
Templars were in possession of the Shroud in their Preceptory
in France, of which Geoffrey de Charny was in charge. The
King may have hoped to capture the Shroud in this secret raid
while incarcerating the Templar leaders. His charge of "idol
worship" seems to support that he was aware of some object
in the possession of the Templars. The King demanded an
inventory of all Templar wealth, but could not find the Shroud
listed among their possessions. The Templars were careful to
protect the Shroud, their most prized possession, from the
King.

Many members of the Order were tortured and forced
to confess to a variety of alleged crimes. The lands of the
Templars were seized. Among the leaders captured were
Jacques de Molay, the twenty-second and last Grand Master,
and Geoffrey de Charny, Preceptor of Normandy. In 1314,
these two leaders were burned at the stake. Wilson suggests
that Geoffrey de Charny was the ancestor of Geoffrey I de
Charny (Porte Oriflamme) and that this original Geoffrey, as
Preceptor of Normandy, had possession of the Shroud which
he stowed in the family castle for forty-one years until his suc-
cessor, and possible grandson, Geoffrey II de Charny, moved
it to the Church in Lirey and publicly exhibited it in 1357.
Interestingly, Geoffrey de Charny told his inquisitors that he
had been received into the Order forty-two years earlier (in
1265) by none other than Amaury de la Roche, Master in
France.[33] Amaury de la Roche may well have been a relative
of Otto de la Roche who took the Shroud to Athens in trust
for Boniface after the attack on Constantinople.

Templars Charged with Idol Worship

The charge of "idol worship" involved the Templars' secret worship of a "bearded head" which one of the Templar
leaders, Purred, admitted was made of wood. The brothers

were accused of worshipping this head at secret Chapters. During the efforts to defend the Order, one of its members, Jean de Montreal, presented a document in which he spoke of the Order's foundation, its great efforts to fight the Saracens, its carrying of the Cross and the Thorns of the Crown of the Savior, and the fact that they had been able to acquire a great collection of relics."[34] Another Templar, Jean Taylafer de Gene, told his inquisitors that "on the day of his reception 'a certain head' had been placed on the altar of the chapel and he was told to adore it... it appeared to be an effigy of a human face, red in color and as large as a human head."[35]

The Templecombe Image

What could this wooden, bearded effigy of a human head have been and how may it have been related to the Shroud? The answer to this may well have been found in modern times in the village of Templecombe in Somerset, England, and a site that was the former Preceptory or Commandery of the Knights Templar in England. In 1945 a painting of the head of Christ on a wooden panel was discovered. It is strikingly similar to the face of the Shroud. Australian sindonologist Rex Morgan indicates that the presence of a keyhole and hinge marks on the wooden panel suggest it was the lid to a chest that once likely held the actual Shroud — somewhat like the Grail. The Templars, then disbanded in France, took the Shroud to England in this chest, where Geoffrey I de Charny acquired the Shroud in 1350 when taken prisoner by the English.[36]

The Templecombe image as a repository of the Shroud could well contain on its lid the picture of the wooden, "bearded image" worshipped by the Templars. There may have been an actual wooden image of the head, or series of wooden heads, reproducing the face on the Shroud which circulated within the Templar communities to remind them that the Order possessed the Holy Shroud. After the trials of the Templars were completed, the Order was disbanded. However, the Shroud reemerged almost forty-one years later in the possession of Geoffrey II de Charny in Lirey, France.

The Genealogical Link and the Shroud "Mafia"

All three Geoffreys de Charny and other families associated with the Shroud appear to have been closely associated with, or members of, the Knights Templar. Rex Morgan believes that the Knights could have collaborated with powerful French families to conceal the Shroud. This is supported by Noel Currer-Briggs who presents intriguing information. He has tracked the genealogical chart of Boniface de Montferrat (leader of the Fourth Crusade) and his wife Mary Margaret and demonstrated (see Genealogical Chart) that the family of Louis, Duke of Savoy and his wife, Anne de Lisugnam-Chypre, were related to Boniface. It is hardly coincidental that there was a relationship between Boniface de Montferrat, who confiscated the Shroud in the conquest of Constantinople in 1204, and the family that inherited the Shroud from Marguerite de Charny some 250 years later. Somehow, the Shroud remained the closely guarded secret of these French families, primarily families from the regions of Burgundy and Champagne.[37] These families, linked to the Knights Templar as we shall see, utilized the Knights Templar, with their wealth and power, to confiscate and protect the sacred cloth until the Templar dispersion after the trials in the early 1300's. The Shroud then moved under the protection of the powerful and rising House of Savoy. These families, principally the Vergys, the Joinvilles, the Briennes and the family of Mont St. Jean included the de Charny family. Currer-Briggs relates the genealogy of Otto de la Roche, the right-hand man of Boniface, to Humbert de la Roche-Saint Hippolyte and to Marguerite de Charny, his wife. These French families, whom Currer-

MONTFERRAT / HOHENSTAUFEN / SAVOY / COMNENUS / ANJOU (JERUSALEM)

```
BONIFACE OF = (1)Elena        Thomas I, = Beatrix de Gondre   WILLIAM OF MONTFERRAT =   CONRAD OF MONTFERRAT =   Rainier=Maria Comnenus
MONTFERRAT    di Buoca        Count of Savoy (1177-1233)      SIUTILLA of Jerusalem     Isabella of Jerusalem
              (2)MARY MARGARET

William of = (1) Sophie von         Amadeus IV        Thomas II          Umberto, killed            MARIA OF MONTFERRAT
Montferrat       Hohenstaufen       Vicar General     Prince of Achaea   in Hungary                 Queen of Jerusalem
(d. 1225)                           of the Empire (1197-1253)
           = (2) Herta di Clavesans
               (m. ca. 1201)

                                                       Amadeus V = (1) Sibylle de Bourg-en-Bresse
                                                       (1249-1323) =  (2) Marie de Brabant
Boniface II of Montferrat = Margaret of Savoy                     =   (3) Alix de Viennois
(d. ca. 1253)

                                                       Margaret = John of Montferrat     Andronicus Palaeologus = Anne of Savoy
                                                                                          Byzantine Emperor
EDWARD =  BLANCHE of        Ayson =  Yolande of Montferrat
(1284-1329)  Burgundy       (1291-
             (m. 1307)      1344)

                   Amadeus VI = Bonne de Bourbon

                         Amadeus VII = Bonne de Berry

                               Amadeus VIII = Marie of Burgundy

                                     LOUIS, DUKE OF SAVOY = ANNE DE LUSIGNAM-CHYPRE
                                                            (1402-1465)
```

Chart of Noel Currer-Briggs showing the relationship between Boniface of Montferrat (leader of the Fourth Crusade that confiscated the Shroud) and Louis, Duke of Savoy who received the Shroud from Marguerite de Charny. This chart covers the period from 1204 (when the Shroud disappeared) through the early 15th century (when it came into the hands of the Savoy family).

Briggs calls the "Shroud Mafia" guarded a powerful secret over the years.[38] But what is the link with the Knights Templar?

Linking the French Families to the Templars

Authors Lynn Picknett and Clive Prince have provided additional evidence to show that these same families had links to the foundation of the Knights Templar in 1118.[39] These authors point out that the members of Currer-Briggs' "Shroud Mafia" were involved in secret dealings surrounding the formation of the Knights Templar. They state: "It also struck us as significant that the families involved in the origins of the Templars should have been involved in the equally mysterious events surrounding its end."[40] There was an intertwining of families and they go on to say that "Guillaume de Champlitte, the part of the 'clique' surrounding Boniface de Montferrat during the Fourth Crusade — and married into the Mont St. Jean / de Charny family — was descended from Hugues, count of Champagne, the prime mover in the establishment of the Templars."[41]

Currer-Briggs pointed out that the "Shroud Mafia" was all "families descended from or linked with Fulk of Anjou" who died in 1143. Fulk became King of Jerusalem in 1131 and through intermarriage of his grandchildren eventually brought the title of Jerusalem to the House of Savoy. While I part company with Picknett and Prince in their efforts to prove the Leonardo da Vinci theory, the search for the Ark of the Covenant and other matters beyond the province of this book, This author agrees that there were family links between the founding of the Templars in 1118, the visit of the Templar leader Philip de Milly with King Amalric I to Constantinople in 1171, the viewing of the Shroud and the plot involving the Templars to capture the Shroud in 1204 and transport it to Europe.

The links were in the powerful French families orchestrating events who were involved in the founding of the Knights Templar; the engineering of the Fourth Crusade and the confiscation/protection of the Shroud until it emerged in the public exposition at the Church of Lirey by Geoffrey II de Charny in 1357. Basically, it shows the involvement of the powerful Knights Templar with the Shroud from their inception in 1118 until the Shroud came into the hands of the Dukes of Savoy. Essentially, the Templars and the French families had the *motive* (desire to possess the Shroud and enhance their power and stature in Europe); the *method* (military force of the Crusaders and Templars) and the *opportunity* (occupation of Constantinople during the Fourth Crusade) to hatch and execute their plan to remove the Shroud from Constantinople via Athens to Europe.

Modern History of the Shroud

The history of the Shroud after 1453 is well documented. In 1471 Pope Sixtus IV in his monograph *The Blood of Christ* states that: "the Shroud in which the body of Christ was wrapped... is now preserved with great devotion by the Dukes of Savoy and it is colored with the blood of Christ."[42] Shortly thereafter, in 1502, it was deposited in the Chapel of Chambery Castle in France and in 1506 Pope Julius II approved a special Mass and Office, allowing the public veneration of the Shroud.

The Great Fire of 1532

On the eve of December 4, 1532, a fire was accidentally set, most likely by a candle in the Sacristy of the Chapel of Chambery, and the fire was quite intense, engulfing part of the castle and chapel. Philip Lambert, the counselor to the Duke of Savoy, along with two Franciscan priests rushed into the chapel, broke through the grille protecting the Shroud and carried the Shroud in its silver casket to safety. The intensity of the fire, some 900-960 degrees centigrade, was so great that the fire melted part of the silver Reliquary in which the Shroud was kept, and the melting silver created burn holes in the Shroud which are still visible today.

The intense heat caused scorch marks along the longitudinal folds. The Shroud was rescued and during its rescue the Shroud was stained by water. The marks of the fire are visible on the Shroud today: the scorches, water stains, patches  and burn holes. The Poor Clare Nuns patched and darned areas of the Shroud. Many scholars today believe that the intensity of the heat of this fire in 1532 and the carbon produced by the fire chemically altered the linen and had a serious impact on distorting the accuracy of the Carbon-14 testing in 1988 by adding carbon atoms to the Shroud, thereby giving it a "younger" appearance. This will be discussed in detail in a later chapter.

Fire of 1997

Readers will recall a recent fire (April 11, 1997) involving the Shroud. The *New York Times* (Sunday, April 13, 1997, p. 4) reported that an electrical short circuit caused a fire in the Cathedral which was heavily damaged. Firefighters rescued the Shroud without damage to the fabric. Firefighter Mario Trematore used a hammer to break through four layers of bulletproof glass protecting the reliquary while other firefighters poured water on the vessel to keep it cool. It took almost 200 firefighters to extinguish the blaze. Turin police indicated that the cause appeared to be a short circuit, and did not believe sabotage was involved, but were continuing the investigation. The state-run Italian television network reported that the fire apparently started in the Cathedral's 314-year-old wooden dome which was scaffolded for restoration work. Archbishop Saldarini stated that the cloth was intact and that church authorities would go ahead with a rare public viewing in 1998.

Further History

In 1535, to get it out of harm's way during a war, the Shroud was sent to Nice and thereafter to Vercelli where it remained until 1561 when it was returned to Chambery. In 1578, the Shroud was moved to the Cathedral of St. John the Baptist in Turin where it has remained ever since. It was venerated by notables of the day, including St. Charles Borromeo. In 1613, St. Francis de Sales held the cloth before the people at a rare exposition. In 1694 the Shroud was placed in the Royal Chapel in Turin designed by Guarino Guarini on an altar designed by Antonio Bertola. It was given a new back lining cloth. Over the following years, there have been several limited expositions, the latest being in 1978.

The officials in Turin rarely agree to expose the Shroud because each exposure appears to cause environmental damage to the ancient cloth. Giovanni Cardinal Saldarini has written:

> Current efforts are underway by the scientific community to find better ways of preserving the images on the Holy Shroud and keeping them from fading. With each exposition, there seems to be some damage as a result of exposure to the elements and there is great concern that the Shroud be carefully preserved perhaps by utilization of inert gases in a carefully sealed bullet-proof container (there has been deep concern for potential terrorist efforts to capture or destroy this sacred relic).

Cardinal Saldarini is working to put together records from around the world as archives for future reference. The Cardinal notes that part of the purpose of this gathering of information is to assist in a "series of decisions... the most pressing of these decisions regard the steps to be taken in the conservation of the Shroud itself, and a study of the precious fabric."[43] (See Appendix for full text of the Cardinal's letter).

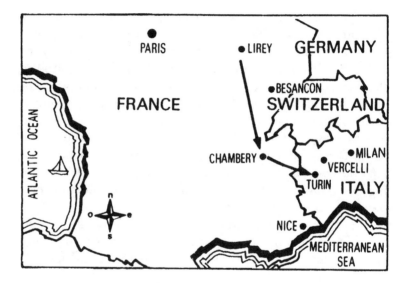

CHAPTER EIGHT

Art and the Shroud

"While the technology of our own age has mastered outer space exploration, we are still at a loss to explain the image on the Shroud or make another Turin Shroud. It is not the result of invention."

Artist Isabel Piczek

There is no information in the Gospels and Epistles that can serve as a guide to Jesus' physical or earthly appearance. We have no written description by His followers that tells us His height or weight, the color of His eyes or hair; not even the slightest clues appear to be provided by the writers for future generations. However, the Shroud itself does provide numerous physical and visual clues to Jesus' earthly appearance. Additionally, study of the Shroud by artists has helped to eliminate any question that the Shroud was "painted" — the formation of the images remaining as a great mystery. We will now focus on the images on the Shroud and on Christian art depicting Jesus in both the Eastern and Western Churches to see what information they provide us about the cloth and about Jesus Himself.

When the Apostle John reached the tomb with Peter on Easter morning, the Gospel tells us that "then the other disciple (John), who had reached the tomb first, went in, too, and he saw and believed" (Jn 20:8). Kenneth Stevenson considers verse eight, relating to John's entry into the tomb where he saw and believed, as one of the most powerful statements in the New Testament leading to speculation as to what actu-

145

ally inspired John to believe. Stevenson contends that "seeing the image we now see on the Shroud would explain John's sudden acceptance of the Resurrection."[1] Josh McDowell likewise concludes that something about the grave cloths themselves convinced John that Jesus had risen from the dead.[2] It is possible that when Peter and John entered the tomb early that Easter morning, they witnessed the images on the *sindon* — an actual startling photo imprinted by some mysterious process that left them and all future generations a life-sized image of their Lord.

The Legend of Peter as an Artist

In the early Church, there developed the legend of Peter as an artist. St. Peter eventually left Jerusalem and journeyed to Rome. Rev. Albert Dreisbach of Atlanta established a continuous historical chain of evidence from the early Church affirming Peter's awareness of the images of the Shroud.[3] Werner Bulst suggested that Peter took the Shroud out of the tomb and brought it to Rome where it inspired copies known as Veronicas. The Veronicas refer to the early legend of St. Veronica (which literally means *vera icon* or true image), the woman who allegedly wiped the face of Jesus during His journey to the Cross and is now memorialized in the Stations of the Cross. However, if one accepts the legend of Peter as an artist, it would appear that Peter drew the images precisely because *he did not have the authentic Shroud with him in Rome.* Thomas had authorized its transfer to Edessa via the disciple Thaddaeus.

One legend tells us that when Peter arrived in Rome he visited the home of Prudens (a Roman Senator) and Claudia, his wife. Their daughters, Saints Prasside and Prudentia, asked Peter to show them what Jesus looked like. Peter, the legend relates, took a handkerchief and drew on it with ink and stylus. Peter's drawing became a pattern. Copies were made on cloth and later used to cover faces of martyrs of the Neronian persecution.[4] Possibly, this handkerchief, its whereabouts having been lost in the annals of history, was also used as a model for paintings of the face of Jesus on the walls of the catacombs. The significance, according to Rev. Albert Dreisbach, is that *Peter is associated with an image of Jesus reproduced on a cloth.*

The Image Disappears

Earlier, we referred to the disappearance of the image from men's minds after the reign of King Abgar. The tenth century historians of the court of Constantinople tell us in their *Narration on the Image of Edessa* that the Image of Edessa (identified as the Shroud) was preserved by King Abgar and his son. However, in later years (50-57) Abgar's grandson Ma'nu VI sought to destroy the cloth in his persecution of the early Church. As the tenth century document relates, the bishop of the region:

> lit a lamp in front of the image and placed a tile on top. Then he blocked the approach from the outside with mortar and baked bricks and reduced the wall to a level appearance. Then a long interval of time elapsed and the erection of this sacred image and its concealment both disappeared from men's memories.[5]

The Shroud was "doubled-in-four" to reveal only the face mounted on a board and embellished with a trellis and then hermetically sealed in the wall of Edessa for protection. Over time, this caused people to forget that behind the face was a full-body image rediscovered many centuries later.

Image of Edessa Rediscovered in the Sixth Century

Early in the sixth century, between 525-544 according to Ian Wilson, a very significant event occurred, namely the rediscovery of the Image of Edessa in the walls of Edessa. The Icon was rediscovered either during the great flood of Edessa in 525 when the walls were being repaired, or later in 544 when the Persian King Chosroes was attacking the city and the Edessans built a tunnel to undermine the Persian defenses. In either case, the cloth was rediscovered during this period. The rediscovery of the cloth has had a profound impact on the history of Christian art. Ian Wilson is credited with making the remarkable discovery that links the Image of Edessa with the Shroud. We noted earlier that Wilson describes at length the impact of this rediscovery on the art of the period. It bears repeating at this point. Prior to the rediscovery, the common images of Jesus were of *a young, beardless, Apollo-like man with short hair pictured usually in profile. Jesus was most often depicted as a shepherd and teacher. The themes were mostly of the risen glorified Christ.* Wilson tells us that after the rediscovery of the Image of Edessa, Christian art takes a radical turn. Jesus' images in art appear remarkably similar to that of the Shroud of Turin, with Jesus as *a bearded man with long hair, pictured frontally.* He notes particularly *that the Image is a full facial Image.* An example of this is the fourth century face of Christ from a mosaic pavement found at Hinton St. Mary in Dorset, England, and now in the British Museum.[6] Shroud Historian Robert Drews points out that portraits from the third and fourth century show Jesus as *a teacher, miracle worker, shepherd or Christ in triumph, but do not depict the passion and death of Jesus.* He cites six examples, including the Tomb of the Aurelii.[7]

Wilson relates that from this point on, a consistent Shroud-like, long-haired, fork-bearded, front-facing likeness of Christ appears in Christian art. The front view is striking as opposed to the profile images of most of the depictions of

Jesus in earlier Christian art. Wilson's important discovery was that "the universally recognized source of the true likeness of Jesus in art was an apparently miraculously imprinted image of Jesus on cloth, the so-called Image of Edessa or Mandylion."[8] The rediscovered image, sealed for centuries in a niche above the city's gate of Edessa, had become the model for future artists.

The apocryphal letter of Lentulus, written in Greek and translated into Latin during the fourteenth century, agrees with the so-called Abgar picture of our Lord:

> There has appeared in our times, and there still lives, a man of great power (virtue), called Jesus Christ. The people call him prophet of truth; his disciples, son of God. He raises the dead, and heals infirmities. He is a man of medium size (*statura procerus, mediocris et spectabilis*); he has a venerable aspect, and his beholders can both fear and love him. His hair is of the color of the ripe hazel-nut, straight down to the ears, but below the ears wavy and curled, with a bluish and bright reflection, flowing over his shoulders. It is parted in two on the top of the head, after the pattern of the Nazarenes. His brow is smooth and very cheerful, with a face without wrinkle or spot, embellished by a slightly reddish complexion. His nose and mouth are faultless. His beard is abundant, of the color of his hair, not long, but divided at the chin. His aspect is simple and mature, his eyes are changeable and bright. He is terrible in his reprimands, sweet and amiable in his admonitions, cheerful without loss of gravity. He was never known to laugh, but often to weep. His stature is straight, his hands and arms beautiful to behold. His conversation is grave, infrequent, and modest. He is the most beautiful among the children of men.[9]

Depictions of Jesus in the Catacombs

Going back in time, Shroud historian Rex Morgan of Australia, through his study of the nineteenth century artist Thomas Heaphy's renditions of catacomb paintings, makes the case that there are some paintings and frescoes in the catacombs with Shroud-like images. For example, Heaphy's painting of a fresco in the Catacomb of Saint Domitilla (dated to Apostolic times) which is now called the Catacomb of Saints Achilleus and Nereus (dating from the first century) and other catacomb renditions by Heaphy show Jesus *having dark hair to the shoulders, hair parted in the middle and a short beard.* Morgan makes the case that these earliest catacomb paintings may have been made by artists who directly witnessed Jesus or who had met people who knew Jesus. Perhaps, as Dreisbach points out, they were copies of Peter's drawing with ink on cloth described earlier. Although these were most likely paintings made independent of the Shroud, they support the Shroud image as an authentic image of Jesus as long-haired and bearded, and, according to Morgan, "could arguably represent the same person."[10] Morgan states:

> I formed the theory early in 1984 that if these paintings could be judged to be similar in their characteristics to the image on the Shroud, then both sources were representations of the same man, which in turn suggested that the image we have on the Turin Shroud is, indeed, that of Christ as depicted in the earliest catacomb representations.[11]

Not only the image on the Shroud, but the paintings discovered by Heaphy in the catacombs, as well as the legend of Peter as an artist, depict early on the image of Jesus as known to His disciples and their followers. These images were early witnesses, and *when the catacombs were sealed by the Emperors, and the Image of Edessa sealed up in the walls of Edessa, the actual image of Jesus was lost in the memory of the growing Church for a period of time.* The more youthful, Apollo-like Roman image of Jesus as a beardless teacher and shepherd depicted mostly in profile came to dominate early Christian art.

The Roman Catacombs

The Roman catacombs are ancient burial grounds outside the original city some two or three miles. The volcanic soil, as Morgan points out, is soft enough for the excavation of tombs. However, the catacombs were not just burial grounds but also meeting places for worship for the earliest Christians. As Morgan points out: "These early Christians simply used their legal right to bury their dead rather than the Roman tradition of cremation, and used a form of burial similar to that of the Jews."[12]

It appears that the very earliest artists in the catacombs painted the image of Jesus from having directly witnessed Him, or, more likely from the guidance of those who traveled to Rome and who knew Jesus (such as Peter). Frank Tribbe points out that perhaps, since the Shroud was not yet hidden between approximately 33-50 (when the Image of Edessa was bricked up in the vault over the gate in the wall) copies may have been made in the catacombs and elsewhere directly from the burial cloth.[13]

The Vignon-Markings

Wilson's theory linking the Image of Edessa with the Shroud receives strong support from the work done previously by the famous sindonologist Paul Vignon in the 1930's. Vignon pointed out that, among the family of post-sixth century portraits of Christ, there was a recurrence of certain unusual markings seemingly derived from the Shroud. Tribbe notes that "in each of these cases, the artist, wishing to be totally faithful to the original, incorporated these oddities even though they are irrelevant to or detract from the naturalness of the face." He goes on to say that "all these artists must have copied from the same original, and all of them misunderstood the nature of these imperfections." However, because of the sacred status of the *acheiropoietas*, it was very important that every detail, even if odd or unusual, be faithfully duplicated by the Byzantine artists.[14] Wilson, following Vignon, cites fifteen such oddities or anomalies which have come to be known as the Vignon-Markings:

Starkly geometric topless square (3-sided) visible between the eyebrows on the Shroud image.

V-shape visible at the bridge of the nose.

A transverse streak across the forehead.

A second V-shape inside the topless square.

A raised right eyebrow.

An accentuated left cheek.

An accentuated right cheek.

An enlarged left nostril.

An accentuated line between the nose and upper lip.

A heavy line under the lower lip.

A hairless area between the lip and beard.

The fork in the beard.

A transverse line across the throat.

The heavily accentuated "owlish eyes."

Two loose strands of hair falling from the apex of the forehead.

The late Professor Kurt Weitzmann of Princeton University noted that "the pupils of the eyes are not at the same level, the eyebrow over Christ's left eye is arched higher than over His right. One side of the mustache droops at a slightly different angle from the other, while the beard is combed in the opposite direction."

The Polarized Image Overlay

Former Professor of Psychiatry and long-time sindonologist Dr. Alan Whanger of Duke University developed the technique, noted earlier, called the Polarized Image Overlay, to point out these many oddities and anomalies relating the Shroud with post-sixth century Christian art. The technique basically utilized two polarized filters at right angles to each other and enabled Whanger to superimpose two images over each other and shift back and forth to discover similarities or anomalies. He discovered that *many images of later (post-sixth century) art must have been made directly from the Shroud or a copy of it based on the high number of congruencies between the images.* He studied many portraits, mosaics, frescoes and coins and compared them, via the Polarized Image Overlay, to the Shroud images. He concludes that *a consistent, shroud-like, long-haired, fork-bearded, front-facing likeness of Christ can be traced back through numerous works in the Byzantine tradition dating many centuries before the time of Geoffrey de Charny (1357).*[15] Wilson had noted the same thing, citing as an example the Christ Pantocrator (meaning having power over all the universe) from Cefalu, Sicily. He also notes, a century earlier, the Pantocrator of the Dome of the Church of Daphni, near Athens (a city that once served as the temporary home of the Shroud from 1204-1207); the "Christ Enthroned" in the church of St. Angelo in Formis, near Capua, Italy in the tenth century; and a similar Christ portrait from the eighth century found in the depths of the Pontianus Catacomb near Rome.

In the sixth century, the Christ portrait appears on a silver vase found at Homs, in present-day Syria and on the beautiful icon of Christ Pantocrator from the Monastery of St. Catherine in the Sinai desert. As Wilson states: "Despite stylistic variations, each of these works seems inspired by the same tradition of Jesus' earthly appearance. And each has a strong resemblance to the face visible on the Shroud."[16] We can add to this list the seventh-century coins, the *tremisses* and *solidus* coins, minted by Justinian II with shroud-like images; the Spas Nereditsa fresco (Savior of Neredica) in 1199 and the icon in the Church of St. Bartholomew of Armenia in Genoa, Italy.

The *Epitaphioi* — Embroidered Cloths

In the tenth and eleventh centuries there developed the *epitaphioi* in Byzantine art. These are large embroidered cloths used in the Good Friday liturgy explicitly symbolic of the Shroud. The body of Jesus is depicted frontally with hands crossed such as the *epitaphioi* of King Uros Milutin. All of these seem to point to the rediscovery of the full-length of the Shroud in Constantinople in the tenth and eleventh centuries. The Image of Edessa, when brought to Constantinople, was apparently removed from the board on which it was folded and mounted, revealing its full length and hence the full-body images (front and rear) and bloodstains.

The Hungarian *Pray* Manuscript: Four Fingers and Four Circles

On the Shroud today one notes that, in addition to the distinctive marks of the 1532 fire, there are *four sets of triple burn holes* that are the result of some incident previous to the famous fire that damaged the Shroud. This prior existence is known because a painting of 1516 from the Church of Saint Gommaire, in Lierre, Belgium, clearly shows the four sets of triple holes. In 1986, the French Dominican Father A.M. Dubarle, corresponding on the subject of the Shroud-like figure on the Hungarian *Pray* Manuscript (1192-1195), had his attention drawn to some curious holes noted on the Shroud in the illustration. Wilson points out that "clearly visible on the sarcophagus in the scene of the three Marys visiting the empty tomb was a line of three holes, with an extra one offset to one side."[17]

Even more curious, though almost vanishingly tiny, was a similar set of three holes to be seen on the Shroud or napkin-like cloth depicted rolled up on the sarcophagus. It appears that the artist of 1192 who illustrated the Hungarian *Pray* Manuscript was aware of the "burn-holes" on the Shroud in his day. If correct, it would set the Shroud's date nearly a hundred years earlier than the very earliest date allowed by Carbon-14 dating. Significantly, Jesus is depicted as naked and laid on a Shroud. His arms are crossed, with the right hand placed over the left, and the hands show only *four fingers*. There is a herring-bone weave in the lower illustration. There is an imprint of a body on the inside and not on the outside of the Shroud. However, on the illustration there are *four circles* that appear to be burn holes on the Shroud. The *othonia* (other burial cloths) are rolled up separately.

The appearance of only four fingers and four circles on the illustration and matching the same on the Shroud is highly significant. Pathologists studying the Shroud noted that only four fingers appear to the viewer, and the thumb is not seen, as we noted earlier. Moreover, the four burn holes seen in the Hungarian *Pray* Manuscript correlate to four holes found in the corresponding area of the Shroud and predate the fire of 1532. Much speculation has been devoted to how these holes were created. Dreisbach notes that most likely the holes were made by fragments of hot coal or burning incense that fell on the Shroud.

No Paints, Pigments or Dyes

In 1978 the S.T.U.R.P. team was permitted a brief five-day, 120 hour nonstop period to examine the Shroud in Turin first-hand with the most sophisticated scientific equipment. Their findings have been published in many scientific journals, and have tended to support the antiquity and authenticity of the Shroud. Among the many findings of S.T.U.R.P. were those related to art. These scientists discovered, for example, that there are absolutely no pigments, paints or dyes which in any way contributed to the formation of the image and no capillary action. Nor did they find any medium by which pigments would traditionally be applied. The ultraviolet and infrared evaluations as well as the X-ray fluorescence and microchemistry of the fibrils preclude the possibility of paint being used as a medium for creating the images.

A Surface Phenomenon with No Brush Strokes

Tests indicated no brush strokes and no "directionality" of any type which would be characteristic of an artist's painting. In addition, there is no penetration or saturation of the fibrils by any paint or solution, and the image itself is mysteriously limited to only the very top fibrils of the flax, or linen fibers. The image is such that it tends to disappear when one looks at it closely and scholars point out that any artist would have had to work from a long distance away from the cloth to create such an image. The Shroud, as the team officially recognized, is certainly no painting.

No Outline or Style

Internationally renowned artist Isabel Piczek of Los Angeles has said that the Shroud of Turin shows no affinity whatsoever with any of the styles which were practiced through the cultured world in the Middle Ages. She notes that the Shroud image has no outlines and states that "art always exhibits the mandatory use of the outline, the event horizon in art."[18] The S.T.U.R.P. scientists point out that the image, far from being a painting, appears to be a sort of scorch. The coloring is sepia, or a sort of straw-yellow. Their conclusion is that the image was produced through some unidentified process (most likely involving heat or light) which caused an accelerated dehydration, oxidation and degradation (rapid aging) of the cellulose fibers of the linen. This is similar to what might happen if a hot iron scorched a linen, dehydrating the linen fibers rapidly causing the fibers of the linen or flax to change color to a sepia. What constituted the mysterious process that caused the accelerated aging of the linen? We reserve the question to Chapter Ten.

As Isabel Piczek states:

> The practiced arts come to the conclusion: the Turin Shroud does not fit into the milieu of the Middle Ages. Whatever happened before, during or after the Carbon-14 testing of the Shroud, the test results are at great odds with the conclusive results drawn by the practiced arts — namely that the Shroud is definitely not a painting or the result of manipulations by a medieval artist.[19]

CHAPTER NINE

Credibly Discrediting
The Carbon-14 Test on the Shroud

*"There seems to be an unhealthy consensus approaching the level
of dogma... that C-14 dating will settle the issue... This attitude
simply contradicts the general perspective of field archaeologists and
geologists who view contamination as a very serious problem."*
Archaeologist William Meacham

After the 1978 studies by the Shroud of Turin Research Project
(S.T.U.R.P.), several scientists, in spite of warnings from such
renowned archaeologists as William Meacham not to rely too
heavily on the Carbon-14 test, believed that only the C-14 test
could definitively establish the age of the Shroud. The
S.T.U.R.P. team, which included Catholics, Protestants, Jews
and agnostics, supported authenticity and some warned of the
pitfalls of Carbon-14 testing.

The Vatican was hesitant to utilize the procedure at the
time because the Carbon-14 test, prior to the 1980's, required
a relatively large piece of cloth (almost the size of a handkerchief) to be, and the test would result in the destruction
of the sample of cloth. Cardinal Anastasio Ballestrero of Turin,
then Papal Guardian of the Shroud, refused to allow this test
because he could not justify destroying a substantive piece of
the sacred cloth to prove authenticity. However, in the 1980's,
great strides were made with the improvement of the Accelerated Mass Spectrometer (AMS), the equipment used to
measure Carbon-14 levels, which would allow the same test to

be done on a postage size piece of cloth. When this capability was demonstrated, the Vatican permitted samples to be taken from the Holy Shroud.

Carbon-14 — What is it?

Scientists tell us that life on earth is carbon-based and that in the food chain, all living things, whether human, animal or plant, ingest carbon, especially Carbon-12 and Carbon-13 (which are stable atoms, that is, atoms likely to hold on to their electrons) and unstable, radioactive Carbon-14 in much smaller quantities. While something is alive, it contains C-12 and C-13 in high quantities and C-14 in very small quantities. Of significance is the fact that there is a constant measurable ratio of C-12 to C-14 in the organism as long as the creature is alive and participating in the food chain.

However, when the living object dies, it slowly begins to lose its C-14 (a process called "atomic decay") and the unstable C-14 atoms decay at a certain rate, called its "half-life," or the period of time it takes for the creature or object to lose half the C-14. The "half-life" of C-14 is approximately 5,730 years. In other words, in 5,730 years a human, animal, tree trunk, perhaps a fossil bone of a dinosaur, and so forth, will lose one half of its C-14, thereby altering the ratio that exists between the stable C-12/C-13 and the unstable C-14. Since the initial ratio between C-12 and C-14 is known in living creatures, the object can be measured to determine the degree of decay or ratio left between the C-14 and C-12 and a date is then assigned to it.

For example, if a fossilized animal is measured and the animal has only one half of the C-14 left, then scientists can date the creature as being approximately 5,730 years. However, if there is only half of that half, or one quarter of the C-14 left, the creature could be twice as old, or 11,460 years old, and so on. This assumes, however, that no other factors have interfered to alter the ratio over time, for example, by exposure to radioactivity from other sources or other contaminants, which can then seriously affect the accuracy of the dating.[1]

With regard to the amount of C-14 in proportion to C-12, scientists advise that it is extremely small. Paul E. Damon, a University of Arizona geochemist and principal co-investigator with the University's Laboratory of Isotope Geochemistry, tells us that "at death, the organism no longer takes up carbon dioxide and the various types of carbon isotopes decay at different rates. The task will be especially difficult because only about one out of every trillion carbon isotopes is Carbon-14. It is like you had an acre of blue marbles, three feet deep, with one red marble mixed in with the blues. Your job would be to find the red marble."

Credit for the discovery of the Carbon-14 test goes to Willard Frank Libby who won the Nobel Prize in Chemistry in 1960 for "his method of using Carbon-14 for age determination in archaeology, geology, geophysics and other branches of science."[2] His first presentation or first formal public lecture describing the C-14 method was before a group of archaeologists and anthropologists in January 1948 in New York City. It was an historic moment. Scientists consider the use of the C-14 method a landmark in the history of archaeology, particularly in prehistoric studies. Since the Shroud is made of linen, that is, cellulose fibers from the flax plant, scientists reasoned that the Shroud would be able to be dated using the C-14 test.

Shroud Submitted to the C-14 Test in 1988

After reviewing the credentials of seven laboratories that utilized the Accelerated Mass Spectrometer to perform the C-14 test, the Vatican selected three laboratories in different parts of the world. The Carbon-14 test was performed on July 29, 1988 at Oxford as well as the Federal Polytechnic Institute of Technology of Zurich and the University of Arizona at Tucson. A piece of cloth 3/8 of an inch by 2 1/4 inches was cut in the presence of Cardinal Ballestrero, then Papal Guardian of the Holy Shroud; Professor Luigi Gonella (Dept. of Physics, Turin Polytechnic and scientific advisor to the Archbishop); Professor F. Testore and G. Vial — two textile experts; Dr. Michael S. Tite of the British Museum; Giovanni Riggi (who removed the sample from the Shroud) and five representatives of the three radio-carbon dating laboratories (Professors P.E. Damon; D.J. Donahue, E.T. Hall, Dr. R.E.M. Hedges and W. Woelfli). They divided the sample into four parts; three were given to the laboratories and one was kept separately by the Vatican scientific advisor. The British Museum agreed to function as record keeper. The three laboratories were given two other dated fabrics as controls. The results were to be given to Professor Luigi Gonella. Dr. Michael Tite of Oxford was asked to be the coordinator of the radio-carbon dating tests.

The Actual Test Procedure

It is worthwhile describing the method used to break down the Carbon-14 sample, as it will help the reader to understand concerns raised over the application of the C-14 test to the Shroud. An article in *National Geographic* described the process as follows:

> Three laboratories received a snippet of linen from the shroud. Each was thoroughly cleaned and burned to produce carbon dioxide and then pure carbon, whose atoms were electrified. A high-energy mass spectrometer separated the carbon isotopes and counted their atoms. From their ratio came the fabric's age.[3]

The *New York Times* described the process as follows:

In the technique used by all three institutions, carbon and other atoms and molecules extracted from the sample are electrically charged and hurled through a series of magnetic fields by a special nuclear accelerator called a tandem accelerator mass spectrometer. These fields deflect atoms of varying mass and electrical charge so they strike different regions of a detector target. Heavier atoms are deflected less by the magnetic fields than are lighter atoms and this difference separates the trajectories of atoms according to their masses. By counting the atoms that strike any given part of the detector, the apparatus can estimate their abundance.[4]

Postage-stamp size samples of the Shroud were utilized. The linen was first carefully cleaned, using both chemical and mechanical methods, according to Dr. Douglas J. Donahue. Next, the sample was burned in oxygen thereby converting the carbon in its molecules into carbon dioxide gas. The gas was then reduced to pure carbon in the form of graphite by heating the gas in the presence of iron powder. In the next stage, the graphite derived from the Shroud sample, consisting of a mixture of stable carbon isotopes with radioactive C-14 was bombarded by heavy cesium atoms. This process knocked carbon atoms loose from the graphite, endowed some of them with electric charges and sent them toward the accelerator.

By passing accelerated carbon atoms through argon gas, the instrument next stripped electrons from the carbon atoms, thereby giving them positive charges. In the process, "background" molecules having the same masses as carbon atoms were removed, eliminating a potential source of error. Finally, the electrically charged carbon atoms emerging from the accelerator were sorted out by magnetic fields, permitting precise measurement of the ratio between Carbon-14 and Carbon-12.[5]

The C-14 Laboratory Test Results

Unfortunately, as often happens, the newspapers printed the results prematurely. The *London Times* stated on August 27, 1988 that Oxford scientists had leaked the results. Shortly thereafter, the Vatican made an announcement in Turin, Italy on October 13, 1988. The results of the test were first officially published in an article entitled "Radiocarbon Dating of the Shroud of Turin" in 1989 in *Nature* Magazine.[6] The official report stated that the Shroud of Turin was dated between 1260-1390, and this would make the Shroud between 607 to 737 years old.

Test Conclusion

The report stated the following conclusion: "The results of radiocarbon measurements at Arizona, Oxford and Zurich yield a calibrated calendar age range with at least 95 percent confidence for the linen of the Shroud of Turin of A.D. 1260-1390. These results therefore provide conclusive evidence that the linen of the Shroud of Turin is medieval."[7] Headlines all over the world jumped on this report and, ignoring the vast body of evidence to the contrary, and the warnings of the perils of the C-14 test, prematurely accepted the results of this one test to condemn the Holy Shroud as a "fake or fraud." Sensationalism was the operative word. The newspapers in New York, as an example, capitalized on the negative test results of the Holy Shroud. Some headlines read as follows:

"Test Shows Shroud of Turin to be Fraud, Scientist Hints," read the *New York Times* on September 22, 1988.

"Turin Shroud Made After Crucifixion," was the Associated Press headline in the *Daily News*, September 28, 1988, which went on to explain that the Shroud was created almost a millennium after the death of Jesus.

"Shroud of Turin Legend in Tatters: Carbon Tests Date it to the 14th Century," was the headline in the *New York Post* on September 28, 1988.

It was truly a bleak period for the Holy Shroud — no stranger to difficult periods — and for scientists who had carefully studied the "preponderance of evidence," as Dreisbach calls it. They knew that the mass of evidence supported the probable authenticity and antiquity of the Shroud while one test contradicted this evidence. Unfortunately, the press, in a highly unbalanced approach, simply ignored the body of evidence and never questioned the reliability of the Carbon-14 test. The Vatican, to the dismay of sindonologists, exercised poor "spin-control" on the one-sided view of the press and lent credibility to the C-14 tests by failing to question the reliability of the tests.

Since 1988, however, a number of scientists have carefully examined the results of the C-14 test and have seriously challenged its results, claiming that the tests were performed in such a manner as to call into question the reliability of the data. The C-14 test, normally reliable under very controlled circumstances, was studying an object subjected to many historical events and highly contaminated. This C-14 test was out of balance with many other scientific tests that confirmed the antiquity of the cloth. The data was now subjected to serious scrutiny by the scientific community. What accounts for the discrepancy? As Dr. Anthony N. Paruta observed: "There is a vast array of coherent scientific data and information from other fields that points to its authenticity. In the case of the Shroud, one piece of seemingly contradictory data is certainly over-balanced by all of the favorable data that has been determined on the Shroud that undergirds its authenticity." (Reported by Father Joseph Marino, O.S.B. in the newsletter "Sources for Information and Materials on the Shroud of Turin.")

A Conspiracy Theory?

Before elaborating on several more credible and promising theories concerning the C-14 count, I would like to address the recent work of Holger Kersten and Elmar Gruber, *The Jesus Conspiracy*. The authors attribute the C-14 medieval dating to the manipulation of certain Vatican scientists and overseers of the C-14 test, who they claim, deliberately substituted the samples of the Shroud with samples of a known medieval cloth. The authors fallaciously build the case throughout their book that Jesus never really died on the cross, but was drugged and later revived, thereby pretending to be resurrected. They claim that the Vatican, fearing that intensive study of the Shroud would reveal that Jesus was not really dead, but only sleeping, needed to discredit the Holy Shroud. These authors claim that certain Vatican officials, including Archbishop Ballestrero, scientific advisor Luigi Gonella, Professor Giovanni Riggi and Dr. Michael Tite of the British Museum, cut samples and went into the sacristy behind closed doors to switch samples in order to deceive the various laboratories around the world.[8]

It should be noted that all of the scientists who have studied the actual Shroud and/or photographs of it, primarily the surgeons and forensic pathologists with the most sophisticated scientific equipment, agree that the body in the linen was truly dead, and not just sleeping or drugged. The intense blood flows are real. The signs of rigor mortis, the manner of venous and arterial blood flow, the blood-clotting and separation of serum evident from the lance-wound, and many other clues point to the true death of Jesus. The Roman centurion did not break the legs of Jesus precisely because He was dead, assured as such by a lance thrust through the fifth and sixth ribs into the heart, allowing "blood and water" to flow out, as noted earlier. The "Jesus was not truly dead" is a radical conspiracy theory and one need not look to such an explanation to call into question the accuracy of the Carbon-14 test. The Carbon-14 test as applied to the Shroud falls on its own sword without specious theories.

Further, the theory that the Church needed to participate in an elaborate conspiracy to hide the "truth" that the Shroud showed Jesus to be really alive is simply divorced from reality. The Church has had the Shroud in its direct possession for centuries and had more than ample opportunity to destroy or discredit the Shroud, including allowing it to perish in the fire of 1532, but chose instead to rescue the Shroud, build a special Church to house it and display it publicly many times. Many Pontiffs, including the current Pope, John Paul II, have professed their personal belief in the Shroud's authenticity. In addition, Vatican officials permitted a team of scientists in 1978 to intensely study the cloth. This team consisted of Jews, agnostics, Protestants and Catholics — hardly a way to hide the "truth." An earlier team, the Turin Commission, was permitted studies in 1969 and 1973. If the Church was guilty of anything, I believe it erred in accepting the Carbon-14 test unquestioningly, without understanding the errors inherent in the test, especially with regard to linen, as will be demonstrated. In this respect, the Church was in good company since the world press and many members of the world scientific community also accepted the initial results without putting the information in the broader context of many other pieces of evidence supporting authenticity and antiquity.

A Litany of Contaminants Affecting the Test

The scientists who conducted the Carbon-14 test were very concerned with the potential of foreign elements that might affect the test on the Shroud, as was noted in the report in *Nature* Magazine. Throughout history, the Shroud was exposed to many and varied contaminants. The exposure of the Shroud linen to washing and soap prior to its being used as a burial cloth and many other contaminants combined with questionable cleaning of the test patches, likely threw off the test results. Such contaminants as ointments (aloes and myrrh), sweat, blood, saliva, candle wax and smoke from candles, finger oils from continued handling by the faithful in earlier years, atmospheric dust, limestone dust from the tomb (calcium carbonate), dirt (travertine argonite), pollen, mites, mold/mildew and the smoke, soot and steam water from the 1532 fire — all contribute to the litany of contaminants that left their marks on the Shroud over two thousand years.

William Meacham pointed out in the 1986 Hong Kong Shroud Symposium:

> There appears to be an unhealthy consensus approaching the level of dogma among both scientists and lay commentators that C-14 dating will settle the issue once and for all time. This attitude simply contradicts the general perspective of field archaeologists and geologists who view possible contamination as a very serious problem in interpreting the results of radiocarbon measurement.... I find little awareness of the limitations of the C-14 method.... Statements quoted from Shroud researchers, both pro and con, reveal an unwarranted trust in radiocarbon measurement to produce an exact calendar date.... I doubt anyone with significant experience in dating archaeological samples... would dismiss... the potential danger of contamination and other sources of error. No responsible field archaeologist would trust a single date, or a series of dates on a single feature, to settle a major historical issue.... No responsible radiocarbon scientist would claim that it was proven that all contaminants had been removed and that the dating range was... its actual calendar date.[9]

This is a very strong statement regarding the impact of

contaminants on C-14 dating. His opinion is shared by Dr. Herbert Haas of the prestigious radiocarbon laboratory at the Institute for the Study of Earth and Man at Southern Methodist University. Fr. Joseph Marino, O.S.B., a sindonologist at the Benedictine Abbey in St. Louis, points out that "the sample was taken from the lower left corner of the portion of the cloth containing the frontal image; this corner is the most contaminated area of the Shroud. This is the area that has been constantly handled whenever the Shroud has been taken out for exhibits and private showings."[10]

The 1994 Fire-Simulating Laboratory Model

Dr. Dmitri A. Kouznetsov of the Biopolymer Laboratory in Moscow developed a laboratory model in 1994 to simulate the physical/chemical conditions of the 1532 Chambery fire. His findings (reported in the *Journal of Archaeological Science*, January 1996, Volume 23) maintain that a chemical modification of the textile cellulose of the Shroud (carbonization via the introduction of carboxyl COOH) resulting from the 1532 fire, impacted the C-14 dating. This "rejuvenation" of the linen was caused when the intense heat (960 degrees Celsius) generated by the fire, and the super steam vapor caused from the dousing with water created a chemical action of the melting silver from the reliquary and the silk backing of the Shroud with cellulose of the linen fibers, adding carbon-14 isotopes and thereby suggesting a younger, rejuvenated cloth. Kouznetsov was supplied with a linen sample from approximately 100 B.C. to 100 A.D. excavated at En Gedi, Israel by the Israel Antiquities Authority through Professor Mario Moroni in Italy. The AMS Laboratory of Tucson, Arizona had radiocarbon-dated the Israeli textile between 386-107 B.C. (a trifle older than the dig would indicate it really was, but fairly close). The test textile was cleaned as was the Shroud of Turin, and submitted to similar conditions of the 1532 Chambery fire. It was then submitted to testing in the MK80 Mass Spectrometer in Russia and the new date arrived at was between 1044 and 1272 A.D. (much, much younger by 1,000 years). Kouznetsov reports that:

> The results of our measurements and the interpretation of the dates drawn from them... point to the high probability of *a very serious error* in the radiocarbon dating of the textile... which is a consequence of the "fire-induced" textile cellulose carboxylation. Thus... the dating error is perhaps about twelve centuries. The Shroud... should be dated using a multidisciplinary approach including radiocarbon dating with special correction for at least both biological fractionation of C-isotopes and that takes into account (that) the Chambery fire induced a carboxylation of the Shroud textile cellulose and consequent enrichment of the latter by C-13 and C-14. Biofractionation and fire-induced carboxylation corrections modify the conventional radiocarbon methods, and... the use of this modified corrected method *leads us to conclude that the actual calendar age of the Shroud of Turin would be closer to the first or second century, A.D.*

Test Samples Taken from the Restored Area?

As noted earlier, at some point in the history of the Shroud, a selvedge was added to the entire length of the Shroud, most likely to center the image on the cloth. Some scientists have pointed out that the sample may have been taken from this selvedge where there could have been intense handling and wear and possible fraying and reweaving or patches placed there in medieval times. The sample from the Shroud that was carbon-dated was next to the selvedge woven into the fabric of the Shroud. The history and contamination of this selvedge are unknown. Fr. Joseph Marino quotes Gillian Eastwood, a specialist in Near Eastern archaeological textiles: "The existence... of some form of end or selvedge needs to be determined and properly documented. Similarly, the published works concerning the Shroud make no reference to the type of seam used.... It may have constituted an original extension or it may derive from a later repair."[11]

Meacham also noted that the repair area from the fire may actually contain fibers woven in by a restorer in the Middle Ages. Professor Giovanni Riggi, who actually removed the samples from the Shroud for the C-14 dating, stated: "I was given permission to cut about eight square centimeters from the cloth in the same area where in 1973 a sample was taken by Professor Raes. This was eventually reduced to about seven square centimeters due to contamination of the cloth with threads of different origins, which even in small quantities could cause variation in the dating due to their being of later addition."[12]

Problems with the Carbon-14 Dating of Other Linens

The laboratories involved have demonstrated inaccuracy of C-14 in recent tests, thereby further reducing the credibility of the test. This fact was alluded to in a warning by archaeologist William Meacham that field archaeologists and anthropologists exercise great skepticism in the C-14 test *unless a sample has been left completely undisturbed in its environment* — a statement certainly not true of the Shroud. Kenneth Stevenson pointed out that, before the laboratories could participate in the testing, they must first successfully date a sample of known origin. During this test, one of the selected laboratories was off by over a thousand years![13]

As reported in the Journal *Radiocarbon* in 1986, scientists used C-14 to date an Egyptian Bull Mummy linen (the wrappings from an ancient Egyptian burial) as well as two Peruvian linen cloths. The new accelerator method was used. It demonstrated that the method is somewhat wanting in accuracy with regard to linen. On the Egyptian Bull Mummy linen, the dates ranged from 3440 to 4517 B.C. — spanning 1,100 years. The known age of the cloth was 3000 B.C. and the closest date C-14 could produce was 2528 B.C. — requiring a calibration of 472 years to correct it.[14]

Bio-Plastic Coating Theory

Dr. Leonico A. Garza-Valdéz, a microbiologist at the University of Texas in San Antonio, delivered a scientific paper along with Dr. Faustino Cervantes Ibarola of Mexico to the International Scientific Symposium on the Shroud in Rome in 1993 entitled "Biogenic Varnish and the Shroud of Turin." Garza-Valdéz, working with microbiologist Dr. Stephen J. Mattingly, reported that, at some point in its history, *a fungus and bacteria were introduced to the Shroud that formed a symbiotic relationship creating a bio-plastic coating (a varnish or patina) which coated the linen fibers and interfered with proper dating of the linen. This coating (or polymer) rejuvenated the linen and made it appear younger than it is believed to be.*

Garza-Valdéz was provided fibers by Professor Giovanni Riggi of Turin which Riggi had obtained during the 1988 cutting of four samples of the cloth. Some remaining fibers were vacuumed and/or picked up by sticky-tape and kept by Professor Riggi. The Shroud fibers' bio-plastic coating is a mixture of a micro-colonia black fungi (*Lichenothelia*) and bacteria (*Leococcus Albus* and *Leobacillus Rubus* along with some *Natronococcus* bacteria). The fibers were taken from the area immediately adjacent to those actually dated by the C-14 labs. He subjected them to the same cleaning sequence used by these labs. Drs. Garza-Valdéz and Mattingly conclude that *the*

C-14 laboratories were not dating the pure Shroud linen. He notes that the bacteria is still growing within the lumens of the flax fibers.

Dr. Daniel Scavone advised in a recent paper of October 13, 1995 that Dr. Garza-Valdéz is working with the Department of Microbiology at the University of Texas Health Science Center at San Antonio; the University of Munich; the Pasteur Institute; Southwestern Research Institute; Washington State University and with Dr. Harry Gove, Emeritus Professor of Physics of the University of Rochester and co-developer of the AMS radio-dating process, to refine his understanding of the symbiotic activity of the fungus *Lichenothelia* and the bacteria *Rhodococcus.*

The Biological Fractionation Theory

Russian physicist Dr. Dmitri Kouznetsov has postulated another theory receiving much attention currently, called the "biological fractionation of carbon isotopes." He points out that living green plants such as flax, can fractionate or redistribute different varieties of carbon atoms (isotopes) between the different classes of biomolecules contained within the plant's cellular structure. As a result, this phenomenon can concentrate more than 60 percent of all C-14 atoms within the cellulose part of the flax plant. He notes that "during the manufacturing process of linen production, cellulose is removed from the flax and that gives the linen textile an enriched amount of C-14 relative to the total flax plant."[15] Kouznetsov points out that this significant detail was not taken into account in the well-publicized 1988 radiocarbon dating of the Shroud.

To explain his theory, he draws an analogy to the human body. The body concentrates calcium into one of its component parts, namely the skeleton, in the same manner as the flax concentrates C-14 into one of its component parts, namely cellulose. If we did not realize that calcium was concentrated in the bones and we were to assume that calcium was uniformly distributed throughout the entire body, we would make a significant mistake. With the Shroud, the laboratories did not realize that C-14 was redistributed by the flax plant to concentrate it in the cellulose (now used to make the linen). They thus made a similar assumption that the linen of the Shroud contained the same C-14 concentration as the total flax plant from which it had been extracted during the manufacturing process. Thus, they interpreted (erroneously) the measured amount of C-14 in the linen as an indicator of the age of the Shroud. The Shroud then appeared younger because of the concentration of C-14 redistributed into the cellulose by the flax plant. If one factors in a biological fractionation correction, Dr. Kouznetsov computes a corrected radiocarbon date for the Shroud that makes the Shroud much older than the date of the 1988 study.

The California Test

Stevenson points out that potentially the most damaging single piece of evidence to controvert the 1988 test results comes from the reported disclosure that there was a secret dating of the Shroud conducted at a California nuclear accelerator facility in 1982. Separate ends of a single thread were dated, with one end dating 200 A.D. and the other 1000 A.D. The wide divergence in dating on the same thread should, he notes, be alarming to those who consider the 1988 test definitive. In addition, the one end of the thread would place the dating closer to the time of Jesus. Stevenson concluded that the 1982 results should "at least lessen dogmatism over the conclusiveness of the 1988 dating." Rev. Robert Dinegar, Ph.D. of Arizona, and S.T.U.R.P. scientist, notes, however, that the sample is too small to have statistical significance and that, in addition, the test was unofficial and unauthorized. Note: In a press release of June 7, 1997 from the Turin Shroud Center in Colorado, theoretical physicists Dr. John Jackson and Dr. Keith Propp, supporting the work of Dr. Dmitri Kouznetsov, reported the results of their own experiments. They noted that, at elevated temperatures such as those expected in the 1532 fire, linen chemically reacts with carbon-containing molecules from the air (especially C-14 more than C-12 or C-13) thereby enriching the linen with C-14 and rejuvenating the Shroud. (See the *Proceedings of the 1997 Conference on the Shroud* in Nice, France.)

The Impact of Image Formation on Carbon-14

An even more intriguing theory relative to the formation of the image that some physicists believe likely interfered with the results of C-14 will be addressed in the next chapter. Over the past years since the 1988 test, scientists have carefully reviewed the process and procedures and the results on testing of other linens, as well as the factors that likely affected the results. A strong conviction has emerged among scientists that the test dates were thrown off by factors contaminating the linen and by other factors (such as the 1532 fire) that added carbon isotopes to the Shroud, thereby "rejuvenating it" and giving it a dating younger than its true age. It is now appropriate to consider perhaps the most fascinating aspect of the study of the Holy Shroud: namely, the question of how the mysterious images were formed.

Chapter Ten

How Were the Mysterious Images Formed?

"I am forced to conclude that the image was formed by a
burst of radiant energy — light if you like."
Ray Rogers, Physical Chemist of the S.T.U.R.P. Team

Perhaps the most intriguing aspect of the study of the Shroud is the question of what mechanism actually formed the mysterious images on the linen. Despite exhaustive investigation by scientists from all disciplines, no one has yet been able to provide conclusive proof of the process of image formation.

Is the Shroud a Painting?

Let us first reexamine some facts about the images. The images are of the frontal and dorsal side of Jesus crucified and laid out in an attitude of death according to Jewish burial custom. The image itself appears to be sepia or straw-yellow in color, as one might expect from a scorch on linen. Significantly, the image is limited to the very top fibrils on the linen fiber. There is no penetration or saturation such as one might expect from a paint or dye. It is called a "surface phenomenon." There are no brush strokes or directionality of strokes such as would be normally characteristic of any artist, nor any outline formed by an artist. Further, *there is an inverse relationship between the cloth-body distance and the intensity of the image. The farther the cloth would have been from the body it covered, the less intense the image.* No artist could create such a perfect relationship between cloth-body distance and intensity of image, especially in negative reverse.

Where there is blood, there is no image, leading to the conclusion that the blood was on the Shroud first before whatever mechanism forming the image took place. The blood interfered with the image formation process on those particular spots. Those who have worked directly with the Shroud say that the closer one gets to the image, the harder it is to see, being best viewed from a distance of six to ten feet — a distance that is not realistic for an artist to have painted the Shroud. This also refutes the theory that an artist painted the image and then added real human blood for effect. The reverse is true: the images had no outline, and the blood was there first and then the image formed on a horizontal landscape versus a vertical portrait shaped linen. This is not the way an artist would have worked.

In a 1981 meeting at New London, Connecticut, scientists reported:

> No pigments, paints, dyes or stains have been found on the fibrils. X-Ray fluorescence and microchemistry on the fibrils preclude the possibility of paint being used as a method for creating the image. Ultraviolet and infrared evaluation confirm these studies.[1]

The late Dr. John Heller, then Professor of Medical Physics at Yale and Director of the New England Institute of Medicine, noted that "at the end of months of work, we had pretty well eliminated all paints, pigments, dyes and stains. Where did this leave us? There were images of a man that produced 3-D read-outs in a VP-8 Image Analyzer and the images were not the result of any colorant that had been added."[2]

The Rise and Fall of the Iron-Oxide Theory

Dr. Walter McCrone, a noted microanalyst with his own research laboratory, Walter C. McCrone Associates, Inc. in Chicago, Illinois noted the presence of some flecks of iron oxide on the Shroud and reached the conclusion that this was some sort of paint. McCrone had an international reputation from his discovery of the Vinland Map forgery. In 1957, an American book dealer found a map apparently dating from the fifteenth century and copied from an earlier Viking map, showing parts of North America. Speculation arose that the Vikings beat Columbus to North America by some 500 years. Walter McCrone received the map for Yale University and studied it, only to discover in 1974 that the ink contained anatase (titanium dioxide), which had only been invented in the 1920's. He declared the map a forgery. However, as is pointed out by Picknett and Prince, McCrone's findings have been called into question. In 1987, physicists at the University of California examined the map using a method of particle induced X-ray emission and found only minute amounts of titanium — more than 1,000 times less than that claimed by McCrone, which, as they point out, one would expect to find in medieval ink. Perhaps the Vinland Map is genuine after all. More importantly, McCrone's judgment regarding the Shroud was further called into question.

McCrone had not been with the team that examined the Shroud first hand, and he claimed that the pigment Venetian red, made by grinding iron oxide into a powder, was solely responsible for the Shroud image. However, the S.T.U.R.P. scientists who examined the cloth directly reported that, *while there were some isolated flecks on parts of the cloth, these flecks had nothing to do with the formation of the images.* It was pointed out that often in the long history of the Shroud other paintings would be laid over the Shroud to somehow sanctify such paintings and that this process left an occasional microscopic trace of paint or pigment on the cloth. In addition, chemists noted that some flecks could have been from the blood. With the folding and rolling up of the Shroud over the years, some flecks of iron oxide from the blood could easily have fallen on other parts of the Shroud. Other specialists noted that iron oxide is involved in the manufacture of the linen itself, specifically in the retting process or soaking in water containing iron.

Further, apart from the scientific evidence, it is highly unlikely that any medieval artist would have painted (or created by some as yet unknown process) an image of a naked Jesus. Further, as noted earlier, no medieval painting has ever shown Jesus nailed through the wrists or capped with thorns. All known paintings were of nails through the center of the palms and with a crown, not a cap, of thorns. The Shroud goes against any medieval style of any known artist and even against the mindset of the period.

What Caused the Image?

The Shroud is a linen cloth. Linen is composed of cellulose fibers that in turn are composed of carbon, oxygen and hydrogen. Scientists who have studied the Shroud directly utilizing many tests concluded that *the image was formed due to an accelerated dehydration, oxidation and degradation (rapid aging) of the Shroud's topmost cellulose fibrils from an energy source (heat or light) causing a scorch-like effect. This rapid removal of water caused discoloration creating a straw yellow, sepia one-tone color.* However, the question remains: what process caused this rapid and accelerated dehydration or scorch-like effect?

A Natural Process?

Could some natural process have created the image? We will review some theories along this line. However, contradicting this theory, as Stevenson points out, is the fact that, if the image was created by some process of nature why is there no record of any other image among the many burial cloths remaining from antiquity? There are many Egyptian funerary cloths, for example, in museums and other locations throughout the world. At most, a very limited few have some marks on them, primarily from decomposition of tissue of the deceased. But none has anything like an image — and certainly not approaching the clarity of the full-body images on the Shroud.[3] In addition, there is no sign of decomposition on the Shroud. The New Testament tells us that Jesus was not in the tomb very long (perhaps about thirty-six hours) and in Acts 2:22-32 we read that Jesus' body did not experience corruption but was resurrected instead. Could some other natural process provide a clue?

The Vaporgraph Theory

In 1902, biologist Paul Vignon, who devoted much of his life at the Sorbonne and the Institut Catholique de Paris to the scientific study of the Shroud, hypothesized that a natural process, namely, the presence of sweat, ammonia, blood and the burial spices (aloes and myrrh) combined with the heat of the body to create a chemical gas that diffused upward toward the cloth and accounted for the image.[4] As Tribbe points out, dying in great agony produces febrile sweat containing urea, which ferments into carbonate of ammonia giving off an ammonia vapor. In the time frame of the grave, such a vapor could cause a light brown stain on linen.[5]

Vignon's work was taken up by Michel Adgé, professor of chemistry and by Giovanni Imbalzano, professor of mathematics and physics as well as by John D. German of the USAF Weapons Laboratory. John A. De Salvo of Northwestern College of Chiropractics in his *Revised Vaporgraphic-Direct Contact Hypothesis* placed a great deal of importance on the presence of lactic acid in perspiration as a factor in the production of the image. Robert Wilcox (as quoted by Stevenson) summarized the objections to the theory saying that "as far as chemicals being able to make such an image, lab tests have shown that chemicals diffuse and run through linen fibers, and thus produce a blurry, and certainly non 3-D image." This may rule out Dr. Eugenia Nitowski's "post-mortem fever" theory of image formation.[6] Vaporgraphs do not account for a three-dimensional image. In addition, the Shroud image is a surface phenomenon and gases penetrate and permeate the cloth. Stevenson notes that vapor does not travel upward in a straight or parallel line, but diffuses and creates an unclear image. Finally vaporgraphic theories cannot account for the transfer of images of hair or coins. S.T.U.R.P. physicist Dr. Eric Jumper noted that the process was an "image forming process" that acted through space, not by contact. Further, there is a relationship between "intensity versus distance," that is, the closer the body to the cloth, the more intense the image. Finally, Jumper notes that the images were not "pressure sensitive," that is, the image on the back of the body has the same shading characteristic and lack of saturation as the front even though the body was lying with full weight on the cloth.[7]

The Volckringer Effect

Dr. Jean Volckringer, formerly Chief of Apothecary at St. Joseph's Hospital in Paris and member of the French Academy of Sciences, discovered that certain leaves, which had been left between the pages of a book for over a hundred years, formed a highly detailed negative image on the paper several pages away. This theory was advanced to potentially explain the image on the Shroud. He noted that the heavy paper covering these plants is not uncommonly imprinted with a striking image of the specimen involved. Some of the parallels of these to the Shroud are remarkable — being sepia in color and featuring considerable observable detail of roots, veins, stems and leaves. The imprints also have inverse relief characteristics becoming fainter the greater the distance of any part of the plant from the paper and yet reproducing without direct contact over the distance.[8] They also have a three-dimensionality when viewed under a VP-8 Image Analyzer. Volckringer noted the important fact that the plant images are formed from an undoubted dehydration, degradation and oxidation of the cellulose of the rag paper in which the plant specimen has been pressed. Somehow, the plants projected or radiated their image to the paper.

The puzzle is that, if the image-formation process on the Shroud was from a natural source such as the Volckringer effect, then why do such images not appear on many hundreds of Egyptian and other burial cloths in possession of our museums throughout the world? The answer may lie in the fact that the Volckringer effect takes time, perhaps decades. Jesus, however, was in the tomb for perhaps twenty-four to thirty-six hours. It is not likely that this process took place in such a short time. But there does seem to be some relation of the process creating the Volckringer effect and the process that created the Shroud image.

The Kirlian Aura

In the late 1940's, Ralph Graeber, a nuclear engineer, spoke of Kirlian photography as a type of radiation possibly involved in the formation of images on the Shroud. In 1939 Semyon Kirlian, then a Soviet electrician, was observing a demonstration of a high-frequency machine being used in electrotherapy. He noticed a tiny flash of light between the electrodes attached to the patient and the patient's skin. Kirlian attempted to photograph this process by holding a piece of film between the two and placed his hand on the film. As Wilcox points out, "although Kirlian got a severe burn for his efforts, he also got a brilliant photograph of his hand, with a luminescence, or halo, or aura, along the contours of the fingers."[9] He then photographed all sorts of objects, inanimate and alive, ranging from leaves, coins, and fingers as well as the entire human body. The results were always the same: a glowing luminescence that seemed to radiate from the subject in a myriad of hues — red, blue, green, yellow and white. Soviet scientists called it "bio-radiation" or an "energy body" that somehow was inside and emanated from all things. *Kirlian photography demonstrated that the human body emits radiation[10] and Ralph Graeber first related such radiation to the images on the Shroud.*

Kirlian Auras and Halos

Jesus' aura or halo, Graeber speculated, was strong enough to leave marks on the cloth when no other bodies that had been put in shrouds ever had. Kirlian photography demonstrated that both mental and physical stress increased the loss of life-energy from the body. Since Jesus suffered from both extreme mental anguish and physical torture, the intensity level of radiation from His body would have been very great in the tomb. Additionally, Graeber points out that as Jesus was the Son of God, His aura was no doubt stronger than that of any other person.

The crucial differences between the two types of radiation (Volckringer and Kirlian) are in the variables of intensity, exposure duration, and possibly development times. The Volckringer images were produced by *a low-intensity exposure over a long period of time.* The Shroud images appear to have been produced by *high intensity exposure over a short period of time.*

Healers And Cures

American researchers Thelma Moss and Kendall Johnson of the University of California in Los Angeles confirmed much about the Kirlian process (called "radiation field photography") and added some new and fascinating data. They studied the aura of a person claiming to be a healer. *Energy flowing out of the healer's body into the body of the patient* is often the explanation healers give of the phenomenon that apparently takes place.[11] The results of the Moss-Johnson tests were reported in the October 16, 1972 issue of *Time* Magazine. They noted that after a cure the healer's aura was significantly diminished and the patient's aura was correspondingly increased. Jesus was the master healer and curer and the intensity of His aura must have been great. The Gospels tell us that Jesus was a man with a power — a power He is specifically recorded to have felt drawn from Him as in the case of the woman with the hemorrhage who touched the hem of His robe. In Mark 5:30 we read: "Jesus Himself, realizing at once that power had gone out from Him, turned around in the crowd and said, 'Who touched My cloak?'"

Volckringer-Kirlian Radiation

Robert Wilcox discussed with Graeber the type of radiation possibly involved in the Volckringer-Kirlian emanations. Graeber suspected it was in the ultraviolet region of electromagnetic radiation. Ultraviolet radiation was close to visible light (which was why some sensitive individuals were able to perceive human auras) and ultraviolet rays could burn, given enough intensity, and therefore could have caused the scorched look that the Shroud images appear to have. But Graeber did not care for the term "scorched" because he believed that *the mysterious radiation tracing on the Shroud was some-*

what analogous to heat but without heat's harshness, perhaps more like light on a photographic plate.[12]

The Hiroshima-Nagasaki Atomic Bomb Blasts

Ray Rogers, a physical chemist of the Los Alamos Laboratory's Design Engineering Division and a S.T.U.R.P. member, says: "I am forced to conclude that the image was formed by a burst of radiant energy — light if you like."[13] *The emphasis is again on radiation from light versus heat.* Professor Alan Adler of Western Connecticut State College concluded that the Shroud images could have been created only by high-level energy which he could not name.[14] *The physical body that lay on the Shroud of Turin must have radiated at a very high intensity for a very short period of time, perhaps milliseconds.* This radiant light, which Tribbe termed a "flash photolysis," has had historical parallels where permanent images were formed by the light and power in the atomic bomb blast at Hiroshima. Dr. Everett James, a radiologist formerly of Vanderbilt University, calls it an *autoradiograph* emanating from within the body.

In 1976 S.T.U.R.P. scientists in the Los Alamos Laboratory (operated by the University of California for the U.S. Department of Energy) issued a public statement suggesting that one scientific hypothesis "draws an analogy between the mysterious images on the Shroud and the fact that images were formed on stones by the fireball radiation from the atomic bomb at Hiroshima."[15] This coincidence was noted by Ian Wilson[16] and others. In 1946, just after the blast, John R. Hersey published an article in the *New Yorker* magazine on the Hiroshima images and elaborated on them in his book *Hiroshima.*[17] U.S. Army and Air Force photographs as well as Japanese photographs provide a variety of views of this phenomenon.[18] Hersey said that "the bomb had, in some places, left prints of the shadows that had been cast by its light." Scientists noted that the blast discolored some concrete to a light reddish tint and scaled off granite surfaces.

The light produced by the Hiroshima-Nagasaki blasts was so brilliant that it cast shadows of upright objects. The radiant energy of the blast was so powerful that it permanently "etched" those shadows onto both flat, horizontal surfaces such as concrete roadways and vertical surfaces and on the side of a gas storage tank.[19] There was even the shadow of a man in a cart posed in the act of whipping his horse. Obviously, the man, cart and horse — just seconds from the epicenter — were incinerated in the blast, leaving only the shadow. Scientists at a conference in Albuquerque, New Mexico sitting just two hours drive from the site of the first atomic bomb blast at Alamogordo in 1945, considered that some kind of thermonuclear flash created the images.

There are parallels with the Shroud that indicate that, rather than a substance, some kind of force seems to have been responsible for the images and that the Shroud was seemingly scorched from within rather than from without by a process of necessity far more controlled than the blast from an atomic bomb.[20] The information of the 1973 Turin Commission report indicated that the image affected only the topmost surface of the fibrils of the fibers, and whatever created it had neither seeped into nor penetrated the fibers, and was insoluble and resistant to acids. It was powerful enough to project the image onto the linen from a distance of up to four centimeters (according to physicists John Jackson and Eric Jumper), yet gentle enough not to cause distortion in the areas where there would have been direct contact as on the dorsal image where the cloth received the full weight of the body.[21]

The image was created with a marked upward-downward direction, without any diffusion and leaving no imprint of the sides of the body or tip of the head. Additionally, the image did not discriminate between registering the body surface as well as hair, blood and inanimate objects — the coins over the eyes and phylactery. Physicist Dr. Eric Jumper argued that any diffusion process would have involved penetration of the fibers and any remotely lingering laser beam would have caused destruction. *Whatever created the images must have been some extremely high intensity, short duration burst (milliseconds) acting evenly upward and downward.*[22]

Radiation and its Impact on Carbon-14

Returning to our discussion in the previous chapter of factors impacting the Carbon-14 test, we now add the additional factor of potential radiation from the body of Jesus impacting the Carbon-14 count by adding carbon isotopes. In the 1960's, British philosopher Geoffrey Ashe suggested that Jesus underwent an unparalleled transformation in the tomb. Ashe wrote:

> It is at least intelligible that the physical change of the body at the Resurrection may have released a brief and violent burst of radiation, perhaps scientifically identifiable, perhaps not, which "scorched" the cloth. In this case the Shroud image is a quasi-photograph of Christ returning to life, produced by a kind of radiance or incandescence analogous to heat in its effects.[23]

Perhaps the process was "Kirlian" related. Some physicists began to suspect that *the Shroud was exposed to a milliburst of radiation (perhaps at the moment of Resurrection) that seared the Shroud with a burst of blinding light rather than heat.* Some of the terms used have been radiation, scorch, searing by thermonuclear flash, a brief burst of radiant energy, flash radiance, flash photolysis which seared or scorched the Shroud, or autoradiograph, creating the images.

Dr. Anthony N. Paruta of Rhode Island states:

I would suggest that the radiation energy that "imprinted" the bodily image onto the cloth (the blood marks are natural) altered the fibers of the cloth and changed the relative number of carbon isotopes on the linen material. This would render radiodating the age of this unique cloth impossible to determine. Transmutation of elements, that is, changing one element into another or an isotope into another isotope of the same element are in the order of 10 to the sixth power to 10 to the eighth power calories and occur with wavelengths of about 10 to the -4 Angstroms. As a matter of fact, it is these kinds of energetic cosmic rays from the sun that are the cause of the formation of Carbon-14 from nitrogen in the atmosphere. Thus the cloth age would have been changed by the radiant energy by altering the carbon isotope ratios. (Reported by Father Joseph Marino, O.S.B. in the newsletter "Sources for Information and Materials on the Shroud of Turin.")

The Neutron-Flux Theory

The Christian Century reported:

The controversy surrounding the Shroud of Turin may not be over after all. Though for centuries the Shroud was alleged to be Jesus Christ's burial garment, recent Carbon-14 tests seemed to prove conclusively that it was made after A.D. 1260. But physicist Thomas Phillips has come forward to dispute those findings. If Christ was truly resurrected, contends Phillips, then the "neutron flux" phenomenon would have distorted the Carbon-14 tests making (the Shroud) seem less antique than it really is "because of additional carbon deposits on the linen." Phillips, who conducted super-collider research at the Enrico Fermi Laboratory in suburban Chicago, conceded that "we've never had a resurrection to measure before."

But the only way to know for sure, he said, is to test further — this time for the presence of chlorine 36 and calcium 41; these substances should not be present except
under exceptional circumstances — such as a resurrection.[24]

The Phenomenon of the Resurrection of Jesus

Physicists began to suspect that *the image itself points toward
a scorch, perhaps a radiation scorch caused by light instead of heat,
that would have added carbon-14 isotopes to the Shroud, thereby giving it the appearance of being younger than it actually was.* This is a
challenging theory that hints that a momentous, unprec-
edented event occurred at the moment of Jesus' Resurrection
— perhaps a milliburst of radiation emanating from Jesus'
body, a brilliant flashing light upon His return to life that
delicately scorched or seared His images on the Shroud. These
theories mount a significant, additional challenge to the
simple reading of the laboratories that the date is medieval.
This is especially so since the Carbon-14, representing only one
test that has now been seriously challenged, flies in the face
of so many other scientific tests that contradict its results.

The Holy Shroud continues to fascinate the scientific
community by pointing to realities beyond our normal experience. *The moment of Resurrection, believed by millions for centuries in faith, has, this author believes, been captured by the precious
Shroud of Turin — a moment in time that altered the future of hu-
manity by showing us the risen Jesus and, thereby, confirming the hope
of our own resurrection.* The "preponderance of evidence" noted
by Dreisbach, or the "bundle of imposing probabilities" noted
by Yves Delage clearly support the antiquity and authenticity
of the Shroud. The Shroud has indeed survived many obstacles
in its long history, from the earliest Christian persecutions in
Edessa to the Machiavellian tactics of the Fourth Crusade; the

medieval and Renaissance forgery theories; the great fire of 1532, and more recently, the Carbon-14 assault.

We encourage the Papal Custodian, Cardinal Giovanni Saldarini, Archbishop of Turin, to permit continued studies on the Holy Shroud and to take additional steps suggested by scientists around the world to protect and preserve the cloth from the deleterious effects of the atmosphere. 1998 will mark the 100th anniversary of the findings of Secondo Pia regarding the photographic negativity of the Shroud and the beginnings of a century of scientific research. We are pleased that the Vatican has announced that the Holy Shroud will be displayed for public viewing by the Archbishop in 1998 and again in the year 2000 so that the world can see for itself the mysterious images of the man who many continue to believe is the Jesus of history and, for Christians, the resurrected Christ of Faith, Savior of the world.

Chronology of Events Surrounding the Shroud[1]

30 A.D. — On the night of April 7, the body of Jesus is placed in a tomb wrapped in "a clean linen shroud." On Easter morning the sheet was found empty.

40-50 A.D. — A special image on cloth of the face of Jesus arrives in Edessa (modern day Urfa in Turkey), and is later sealed in the city walls.

525 — During the restoration of the church of Santa Sophia in Edessa the image of the face of Jesus called the Mandylion is rediscovered. It is an extraordinary image "not made by human hands" identifiable with the Shroud folded in such a way as to allow only the face to be seen.

944 — Byzantine forces, in the course of a military campaign against the Arab Sultan of Edessa, come in possession of the Mandylion and carry it triumphantly to Constantinople on August 16th. Here it is discovered that the Mandylion is in reality the folded Shroud.

1147 — King Louis VII of France venerates the Shroud in the course of his visit to Constantinople.

1171 — Manuel I Comnenus of Constantinople shows the relics of the passion, including the Shroud, to King Amalric I of Jerusalem.

1204 — Robert de Clary, chronicler of the Fourth Crusade, writes that the Shroud had disappeared from Constantinople. It is probable that fear of excommunication caused those who stole the relic to keep it hidden.

1314 — The Knights Templar, warrior monks who wore a habit emblazoned with a red cross, are burned as heretics, accused of a secret cult involving a "bearded Face" which

matches that of the Shroud. One of these knights is
Geoffrey de Charny.

1356 — Geoffrey II de Charny, a crusader and namesake of the
former, consigns the Shroud to the Canon of Lirey, near
Troyes in France. The precious cloth was in his possession
for at least three years.

1389 — Pierre d'Arcis, bishop of Troyes, prohibits the exposition
of the Shroud.

1390 — Clement VII, anti-Pope in Avignon, mentions the Shroud
in two of his Bulls.

1453 — Marguerite de Charny, descendant of Geoffrey, gives the
Shroud to Anna of Lusignano, wife of Ludwig, Duke of
Savoy, who kept the relic in Chambery.

1506 — Pope Julius II approves the Mass and Office of the
Shroud and permits its public veneration.

1532 — A fire breaks out in Chambery on the night between the
3rd and the 4th of December. The silver urn which held
the Shroud became so hot that it seared the cloth along
its folds and several drops of molten metal burned
through its layers. Two years later the Claretian nuns
tried to mend the fabric and their attempts are visible
today.

1535 — To keep it out of harm's way during a war, the Shroud is
sent to Nice and then to Vercelli where it remained until
1561 when it was brought back to Chambery.

1578 — Emmanuel Philibert has the Shroud sent to Turin in
order to shorten the trip of St. Charles Borromeo who
wanted to venerate it in order to fulfill a vow he had
made. The Shroud is put on display at various times for
special celebrations of the House of Savoy or for jubilees
every thirty years or so.

1694 — On the 1st of June the Shroud is given permanent
housing in the chapel erected by the architect Guarino
Guarini, annexed to the Cathedral of Turin. In the same
year Blessed Sebastian Valfrè reinforced the patches and
the mends.

1898 — The first photographs are taken by Secondo Pia between the 25th and the 28th of May. The emotional discovery of the photographic negative reveals with incredible precision the likeness of the Man in the Shroud. Studies and research, especially in the medical and legal areas, are undertaken.

1931 — During an exhibition of the Shroud on the occasion of the marriage of Umberto of Savoy, the Shroud is photographed again by a professional photographer, Giuseppe Enrie.

1933 — The Shroud is put on display to commemorate the 19th Centenary of the Redemption.

1939-1946 — During the Second World War, the Shroud was hidden away in the Abbey of Montevergine in Avellino, Italy.

1969 — From the 16th to the 18th of June the Shroud was examined by a study commission nominated by Cardinal Michele Pellegrino. The first color photographs were taken by Giovanni Battista Judica Cordiglia.

1973 — The first televised exhibition of the Shroud on November 23rd.

1978 — The celebration of the 4th Centenary of the transferal of the Shroud from Chambery to Turin, with a public exhibition from the 26th of August to the 8th of October and an International Study Congress. On this occasion several Italian and other scientists (S.T.U.R.P.), for the most part from the United States, for some 120 consecutive hours, measured and analyzed the relic in order to undertake an in-depth multidisciplinary scientific study.

1980 — A private showing on April 13th for the Holy Father, Pope John Paul II.

1983 — On the 18th of March Umberto II of Savoy dies. In his last will and testament he gives the Shroud to the Vatican. By Papal decree the relic remains in Turin and is placed in the custody of the Cardinal Archbishop, Anastasio Ballestrero.

1988 — A small sample of cloth is taken from the Shroud and subjected to dating by the radiocarbon method. On the basis of this analysis, the Shroud would seem to date back to the Middle Ages, to a period between 1260 and 1390 A.D. The way the tests were done and the reliability of the method for cloth as contaminated as the Shroud are held invalid by a number of scholars.

1992 — On September 7, a group of invited experts suggest initiatives and appropriate interventions in order to guarantee the conservation of the sacred relic.

1993 — On the 24th of February the Shroud is temporarily transferred to a place behind the high altar of the Cathedral of Turin to allow for the restoration of the Guarini chapel.

1995 — The Russian scientist Dmitri Kouznetsov shows experimentally what he had already affirmed in a meeting held in Rome in 1993, namely that the fire of 1532 had modified the quantity of radioactive carbon present in the Shroud, thus altering its date which can be shown to be from the first century A.D. Cardinal Giovanni Saldarini, Archbishop of Turin and Custodian of the Shroud, announces two exhibitions of the Shroud, in 1998 for the centenary of the first photograph, and in 2000 for the Jubilee.

1997 — A fire on April 11th in the dome of the Cathedral in Turin threatens the Shroud once again. Quick action on the part of firefighters saves the relic from destruction.

Epilogue

You, the reader, have now finished a portion of your pilgrimage to the Shroud. For old-timers, it is a succinct and updated review of sindonological studies stretching from the first photography by Secondo Pia in 1898 to the Carbon-14 "dating" of 1988. Along the way, there have been times ranging from its glorious veneration in Edessa to that of its seeming vilification following its alleged medieval dating by Arizona, Oxford and Zurich. If nothing else, you have learned that this sacred burial linen is like a cork on the seas of religious, scientific and academic investigation: there are heavy storms when it seems to have totally disappeared and sunk to the depths of obscurity. But, just when its detractors think they have won the final victory, like the body it once held, it bobs to the surface again to amaze and mystify all with new and startling information.

John C. Iannone has been your escritorial "tour guide" on this fascinating pilgrimage. His love and dedication to "God's love letter in linen to all mankind" have led to years of devoted study and labor which, in turn, have resulted in this book. If you have learned so much as a single new fact or been prompted to ask even one question which has inspired you to continue on this journey, the author has accomplished his goal. Like the late Fr. Peter Rinaldi, S.D.B., who served as mentor, inspirer and friend to so many in the "Shroud Crowd," the goal of this quest is always *"to get beyond the linen to the Lord whose image it bears."*

In "lifting up" the Shroud for your consideration, John can do no more than ask the question originally posed by the

197

Man of the Shroud Himself in Mark 8:29: "Who do you say that I am?" It is you, the reader, who must decide if the image on this linen is simply that of one of countless unfortunate victims of crucifixion or in truth the historic Jesus of Nazareth whom Christians call Lord and Christ. It is the author's hope that if you are prompted to read more and reflect as he has done for over 10 years, you will reach the same conclusion which gave birth to the writing of this book.

The Rev. Albert R. Dreisbach, Jr.
Executive Director
The Atlanta International Center for
Continuing Study of the Shroud of Turin, Inc.
Feast of the Holy Shroud
May 4, 1996

Letter of Cardinal Saldarini

Turin, October 30, 1994
Ref.: Prot. 541/94 - Cat. 81

Dear Sir,

Until now no complete and up-to-date records have been kept of all the work that has been carried out on the Shroud over the years. It is now necessary to recover all the available data about the research that has been done to date, and to do so as quickly as possible.

As the Papal Custodian of the Holy Shroud, I should like to ask you to help us in this matter. This is the beginning of a long and thorough work of putting these records together so that we can provide archives for future reference. Once complete, these records will be the property of the Papal Custodian of the Holy Shroud.

We would be very grateful if you could let us have a list of all your publications, and of all those of the group you work with, on the subject of the Holy Shroud. We would prefer the works to be on floppy disks (MS-DOS, Macintosh, UNIX, etc.), but paper copies are fine as well. We would also very much like to have a list of all the publications on the Holy Shroud that you have in your possession at the moment, even if they are not the work of yourself or your group.

We wish to set up a computer data-base for reference and as a point of departure for a series of decisions that the competent ecclesiastical authorities shall have to make or suggest in the name of and on behalf of the owner of the Holy Shroud.

The most pressing of these decisions regards the steps to be taken in the conservation of the Shroud itself, and any study of the precious fabric. These records will also be extremely useful for all those who, for various reasons, may wish to study the Shroud and who need complete documentation on the subject.

It would obviously be even more useful not only to have the bibliographic lists, but also a copy of all the works themselves. I therefore ask you, if you can, to send not only a list, but also a copy of each of your publications (books, articles, photographs, etc.) on the subject of the Shroud. If you should also send material that you have not yet published or this is still for any reason confidential, this must be accompanied by clear instructions from you yourself about how the material may be used. I would also be very grateful if you could inform colleagues and friends who may be interested in taking part in this initiative, supplying me also with their addresses and telephone numbers.

This survey also aims to carry out a sort of census on the groups and individual experts who work on the subject of the Holy Shroud in the world, and who may be interested in working closely with the Holy See and with the Papal Custodian of the Holy Shroud. I should like, moreover, to maintain these records up-to-date, adding every new publication that will be sent to us in the future.

I hope that you will accept our proposal. In any case, please reply to let us know your answer, whatever it may be. Should you agree with this initiative, I would be very grateful if you would send me the material as soon as possible, together with your address, telephone and fax numbers.

Thank you for your help.

Yours faithfully,
Giovanni Cardinal Saldarini
Archbishop of Turin

The Shroud on the Internet

Readers wishing to pursue information on the Shroud, especially photographic information, are encouraged to view the Shroud Website prepared by photographer Barrie M. Schwortz, original member of the S.T.U.R.P. Team. If you have Internet access, we recommend you view the detailed photographs on the Shroud Website:

HTTP://WWW.SHROUD.COM

* * *

Readers may also wish to seek further information from the HOLY SHROUD GUILD, a long-time, distinguished Shroud organization located at Mount St. Alphonsus Retreat Center in Esopus, N.Y. The organization is affiliated with the Centro Internationale in Turin, Italy. Please contact:

Rev. Fred Brinkmann, C.Ss.R., President
Holy Shroud Guild, P.O. Box 993
Canandiagua, NY 11424
716-394-2606, Fax 716-594-9215
HTTP://WWW.SHROUD.ORG

* * *

Readers may also contact the Council for Study of the Shroud of Turin (CSST) based in Durham, North Carolina by writing Dr. Alan and Mary Whanger, Council for Study of the Shroud of Turin, P.O. Box 52427, Durham, NC 27717, USA or sending e-mail to:

adw2@acpub.duke.edu

ENDNOTES

Chapter One: What is the Shroud of Turin?

[1] Frank C. Tribbe, *Portrait of Jesus?* (New York: Stein & Day, 1983), 30-31.

[2] Ian Wilson, *The Shroud of Turin* (Garden City: Doubleday & Company, 1979), 24.

[3] Emanuela Marinelli, *La Sindone: Un' Immagine "Impossibile,"* (Milan, Italy: Edizioni San Paolo, 1996), 15-16.

[4] Ian Wilson, *The Mysterious Shroud* (Garden City: Doubleday & Company, 1986), 4.

[5] *Ibid.*, 10.

[6] *Ibid.*

[7] Noel Currer-Briggs, *The Shroud and the Grail: A Modern Quest for the True Grail* (New York: Saint Martin's Press, 1987).

[8] Kenneth Stevenson and Gary Habermas, *The Shroud and the Controversy* (Nashville: Thomas Nelson Publishers, 1990), 151.

[9] Wilson, *The Mysterious Shroud,* 16.

[10] *Ibid.*

[11] Stevenson, 67 (also 165-166).

[12] *Ibid.*

[13] *Ibid.*

[14] Heller, *Report on the Shroud of Turin,* 220; Stevenson, 240.

[15] Tribbe, 225.

[16] Professor Gilbert Raes, "Rapport d'Analise," *La S. Sindone* supplement to *Rivisita Diocesana Torinese* (January 1976), 79-83.

[17] John Tyrer, "Looking At the Turin Shroud as a Textile," *Shroud Spectrum,* 6 (1983), 68-69.

[18] Quoted in Wilson, *The Mysterious Shroud,* 17.

Chapter Two: Pollen, Mites and Flowers — A Unique Cloth

[1] Ian Wilson, *The Shroud of Turin* (Garden City: Doubleday & Company, 1979), 293.

[2] Emanuela Marinelli, *La Sindone: Un' Immagine "Impossibile,"* (Milan, Italy: Edizioni San Paolo, 1996), 27.

[3] Max Frei, "Nine Years of Palynological Studies On The Shroud," *Shroud Spectrum International,* 1 (June 1982), 7.

[4] Giovanni Riggi Di Numana, *Rapporto Sindone 1978-1987* (Milan: 3M Edizioni, 1988).

[5] Kenneth Stevenson and Gary Habermas, *The Shroud and the Controversy* (Nashville: Thomas Nelson Publishers, 1989), 65.

[6] Quoted from William Meacham's interview with Rev. Kenneth Stevenson in Tarrytown, N.Y., July 15, 1988. See also: William Meacham, "The Authentication of the Turin Shroud: An Issue In Archaeological Epistemology," *Current Anthropology,* 24 (June 1983) 306.

[7] *Ibid.*

[8] Ian Wilson, *The Shroud of Turin,* 63.

[9] Stevenson and Habermas, 63.

[10] Wilson, 81.

[11] Werner Bulst, S.J. (as quoted by Kenneth Stevenson), "The Pollen Grains On The Shroud of Turin," *Shroud Spectrum International*, 10 (1984).

[12] *Ibid.*

[13] Stevenson and Habermas, 65.

[14] *Ibid.*, 77.

[15] Dr. Alan & Mrs. Mary Whanger, "Floral Coin and Other Non-Body Images on the Shroud of Turin" (Durham, North Carolina: Duke University).

[16] Michael Zohary, *Flora Palaestina* (Jerusalem: Israel Academy of Sciences and Humanities, 1966-1977).

[17] Whanger.

[18] *Ibid.*

Chapter Three: Ancient Roman Coins Over the Eyes

[1] Dr. Eric Jumper, Kenneth Stevenson, Dr. John Jackson, "Images of Coins on a Burial Cloth?" *The Numismatist* (July 1978), 1354.

[2] *Ibid.*

[3] *Ibid.*, 1356.

[4] *Ibid.*

[5] Francis Filas, S.J., *The Dating of the Shroud of Turin from Coins of Pontius Pilate* (Cogan Productions, a Division of ACTA Foundation, January 1984), 3.

[6] *Ibid.*

[7] *Ibid.*, 4.

[8] *Ibid.*

[9] *Ibid.*, 5.

[10] *Ibid.*, 19. In a recent debate between Dr. Alan Whanger, Professor Emeritus-Duke University, and Antonio Lombatti - Italian history professor, Lombatti denies any coins-over-eye custom in Jewish burials, utilizing Dr. L.Y. Rahmani of the Israeli Department of Antiquities, as his source. Whanger accepts that this was not a *custom*, but notes it was done in certain situations. The Shroud, a genuine archaeological artifact, points clearly to their presence. Rahmani and Hachlili note that some coins placed *over the eyes* were found in the skulls of remains, later changing their position to say the coins were *in the mouth* and not over the eyes. However, as Meachem notes, a coin over the eye would fall into the skull (where the coins were found), while a coin in the mouth would find its way to the neck vertebrae. Very few coins were found because tombs were often ransacked, as Rahmani and Hachlili themselves note (coins being a likely objective) and burials were often secondary burials wherein bones were collected about a year after primary burial and placed in ossuaries. Coins may have been removed at this point, or placed with the bones. Whanger notes that coin-like objects are observable over the eyes and they match *leptons* minted by Pontius Pilate. He outlines the evidence of their presence on the Shroud (naked eye viewing, macrophotography, digital enhancement, 3-dimensionality, coronal discharge, Jewish tomb-findings and Polarized Image Overlay) and points to *cadaveric spasm* as a likely reason for placing the coins (to keep the eyes closed). The placement of coins was not idolatrous since the coins did not bear the *image* of Caesar. My wife pointed out that the origin of the "widow's mite" may relate the *lepton* with widowhood and burial.

The following articles address coins found in Jewish burials: "Jason's Tomb," *Israel Exploration Journal*, Vol. 17, No. 2 (1967), pp. 61-100 by L.Y. Rahmani (including finding of *leptons*); "Ancient Jerusalem's Funerary Customs and Tombs" (Part 3), *Biblical Archaeologist*, Winter 1981, pp. 43-53 by L.Y. Rahmani (Jason's tomb); and (Part 4) Spring 1982, p. 109 (ransacking of tombs); "Beliefs, Rites and Customs of the Jews Connected with Death, Burial and Mourning," *The Jewish Quarterly Review*, Volume VII, 1895, pp. 101-118 by A.P. Bender; "Ancient Burial Customs Preserved in Jericho Hills," *Biblical Archaeology Review*, Vol. V, No. 4, July/August 1979, pp. 28-35 by Rachel Hachlili (Herod coins over eyes, pp. 34-35); "Jewish Funerary Customs During the Second Temple Period in the Light of the Excavations at the Jericho Necropolis," *Palestine Exploration Quarterly*, July-Dec. 1983, pp. 109-132 (coins in skull/mouth, pp. 118, 124, 128) by R. Hachlili and A. Killebrew; *The Jewish Encyclopedia* (Vol. III, pp. 434-436, 1925 edition) re: closing eyes of dead; "Burial Cave of the Caiaphas Family," *Biblical Archaeology Review*, Vol. 18, No. 5, September 1992, pp. 29-36 by archaeologist Zvi Greenhut (*lepton* from 42/43 A.D. in skull of a woman); and "On the Archaeological Evidence for a Coin-On-Eye Jewish Burial Custom in the First Century A.D.," *Biblical Archaeologist* 49 (March 1986), pp. 56-61, by William Meachem.

[11] Robert M. Haralick, *Analysis of Digital Images of the Shroud of Turin* (Spacial Data Analysis Laboratory, Virginia Polytechnic Institute and State University, Blacksburg, Virginia 24061, December 1983), 2.

[12] *Ibid.*, 34.

[13] *Ibid.*

[14] Filas, 15.

[15] *Ibid.*

[16] *Ibid.*, 16.

[17] Dr. Alan D. Whanger and Mary Whanger, "Polarized Image Overlay Technique," *Applied Optics* (March 15, 1985), 766.

[18] *Ibid.*, 767.

[19] *Ibid.*

[20] *Ibid.*

[21] *Ibid.*

[22] *Ibid.*

[23] *Ibid.*

[24] *Ibid.*

[25] Filas, 20.

[26] Lynn Picknett and Clive Prince, *Turin Shroud: In Whose Image?* (New York: Harper Collins Publishers, 1994), 19.

[27] Kenneth Stevenson and Gary Habermas, *The Shroud and the Controversy* (Nashville: Thomas Nelson Publishers, 1990), 165.

Additional Sources:

Meacham, William, "On the Archaeological Evidence for a Coin-On-Eye Jewish Burial Custom in the First Century A.D.," *Biblical Archaeologist* 49 (March 1986), 56-61.

Rachel Hachlili and Ann Killebrew, "Was the Coin-On-Eye Custom a Jewish Burial Practice in the Second Temple Period?" *Biblical Archaeology* (Summer 1983), 147-153.

Chapter Four: The Signature of Roman Crucifixion

[1] Ian Wilson, *The Shroud of Turin* (Garden City: Doubleday & Company, 1979), 46.

[2] Kenneth Stevenson and Gary Habermas, *The Shroud and the Controversy* (Nashville: Thomas Nelson Publishers, 1990), 84.

[3] Wilson, 46.

[4] Frank C. Tribbe, *Portrait of Jesus?* (New York: Stein & Day, 1983), 86.

[5] Dr. Robert Bucklin, *The Silent Witness* (Pyramid Home Video, Box 1046, Santa Monica, California 90406) Telephone: 213-828-7577.

[6] Wilson, 47-48.

[7] *Ibid.*

[8] Stevenson and Habermas, 86.

[9] Ian Wilson, *The Mysterious Shroud* (Garden City: Doubleday & Company, 1985), 21-22.

[10] *Ibid.*

[11] Frederick T. Zugibe, *The Cross and the Shroud: A Medical Inquiry into the Crucifixion* (New York: Paragon House Publishers 1988), 36.

[12] Philip McNair, "The Shroud and History: Fantasy, Fake or Fact?" *Face to Face with the Turin Shroud*, ed. Peter Jennings (Oxford: Mowbray, 1978), 35, as quoted in Kenneth Stevenson and Gary Habermas, *The Shroud and the Controversy*, 92.

[13] Dr. Pierre Barbet, *A Doctor at Calvary* (New York: P.J. Kennedy & Sons, 1953; New York: Image Books, 1963).

[14] Zugibe, 62-63.

[15] Dr. John H. Heller, *Report on the Shroud of Turin* (Boston: Houghton Mifflin Company, 1983), 112.

[16] Tribbe, 86-87.

[17] Wilson, *The Shroud of Turin*, 49.

[18] Emanuela Marinelli, *La Sindone: Un' Immagine "Impossibile,"* (Milan, Italy: Edizioni San Paolo, 1996), 50-51.

[19] Wilson, *The Mysterious Shroud*, 16.

[20] "The Shroud: It's Even Changed the Lives of Scientists Studying It," *Globe*, as quoted by Stevenson, 97.

[21] Robert Wilcox, "Fake or Not, Shroud Leaves Mark on Scientists," *The Voice*, as quoted by Stevenson, 97.

[22] Herbert Thurston, S.J., "The Holy Shroud and the Verdict of History," *The Month*, as quoted by Ian Wilson, 53.

[23] Quoted from the New York *Daily News*, June 12, 1997.

[24] Tribbe, 107, quoting *Sindon* (December 1981).

[25] Tribbe, 99.

[26] Heller, 203.

[27] *Ibid.*, 104.

[28] *Ibid.*

Additional Sources:

Robert Bucklin, "The Legal and Medical Aspects of the Trial and Death of Christ," *Medicine, Science and the Law* (January 1970), 14-26.

Robert Bucklin, "The Medical Aspects of the Crucifixion of Our Lord Jesus Christ," *Linacre Quarterly* (February 1958); "The Shroud of Turin: Viewpoint of a Medical Pathologist," *Shroud Spectrum International* 13 (1984), 3-8; and "The Pathologist Looks at the Shroud," *Second International Congress, The Shroud and Science* (Turin, Italy, October 7-8, 1978).

Chapter Five: The Shroud and Ancient Jewish Burial Practices

[1] Rev. Edward Wuenschel, C.Ss.R., "The Shroud of Turin and the Burial of Christ," *The Catholic Biblical Quarterly* (October 1945), 138.

[2] L.Y. Rahmani, "Ancient Jerusalem's Funerary Customs and Tombs," *Biblical Archaeologist*, 45 (Winter 1982), 44.

[3] Rt. Rev. John A.T. Robinson, "The Shroud of Turin and the Grave-Clothes of the Gospels," *Proceedings of the 1977 United States Conference of Research on the Shroud of Turin* (Albuquerque, New Mexico, 1977), 25.

[4] Rahmani, *Biblical Archaeologist*, 44 (Summer 1981), 173-174.

[5] *Ibid.*, 174.

[6] *Ibid.*, 175.

[7] Dr. Eugenia Nitowski, *The Cave-Tombs.*

[8] Rachel Hachlili, "Ancient Burial Customs Preserved in Jericho Hills," *Biblical Archaeology Review*, 5 (July/August 1979), p. 28.

[9] Wuenschel, 412.

[10] Josephus, *The Jewish Wars* (New York: Dorset Press, 1981).

[11] Werner Bulst, S.J., *The Shroud of Turin* (Milwaukee: Bruce Publishing, 1957), 85.

[12] *Ibid.*, 91.

[13] *Ibid.*, 94-95.

[14] *Ibid.*

[15] Rahmani, *Biblical Archaeologist* (Winter 1982), 44.

[16] Raymond E. Brown, "The Burial of Jesus," *The Catholic Biblical Quarterly* (April 1988), 242.

[17] Wuenschel, 173, quoting Paul Vignon, *The Holy Shroud of Turin* (2nd ed, 1939), 167.

[18] Robinson, 27.

[19] *Ibid.*, 26.

[20] F.H. Closon, ed., *Philo*, Volume 7 (The Loeb Classical Library), 571, as quoted by Wuenschel, 420.

[21] Werner Bulst, S.J., *The Shroud of Turin*, 79.

[22] Raymond E. Brown, "The Burial of Jesus (Mark 15:42-47)," *The Catholic Biblical Quarterly*, 50 (April 1988), 234.

[23] Ian Wilson, *The Mysterious Shroud* (Garden City: Doubleday & Company, 1985), 34.

[24] *Ibid.*

[25] Wuenschel, 147.

[26] *Ibid.*

[27] Kenneth Stevenson and Gary Habermas, *The Shroud and the Controversy* (Nashville: Thomas Nelson Publishers, 1990), 138-139.

[28] Bulst, 81.

[29] Bonnie LaVoie et. al., "In Accordance with Jewish Burial Custom, the Body of Jesus Was Not Washed," *Shroud Spectrum* I, June 1982, 8-17.

[30] Bulst, 99.

[31] In the *Revue Internationale Du Linceul De Turin*, No. 4, 1997, pp. 2-9, Mark Guscin provides a brief history and corroborative evidence that this cloth once touched the face of Jesus. He credits the Spanish Centre for Sindonology, especially Guillermo Hermas and Dr. Jose Villalain for the following finds:
  1. The Oviedo Cloth contains bloodstains of the same blood-group (AB) as that found on the Shroud. Guscin notes that "when the cloth was placed on the dead man's face, it was folded over, although not in the middle. Counting both sides of the cloth, there is therefore a fourfold stain in a logical order of decreasing intensity."
  2. There is no image, and the Oviedo Cloth was "simply placed on the face (of Jesus) to absorb all the blood, but not used in any kind of wiping movement." The *sudarium* was first used *before* the dead body was taken down from the Cross as a kind of blotter, then folded and laid aside in the tomb before enshroudment.
  3. The stains consist of one part blood and six parts fluid from a pleural edema. "This fluid collects in the lungs when a crucified person dies of asphyxiation, and if the body subsequently suffers jolting movements, can come out through the nostrils. These are in fact the main stains visible on the *sudarium*."
  4. Stains are superimposed on each other, with different outlines clearly visible. The first stain had already dried when the cloth was stained a second time, and so on. The first stain was made while Jesus was on the Cross; the second stain was made about an hour later when the body was taken down. The third stain was made when the body was lifted from the ground about forty-five minutes later. Dr. Villalain noted that "the marks of the fingers that held the cloth to the nose are visible under the microscope."
  5. Finally, the face in contact with the *sudarium* had typically Jewish features, a prominent nose and pronounced cheek bones. Since the cloth had no monetary or artistic value, Guscin notes that the very fact that the cloth was kept at all is a sign of its authenticity.

[32] Summer 1981, Volume 44, Number 3, 173.

[33] London: D. Nutt, Volume VI, 1894, 317-347, 664-671 and Vol. VII, 1895, 101-118, 259-269.

Chapter Six: Tracing the Historical Journey: The First Thousand Years

[1] Emanuela Marinelli, *La Sindone: Un'Immagine "Impossibile."* (Milan: Edizioni San Paolo, 1996), 75-76.

[2] J.B. Segal, *Edessa: The Blessed City* (New York: Oxford University Press, 1970).

[3] Josephus, *The Jewish Wars*, 21.

[4] Rev. C.F. Cruse, tr., *The Ecclesiastical History of Eusebius Pamphilus — Bishop of Caesarea in Palestine* (New York: Dayton & Saxton, 1842), 43-47.

[5] Steven Runciman, "Some Remarks on the Image of Edessa," *The Cambridge Historical Journal*, III; 3 (1931), 239.

[6] George Howard, tr., *The Teaching of Addai* (California: Scholar's Press 1981), 9-10.

[7] Alexander Roberts and James Donaldson, eds., *The Ante-Nicene Fathers*, Vol. 8 (Michigan: Eerdmans Publishing Company, 1950), 558.

[8] Ian Wilson, *The Shroud of Turin* (Garden City: Doubleday & Company, 1987).

[9] *Ibid.*

[10] Runciman, 243.

[11] Wilson, 138.

[12] *Ibid.*

[13] Evagrius, Bishop of Edessa, *A History of the Church* (London: Samuel Bagster and Sons, London), 220.

[14] Wilson, 93.

[15] St. John Damascene, *St. John Damascene on Holy Images*, tr. by Mary H. Allies (London: Thomas Baker, 1898).

[16] Henry George Liddell and Robert Scott, *A Greek-English Lexicon* (Oxford: The Clarendon Press), 829.

[17] Ian Wilson, *The Shroud of Turin* (Garden City: Doubleday & Company, 1979), 158 & 162-163. Wilson quotes Ernst von Dobschütz, *Christusbilder* (Leipzig, 1899), 134, appendix entitled "Der altere lateinische Abgartext." The second part of the quote is from a translation from Maurus Green, "Enshrouded in Silence," *Ampleforth Journal*, LXXIV (1969), 333.

[18] Robert Drews, *In Search of the Shroud of Turin* (New Jersey: Rowman and Allanheld, 1984), 39 and 47.

[19] Wilson, 235-251.

[20] Liddell and Scott, 1918.

[21] Ernst von Dobschütz, *Christusbilder*, 48.

[22] Dr. Daniel C. Scavone, "The Historian and the Shroud," *History, Science, Theology and the Shroud* (Proceedings of the Symposium, June 22-23, 1991 at St. Louis University, St. Louis, Missouri), 192.

[23] Drews, 39.

[24] Ian Wilson, *The Mysterious Shroud* (Garden City: Doubleday & Company, 1986), 111-114.

Chapter Seven: The Journey Continues: The Second Thousand Years

[1] Kurt Weitzmann, *The Icons: Monastery of St. Catherine* (Princeton: Princeton University Press, 1976), Vol. 1.

[2] Ian Wilson, *The Mysterious Shroud* (Garden City: Doubleday & Company, 1986), 114.

[3] Dr. Daniel C. Scavone, "The Historian And The Shroud," *History, Science, Theology and the Shroud* (St. Louis, Missouri, 1991), 194.

[4] *Roman Codex*, Vatican Library Codex No. 5696, Folio 35, as quoted by Wilson, 146.

[5] Orderic Vitalis, *Ecclesiastical History*, Part III, Bk. IX, 8, as quoted by Wilson, 158.

[6] Count de Riant, *The Sacred Spoils of Constantinople (Exuviae Sacrae Constantinoplitanae)* (Geneva, 1878), as quoted by Wilson, 167.

[7] Noel Currer-Briggs, *The Shroud and the Grail* (New York: St. Martin's Press, 1987), 118. See also William of Tyre, *Historia Belli Sacri*, XX 25, Migne's *Latin Patrology*, Vol. 201, and William of Tyre's *Histoire Generale des Croisades par les Auteurs Contemporains, Guillaume de Tyre*.

[8] Currer-Briggs, 6, 24, 120-125.

[9] *Ibid.*, 12-13.

[10] Wilson, 75 and 115.

[11] Scavone, 195-196.

[12] Villehardouin and Joinville, *The Chronicles of the Crusades*, tr. by M.R.B. Shaw, (Middlesex, England: Penguin Books, 1963), 31. See also: *O City of Byzantium, Annals of Niketas Chroniates*, tr. by Harry J. Magoulias (Detroit: Wayne State University Press, 1984).

[13] *Ibid.*, 33.

[14] *Ibid.*, 42.

[15] *Ibid.*, 76.

[16] *Ibid.*, 92.

[17] Robert de Clary, *The Conquest of Constantinople* (New York: Octagon Books, 1966), 112.

[18] Frank C. Tribbe, *Portrait of Jesus?* (New York: Stein & Day Publishers, 1983), 56.

[19] Clary, 101.

[20] *Ibid.*, 104.

[21] Currer-Briggs, 147-148.

[22] Brother Bruno Bonnet-Eymard, *Catholic Reformation in the XX Century*, 238 (April 1991), 25.

[23] *Ibid.*, 15.

The shroud of Besançon: Noel Currer-Briggs notes in *The Shroud and the Grail* (pp. 50-55 and 62) that in 705, Bishop Arculf, while visiting Jerusalem, was shown an eight-foot piece of linen bearing Jesus' image which he was told was the burial shroud. A similar story is told in 1140 by Peter the Deacon of Monte Cassino who also visited the Holy Land. Currer-Briggs says that this was likely the Besançon shroud, a painted copy of the original which bears only a frontal image and is eight feet long. This copy (one of several including the shroud of Cadouin and the shroud of Charlemagne) made its way from Jerusalem to Besançon, France. Currer-Briggs notes that this goes "a long way to explain the skepticism of Bishop Henri and Pierre of Troyes in the fourteenth century. After all, the eight-foot cloth had been venerated in Jerusalem for eight centuries, and the copy... came to be taken for the original..." It appears that the Besançon shroud was destroyed in 1349 when the Cathedral of Besançon was struck by lightning and burned to the ground.

Pope Clement VII: Although his claim to the papacy was recognized by several European nations, the Church regards Clement VII (headquartered in Avignon) as the first schismatic anti-Pope of the Western Schism, Urban VI being the legitimate Pope.

[24] Desmond Seward, *The Monks of War: The Military Religious Orders* (Archon Books, 1972), 1.

[25] *Ibid.*, 6-7.

[26] *Ibid.*, 20.

[27] *Ibid.*, 25.

[28] Tribbe, 59.

[29] Wilson, 117.

[30] Currer-Briggs, 6.

[31] *Ibid.*, 14-15.

[32] Malcolm Barber, *The Trial of the Templars* (London: Cambridge University Press, 1978), 1.

[33] *Ibid.*, 63.

[34] *Ibid.*, 137-138.

[35] *Ibid.*, 147.

[36] Rex Morgan, "Did the Templars Take the Shroud to England: New Evidence from Templecombe," *History, Science, Theology and the Shroud* (Proceedings of the Symposium, June 22-23, 1991 at St. Louis University, St. Louis, Missouri), 205-232.

[37] Currer-Briggs, 133.

[38] *Ibid.*, 35 and 39.

[39] Lynn Picknett and Clive Prince, *Turin Shroud: In Whose Image? The Truth Behind the Centuries-Long Conspiracy of Silence* (New York: Harper Collins Publishers, 1991), 118.

[40] *Ibid.*, 125.

[41] *Ibid.*, 124.

[42] Tribbe, 75.

[43] Letter from Giovanni Cardinal Saldarini, Archbishop of Turin and Papal Custodian of the Holy Shroud, dated Turin, October 30, 1994 (See Appendix).

Chapter Eight: Art and the Shroud

[1] Kenneth Stevenson and Gary Habermas, *The Shroud and the Controversy* (Nashville: Thomas Nelson Publishers, 1990), 75 and 170.

[2] Josh McDowell, *Evidence that Demands a Verdict* (Campus Crusade, 1979), 228-231.

[3] Albert R. Dreisbach, "Did Peter See More Than An Empty Shroud?" *History, Science, Theology and the Shroud* (Proceedings of the Symposium, June 22-23, 1991 at St. Louis University, St. Louis, Missouri), 344-357.

[4] Rex Morgan, *The Holy Shroud and the Earliest Paintings of Christ* (Australia: Runciman Press, 1986), 53-54.

[5] Ian Wilson, *The Shroud of Turin* (New York: Doubleday & Company, 1979), 280-281.

[6] Ian Wilson, *The Mysterious Shroud* (New York: Doubleday & Company, 1986), 111.

[7] Robert Drews, *In Search of the Shroud of Turin* (New Jersey: Rowman & Allenheld, 1984), 79.

[8] Ian Wilson, *The Mysterious Shroud*, 104-111.

[9] Ernst von Dobschütz, *Christusbilder* (Leipzig: Hinrichs'sche, 1899), 308-329.

[10] Morgan, 16, 120-122.

[11] Morgan, 8.

[12] Morgan, 20.

[13] Frank C. Tribbe, *Portrait of Jesus?* (New York: Stein & Day Publishers, 1983), as quoted by Morgan, 64.

[14] *Ibid.*, 239.

[15] Wilson, 105.

[16] *Ibid.*

[17] *Ibid.*, 112-114

[18] *Ibid.*, 114.

[19] Ian Wilson, *Holy Faces, Secret Places* (New York: Doubleday & Company, 1991), 160-161.

Additional Sources:

André Grabar, *The Beginnings of Christian Art, 200-395* (London: Thames & Hudson, 1967).

André Grabar, *Christian Iconography: A Study of Its Origins* (London: Routledge & Kegan, 1969).

Heinrich Pfeiffer, S.J., "The Shroud of Turin and the Face of Christ in Paleochristian, Byzantine and Western Medieval Art, Part I," *Shroud Spectrum International*, 9 (December 1983).

Kurt Weitzmann, *The Icons: Monastery of St. Catherine* (Princeton: Princeton University Press, 1976).

Chapter Nine: Credibly Discrediting the Carbon-14 Test on the Shroud

[1] "Using Science to Date an Icon of Faith," *National Geographic* (February 1989).

[2] R.E. Taylor, *Radiocarbon Dating: An Archaeological Perspective* (New York: Harcourt, Brace, Jovanovich Publishers, 1987), ix.

[3] *National Geographic.*

[4] Malcolm W. Browne, "How Carbon-14 Was Used to Fix the Date of the Shroud," *New York Times* (October 14, 1988), p. A-10.

[5] *Ibid.*

[6] P.E. Damon, D.J. Donahue, B.H. Gore et al., "Radiocarbon Dating of the Shroud of Turin," *Nature Magazine* (February 16, 1989), 612.

[7] Holger Kersten and Elmar R. Gruber, *The Jesus Conspiracy: The Turin Shroud and the Truth about the Resurrection* (Rockport, Massachusetts: Element Press, 1994), 313-318.

[8] *Ibid.*

[9] Kenneth Stevenson and Gary Habermas, *The Shroud and the Controversy* (Nashville: Thomas Nelson Publishers, 1990), 49.

[10] Fr. Joseph Marino, O.S.B., "The Shroud of Turin and the Carbon 14 Controversy," *Fidelity Magazine* (February 1989), 36.

[11] *Ibid.*

[12] *Ibid.*, p. 37.

[13] Stevenson and Habermas, *The Shroud and the Controversy*, p. 53.

[14] *Ibid.*

[15] Dr. Dmitri A. Kouznetsov, *Journal of Archaeological Science*, January 1996, Volume 23.

Chapter Ten: How Were the Mysterious Images Formed?

[1] Kenneth Stevenson and Gary Habermas, *The Shroud and the Controversy* (Nashville: Thomas Nelson Publishers, 1990), 120.

[2] Dr. John Heller, *Report on the Shroud of Turin* (Boston: Houghton Mifflin Company, 1983), 198.

[3] Stevenson and Habermas, 127.

[4] Paul Vignon, *The Shroud of Christ* (New Hyde Park, New York: University Books, 1970).

[5] Frank C. Tribbe, *Portrait of Jesus?* (New York: Stein & Day Publishers, 1983), 204.

[6] Robert Wilcox, "What Caused Shroud Images?" *The Voice* (March 12, 1982), 10. Dr. Eugenia Nitowski stated in *The Intermountain Catholic* (Salt Lake City, Utah, March 21, 1997 - Barbara Stinson Lee) that medical science bears out that "the body temperature of a person dying of heatstroke can rise to up to 108 degrees, and at the moment of death can rise another nine or ten degrees in what is called a post-mortem fever or caloricity." Nitowski believes that the "intense heat of the body of Jesus and its chemical changes, the rapidity with which he had to be buried according to Jewish custom, and the environment of the tomb itself led to the production of the image on the cloth, which took place, not on the cloth surface, but in the actual cellulose of its fiber." In 1986, Nitowski, with a team of scientists forming the Environmental Study of the Shroud of Jerusalem, used a medical mannequin filled with water at 119 degrees and created an image with some similarities.

However, I do not believe this "similar image" explains the Turin image. Although the burial of Jesus was rapid, relatively speaking, two to three hours elapsed from the moment of Jesus' death on the Cross to His actual enshroudment — time taken to secure permission to remove the body, carry it to the tomb, and prepare the body. It is thus unlikely that the body would be 119 degrees at the time of enshroudment. Further, as shown earlier with the Vaporgraph theory, such chemical fumes diffuse (creating a vague and unclear image), penetrate the fibers and do not produce a three-dimensional image (whereas the Turin Shroud shows no diffusion, no penetration and a clear three-dimensionality). Further, a post-mortem-fever-image would not account for non-body images (coins, hair, phylactery, flowers). In a separate note, Dr. Nitowski reports that in 1978, her team found a "tiny piece of muscle" (microscopic) from the back of Jesus possibly torn away by the cruel flogging. This bears further examination.

[7] Tribbe, 205-206.

[8] Ian Wilson, *The Mysterious Shroud* (Garden City: Doubleday & Company, 1986), 99.

[9] Robert Wilcox, *Shroud* (New York: Bantam Books, 1978), 141-142.

[10] *Ibid.*, 143.

[11] *Ibid.*, 145.

[12] *Ibid.*, 146.

[13] Tribbe, 208.

[14] *Ibid.*

[15] *Ibid.*

[16] Ian Wilson, *The Shroud of Turin* (Garden City: Doubleday & Company, 1979), 209.

[17] *The New Yorker* (August 31, 1946).

[18] *Hiroshima-Nagasaki: A Pictorial Record* (Tokyo: Hiroshima-Nagasaki Publishing Committee, 1978).

[19] Tribbe, 209-210.

[20] Wilson, *The Shroud of Turin*, 209.

[21] *Ibid.*

[22] *Ibid.*, 210.

[23] Peter Rinaldi, *When Millions Saw the Shroud* (1979), 137.

[24] *The Christian Century* (March 15, 1989), 276.

Chronology

[1] Emanuela Marinelli, *La Sindone: Un' Immagine "Impossibile,"* (Milan, Italy: Edizioni San Paolo, 1996), 142-144.

Bibliography

Barbar, Malcolm. *The Trial of the Templars*. Cambridge University Press, 1978.

_____. "The Templars and the Turin Shroud," *Catholic Historical Review*, April 1982.

Barbet, Dr. Pierre, *A Doctor at Calvary*. Garden City: Image Books, 1963.

Bender, A.P. "Beliefs, Rites and Customs of the Jews Connected with Death, Burial and Mourning," *The Jewish Quarterly Review* 6-7 (1894-1895).

Berry, Dr. George Ricker. *The Interlinear New Testament*. Chicago: Follett Publishing Company, 1960.

Bonnet-Eymard, Brother Bruno. *Catholic Reformation in the XXth Century*, 238, April 1991.

Braulo, "Epistle 42," *Iberian Fathers*. Volume 2. Washington, DC: Catholic University Press 1969.

Brown, Raymond E. "The Burial of Jesus," *Catholic Biblical Quarterly*, 50, April 1988.

Browne, Malcolm B. "How Carbon-14 Was Used to Fix the Date of the Shroud," *New York Times* (October 14, 1988), p. A-10.

Bucklin, Dr. Robert. "The Shroud of Turin: Viewpoint of a Forensic Pathologist," *Shroud Spectrum International* 13 (1984).

_____. *The Silent Witness* (Pyramid Home Video, Box 1046 Santa Monica, California 90406) Telephone: 213-828-7577.

_____. "The Legal and Medical Aspects of the Trial and Death of Christ," *Medicine, Science and the Law* (January 1970), 14-26.

_____. "The Medical Aspects of the Crucifixion of Our Lord Jesus Christ," *Linacre Quarterly* (February 1958).

_____. "The Shroud of Turin: Viewpoint of a Medical Pathologist," *Shroud Spectrum International* 13 (1984), 3-8.

_____. "The Pathologist Looks at the Shroud," *Second International Congress, The Shroud and Science* (Turin, Italy, October 7-8, 1978).

Bulst, Werner, SJ. "The Pollen Grains on the Shroud of Turin," *Shroud Spectrum* 10, 1984.

_____. *The Shroud of Turin.* Milwaukee: Bruce Publishing Company, 1957.

Cameron, Averil. *Procopius and the Sixth Century.* University of California Press, 1985.

Clari, Robert de. *The Conquest of Constantinople.* New York: Octagon Books, York, 1966.

Crispino, Dorothy. *Shroud Spectrum,* 28-29.

Currer-Briggs, Noel. *The Shroud and the Grail.* New York: St. Martin's Press, York, 1987.

Dobschütz, Ernst von. *Christusbilder.* Leipzig: Hinrichs'sche, 1899.

Dreisbach, Rev. Albert R. "Did Peter See More than an Empty Shroud?" *History, Science, Theology and the Shroud* (Proceedings of the Symposium, June 22-23, 1991 at St. Louis University, St. Louis, Missouri) 1991.

Drews, Robert. *In Search of the Shroud of Turin.* New Jersey: Rowman & Allanheld, 1984.

Eusebius of Caesaria, *The Ecclesiastical History of Eusebius Pamphilus.* Translated by Rev. C.F. Cruse. New York: Dayton & Saxton Press, 1842.

Evagrius Scholasticus. *The History of the Church.* London: Samuel Bagster & Sons.

Filas, Francis, SJ. *The Dating of the Shroud of Turin from Coins of Pontius Pilate* (Cogan Productions, a Division of ACTA Foundation, January 1984), 3. Also 3rd ed. Youngston, Arizona, 1984.

Frei, Dr. Max. "Nine Years of Palynological Studies on the Shroud," *Shroud Spectrum,* 3, 1982.

Gervase of Tilbury. *Otia Imperialia.*

Grabar, André. *The Beginnings of Christian Art, 200-395.* London: Thames & Hudson, 1967.

_____. *Christian Iconography: A Study of Its Origins.* London: Routledge & Kegan, 1969.

Green, Maurus. "Enshrouded in Silence," *Ampleforth Journal,* 74, 1969.

Hachlili, Rachael and Ann Killebrew, "Was the Coin-on-Eye Custom a Jewish Burial Practice in the Second Temple Period?" *Biblical Archaeologist* (Summer 1983), 147-153.

Haralick, Dr. Robert. *Analysis of Digital Images of the Shroud of Turin.* Spatial Data Analysis Lab - Virginia Polytechnic Institute & State University, 1983.

Hoare, Rodney. *The Turin Shroud is Genuine: The Irrefutable Evidence.* London, England: Souvenir Press, 1994.

Howard, George. *The Teaching of Addai.* Chicago, CA: Scholars Press, 1981.

Jackson Dr. John P. "Foldmarks as a Historical Record of the Turin Shroud," *Shroud Spectrum International* 11, 1984.

John Damascene, St. *St. John Damascene on Holy Images.* Translated by Mary H. Allies. London: Thomas Baker Press, 1898.

Jones, Alexander, ed. *The New Testament of the Jerusalem Bible.* Garden City, NY: Doubleday & Company, 1969.

Jumper, Eric, Kenneth Stevenson and John Jackson. "Images of Coins on a Burial Cloth?" *The Numismatist,* July 1978.

Lampe, Professor. *Lexicon of Patristic Greek.* Cambridge, England.

Liddell, Henry George and Robert Scott. *A Greek-English Lexicon.* Oxford-Clarendon, 1887.

Marinelli, Emanuela. *La Sindone: Un'Immagine "Impossibile."* Milan, Italy: Edizioni San Paolo, 1996.

McDowell, Josh. *Evidence that Demands a Verdict.* Campus Crusade, 1979.

Meacham, William. "The Authentication of the Turin Shroud: An Issue in Archaeological Epistemology," *Current Anthropology* 24, June 1983.

_____. "On the Archaeological Evidence for a Coin-on-Eye

Jewish Burial Custom in the First Century A.D.," *Biblical Archaeologist* 49 (March 1986), 56-61.

Mingana, A., ed. *Woodbrooke Studies.* Volume 2. Cambridge: W. Heffer & Sons, 1928.

Morgan, Rex. *The Holy Shroud and the Earliest Paintings of Christ.* Manly, Australia: The Runciman Press, 1986.

_____. "Did the Templars Take the Shroud to England? New Evidence from Templecombe," *History, Science, Theology and the Shroud.* (Proceedings of the Symposium, June 22-23, 1991 at St. Louis University, St. Louis, Missouri), 1991.

Pfeiffer, Heinrich, SJ. "The Shroud of Turin and the Face of Christ in Paleochristian, Byzantine and Western Medieval Art, Part I," *Shroud Spectrum* 9, December 1983.

Phillips, George, tr. *The Doctrine of Addai, the Apostle.* London: Truber & Company, 1876.

Phillips, Dr. Thomas. *Nature* Magazine 337, 1989.

Picknett, Lynn and Clive Prince. *Turin Shroud: In Whose Image?* New York: Harper Collins Publishers, 1994.

Piczek, Isabel. "Is the Turin Shroud a Painting?" *History, Science, Theology and the Shroud* (Proceedings of the Symposium, June 22-23, 1991 at St. Louis University, St. Louis, Missouri), 1991.

Rahmani, L.Y. "Ancient Jerusalem's Funerary Customs and Tombs," *Biblical Archaeologist* 44-45, 1981-1982.

Raes, Professor Gilbert. "Rapport d'Analise," *La S. Sindone.* Supplement to *Rivista Diocesana Torinese,* January 1976.

Riant, Count de. *The Sacred Spoils of Constantinople (Exuviae Sacrae Constantinopolitanae).* Geneva, 1878.

Ricci, Msgr. Giulio. *Guide to the Photographic Exhibit of the Holy Shroud.* Center for the Study of the Passion of Christ and the Holy Shroud, Milwaukee, Wisconsin, 1982.

_____. *The Way of the Cross in the Light of the Holy Shroud.* Center for the Study of the Passion of Christ and the Holy Shroud, Milwaukee, Wisconsin, 1975. Revised 1978.

Rinaldi, Fr. Peter. *When Millions Saw the Shroud: Letters from Turin.* Don Bosco Publishers, 1979.

Roberts, Alexander and James Donaldson, eds. *The Ante-Nicene Fathers*, Vol. 8. Grand Rapids, Michigan: Wm. B. Eerdmans Publishing Company, 1951.

Robinson, Rt. Rev. John A.T. "The Shroud of Turin and the Grave Clothes of the Gospels," *Proceedings of 1977 U.S. Conference of Research on the Shroud of Turin*, March 1977.

_____. *Face to Face with the Turin Shroud*. Mayhew-McCrommons, 1978.

Runciman, Steven. "Some Remarks on the Image of Edessa," *Cambridge Historical Journal* III, No. 3, 1931.

Scavone, Dr. Daniel C. "The Historian and the Shroud," *History, Science, Theology and the Shroud*. St. Louis, Missouri, 1991.

_____. "The Shroud of Turin in Constantinople: The Documentary Evidence," *Diadalikon*. Waucanda, IL: Bolchazy-Carducci, 1990.

Segal, J.B. *Edessa: The Blessed City*. New York: Oxford University Press, 1970.

Seward, Desmond. *The Monks of War*. Connecticut: Archon Books, 1972.

Stevenson, Kenneth and Gary Habermas. *The Shroud and the Controversy*. Nashville, TN: Thomas Nelson Publishers, 1990.

_____. *Verdict on the Shroud*. Pennsylvania: Banbury Books, 1981.

Tribbe, Frank C. *Portrait of Jesus?* New York: Stein & Day Publishers, 1983.

Tryer, John. "Looking at the Turin Shroud as a Textile," *Shroud Spectrum*, 6 (1983), 68-69.

Vasiliev, A.A. *History of the Byzantine Empire*. Madison: University of Wisconsin Press, 1958.

Vignon, Paul. *The Shroud of Christ*. Westminster: Archibald Constable & Company, Ltd., 1902.

Villehardouin, Geoffroy de and Jean de Joinville. *Chronicles of the Crusades*. Middlesex, England: Penguin Books, 1963.

Weitzmann, Kurt. *The Icons: Monastery of St. Catherine*. Princeton, NJ: Princeton University Press, 1976.

Whanger, Dr. Alan and Mary. "Floral, Coin and Other Non-Body Images on the Shroud of Turin" (Durham, NC: Duke University).

_____. "Polarized Image Overlay Technique," *Applied Optics* (March 15, 1985), 766-772.

William of Tyre. *Historia Belli Sacri.* Migne's *Latin Patrology.* 201.

_____. *Histoire Generale des Croisades par les Auteurs Contemporains, Guilame de Tyr et ses Continuateurs.*

Wilson, Ian. *The Mysterious Shroud.* Garden City, NY: Doubleday & Company, 1986.

_____. *The Shroud of Turin.* Garden City, NY: Doubleday & Company, 1979.

_____. *Holy Faces, Secret Places.* Garden City, NY: Doubleday & Company, 1991.

Wuenschel, Rev. Edward, C.Ss.R. "The Shroud of Turin and the Burial of Christ," *Catholic Biblical Quarterly,* VII, October 1945, and VIII, April 1946.

Zlotnick, Dov. *The Tractate "Mourning" Semahot.* New Haven, CT: Yale University Press, 1966.

Zohary, Michael. *Flora Palaestina* (Jerusalem: Israel Academy of Sciences and Humanities, 1966-1977).

Zugibe, Dr. Frederick. *The Cross and the Shroud.* New York: Paragon House Publishers, 1988.

NAME INDEX

Aaron 7
Abgar, King xvii, 100, 101, 104, 108, 109-110, 120, 147
Achilles 16
Addai (see Thaddaeus)
Adge, Michel 181
Adler, Dr. Alan 65, 66, 186
Aiello, John 37
Aldo, Prof. Marastoni 46
Alexander the Great 49
Alexis I Comnenus, Emperor 120
Alexis, Emperor 125
Alphonsus VI of Leon 91
Amalric I, King of Jerusalem 120, 121, 123, 133, 140
Ananias 100, 101, 103
Andrew of Crete 109
Anna of Lusignano 194
Ashe, Geoffrey 188
Avi-Yonah, Michael 37
Balossino, Dr. Nello 38
Ballestrero, Cardinal Anastasio 159, 162, 166, 195
Ballone, Prof. Luigi Baima 38, 66, 67, 87
Barbet, Dr. Pierre 50, 58, 66, 93
Basil of Jerusalem 110
Beard, Jonathon 10
Bender, A.P. 95
Berard, Rev. Aram, SJ xiii
Bernard of Clairvaux, St. 131, 132
Bertola, Antonio 143
Blanco, Jose Delfin 67
Boniface de Montferrat 125, 126, 127, 134, 138
Bonnet-Eymard, Brother 129
Borromeo, St. Charles 143
Braulio, Bishop 109
Brinkmann, Rev. Frederick, C SsR xiii, 201
Brown, Raymond 85
Bucklin, Dr. Robert 38, 50, 51, 53-55, 59, 62, 63, 93
Bulst, Werner, SJ 23, 81, 82, 90, 146
Caiaphas, High Priest 51
Cameron, Prof. James 38, 56
Caselli, Dr. Giuseppe 66
Cervantes, Dr. Faustino 172

Cesalpino, Andrea 67
Charles VI, King 129
Charney, Geoffrey de xviii, 136, 193
Charney, Geoffrey I de 128
Charney, Geoffrey II de 128, 129, 130, 136, 193
Charney, Marguerite de 129, 130, 138, 194
Charon 38
Chiara, Alberto 68
Chosroes I, King 107, 148
Chretien de Troyes 122
Claudia 146
Clary, Robert de 124, 126, 127, 134, 193
Clement V, Pope 135
Clement VI, Pope 194
Clement VII, anti-Pope 129, 210
Clotilde of Savoy, Princess 4
Constantine the Great, Emperor 49, 69, 113
Constantine V Copronynos, Emperor 113
Constantine VII, Emperor 30
Coon, Prof. Carleton 7
Currer-Briggs, Noel 6, 122, 129, 135, 138, 140, 209
Curto, Silvio 12
Damien of the Cross, Sr. (see Nitowski)
Damon, Paul E. 161, 162
Dandolo, Enrico 124
Daniel-Rops, Henri 7
Danin, Avinoam 20, 30, 95
D'Arcis, Bishop Pierre 129, 194
DaVinci, Leonardo xvii, 45, 69
Delage, Dr. Yves 16, 50, 73, 97
Dembowski, Dr. Peter 127
DeSalvo, John A. 182
Desmond, Seward 131
Dinegar, Rev. Robert, PhD xiii, 174
Dobschütz, Ernst von 110
Donahue, Dr. Douglas 162, 163
Dreisbach, Fr. Albert xiii, xvi, 4, 24, 89, 115, 146, 147, 150, 155, 198
Drews, Robert 148
Dubarle, Fr. A.M. 154
Ducas, Theodore 128
Durer, Albrecht 4

Eastwood, Gillian 171
Enrie, Giuseppe 5, 28, 34, 36, 39, 195
Erbach, Rabbi Eleazor 9
Eschenbach, Wolfram von 135
Eulalius, Bishop 108
Eusebius of Caesarea 101-102, 117
Evagrius Scholasticus 109, 117
Filas, Fr. Francis, SJ 36, 37, 39, 41, 44, 45
Fossati, Cardinal Maurilio 5
Francis de Sales, St. 143
Frei, Dr. Max 13, 19-22, 29, 31, 91, 96, 100, 103, 112, 117
Fulk of Anjou 140
Gambeschia, Dr. Joseph 50
Garza-Valdez, Dr. 16, 94, 172
Gayet, M. 11, 12
German, John D. 182
Germanus I, Patriarch 110
Giordano, Dr. 85
Goldoni, Carlo 67
Gonella, Prof. Luigi 162
Gorrevod, Cardinal Louis de 3
Gove, Dr. Harry 173
Graeber, Ralph 183, 184, 186
Greeman, H. 7
Gregory II, Pope 110
Gregory the Archdeacon 115
Gruber, Elmar 166
Guarini, Guarino 143
Guscin, Mark 91, 207
Haas, Dr. Herbert 169
Haas, Nicu 60, 93
Habermas, Gary 45
Hachlili, Rachel 78, 79, 204
Hadrian, Emperor 7
Hall, E.T. 162
Hall, Herbert 112
Haralick, Dr. Robert 36, 39, 40, 46
Heaphy, Thomas 150
Hedges, Dr. R.E.M. 162
Heliland, Abbot 122
Heller, Dr. John 10, 65, 66, 178
Henri of Flanders 126
Henry of Poitiers, Bishop 129
Henry IV, King 120
Hermas, Guillermo 207
Herod, King 52
Hersey, John R. 187
Homer 113, 144
Horowitz, Aharon 20

Iannone, John 106, 197
Iannone, Kim 78
Imbalzano, Giovanni 181
Innocent III, Pope, 124, 128
Isaac, Emperor 125
Isaac II Angelus, Emperor 134
Isaiah 47
Jackson, Rebecca 107
Jackson, Dr. John 8, 33, 35, 45, 107, 175, 188
James of Antioch 110
James, Dr. Everett 186
James, St. 99
Jerome, St. 99
John Damascene, St. 110, 117
John of Jerusalem 110
John Paul II, Pope xi, xv, 130, 167, 195
John the Apostle, St. 89, 146
John the Good, King 129
Johnson, Kendall 185
Jehohanan ben Ha'galgol 60, 61, 93, 94
Joseph of Arimathea 13, 79, 80, 85, 99
Josephus 73, 79
Judica-Cordiglia, Giovanni Battista 5, 6, 195
Julius Paulus 85
Julia, Empress 38
Julius II, Pope 141, 194
Jumper, Dr. Eric 8, 33, 35, 45, 59, 182, 188
Justinian I, Emperor 30, 113
Justinian II, Emperor 30, 113, 154
Kersten, Holger 166
Killebrew, A. 207
Kirlian, Semyon 183
Kloner, Amos 92-94
Kohlbeck, Dr. Joseph 59
Kouznetsov, Dr. Dmitri 94, 169, 173, 196
Lambert, Philip 3, 141
Lampe, Prof. 105
Landau, Terry A. 68
La Voie, Bonnie 89
Lazarus 84, 92, 95
Lentulus 149
Libby, Willard Frank 161
Liddell, Henry George 110, 113
Lombatti, Pro. Antonio 204
Louis of Savoy, Duke 130
Louis VII, King 120, 193

Ludwig, Duke of Savoy 194
Lynn, Donald 49
Madden, Frederick 36, 37
Maloney, Paul 14, 20
Ma'nu VI, King 147
Manuel I Comnenus, Emperor 120, 133, 193
Map, Walter 122
Marino, Fr. Joseph, OSB xiii, 92, 165, 169, 171, 189
Mary Magdalene 89
Mary Margaret 134, 138
Marx, Michael 36, 37
Mattingly, Dr. Stephen 94, 172
McCrone, Dr. Walter 179
McDowell, Josh 146
McNair, Prof. Philip 13, 58
McPherson, Daniel xiii
Meacham, William 21, 62, 159, 168-169, 204
Meissner, Peter 41
Mesarites, Nicholas 123
Michael III, Emperor 113
Miller, Vernon xiii, 6
Mills, Dr. Allen 83
Milly (see Philip de Milly)
Moedder, Dr. Hermann 50
Molay, Jacques de 126
Molinari, Ida 68
Montferrat (see Boniface)
Montreal, Jean de 137
Moran, Kevin 43
Morgan, Rex 137, 138, 150, 151
Moroni, Prof. Mario 36, 169
Moses 7
Moss, Thelma 185
Motern, William 33
Nero, Emperor 147
Nicephorus, Patriarch 110
Nicholas d'Orrante 128
Nicodemus 67, 86, 99
Nitowski, Dr. Eugenia 77, 79, 211
Orderic Vitalis 120
Origen 62
Otterbein, Rev. Adam, CSsR xiii
Otto de la Roche 126, 127, 134, 138
Paruta, Dr. Anthony 165, 189
Pascal II, Pope 132
Paul of Mt. Latros 116
Paul, St. 99
Payens, Hugues de 130, 132

Pellicori, Sam 59
Pellegrino, Cardinal Michele 6, 12, 195
Peter the Apostle, St. 49, 82, 89, 91, 98, 99, 145
Philip de Milly 121, 123, 133, 134, 140
Philip of Alsace 122
Philip II, King 124
Philip IV, King 135
Philips, Dr. Thomas 190
Philo 73, 84
Pia, Secondo 5, 34, 66, 191, 194
Picknett, Lynn xvii, 45, 46, 140, 179
Piczek, Isabel 145, 156-157
Pierre de Thury, Cardinal 129
Pilate, Pontius 9, 33, 35, 36, 38, 39, 40, 42, 52, 79, 80, 84
Pliny 11
Prasside, St. 146
Prince, Clive xvii, 45, 46, 140, 179
Procopius of Caesaria 107
Propp, Dr. Keith 175
Prudens 146
Prudentia, St. 146
Raes, Prof. Gilbert 13, 14, 31, 171
Rahmani, L.Y. 76, 77, 83, 95, 204
Ricci, Monsignor Giulio 85
Richet, Charles 16
Richmond, Prof. I.A. 57
Riggi Di Numana, Dr. Giovanni 17, 21, 24, 31, 68, 162, 166, 171-172
Rinaldi, Rev. Peter, SND xiii, 197
Robert of Flanders 120
Robinson, Rt. Rev. John 75
Roche, Amaurey de la 136
Roche, Humbert de la 138
Rodante, Sebastian 66
Roger, Ray 177, 186
Romanus Lacapenus, Emperor 115
Runciman, Prof. Steven 102, 107
Saint Omer, Nicholas de 134
Saldarini, Cardinal Giovanni xi, 48, 68, 143, 191, 196, 199-200
Sargon 16
Sava, Dr. Anthony 50
Scavone, Dr. Daniel xiii, 67, 114, 118, 119, 173
Scheuermann, Oswald 25, 28, 30, 43, 46
Schwortz, Barrie, 64, 201
Segal, J.B. 99
Sennacherib 14

Setti, Dr. Levi 60
Sixtus IV, Pope 141
Smith, Dr. Jennifer 68
Soemundarson, Nicholas 120
South, Peter H. 13
Sox, Rev. 86
Stephen III, Pope 110
Stevenson, Rev. Kenneth ix, xii, 7, 9,
    19, 21, 22, 24, 25, 45, 48, 57, 88, 90,
    145, 171, 174
Strange, James 24
Tacitus 49
Tamburelli, Giovanni 35
Taylafer de Gene, Jean 137
Testore, Prof. F. 162
Thaddaeus (Addai) 103, 104, 117
Thomas the Apostle, St. 57, 101-102
Thurston, Herbert, SJ 65
Tiberius, Emperor 36, 37
Tite, Dr. Michael 162, 166
Trematore, Mario 142
Tribbe, Frank 10, 60, 66, 130, 133, 151,
    181
Trosello, Franca Pastore 91
Tryer, John 14
Tryon, Dr. Victor 67, 68
Tzaferis, Vasilius 60
Ulpian 85
Umberto II, King xv, 12, 130, 195
Urban II, Pope 132

Uros Milutin, King 154
Vergy, Jeanne de 128
Vial, Prof. G. 162
Vignon, Paul 12, 83, 87, 151-152, 181
Villalain, Dr. Jose 207
Villehardouin, Geoffrey de 124, 126
Volckringer, Dr. Jean 182, 185
Wedenissow, Dr. Ugo 63
Weitzmann, Kurt 119, 152
Werfel, Franz 1
Whanger, Dr. Alan 9, 20-21, 25-31, 38,
    41, 42, 46, 87, 91, 96, 153, 201, 204
Whanger, Mary 26, 201
Wilcox, Robert 10, 11, 12, 65, 182, 184,
    186
William of Tyre 120, 122
Willis, Dr. David 50
Wilson, Ian 2, 6-8, 14, 22, 33, 35, 48,
    60, 64, 86, 103, 107, 108, 116, 119,
    134-136, 148-149, 151, 154-155, 187
Woelfli, W. 162
Wuenschel, Fr. Edward, CSsR 73, 82,
    83
Yarbrough, William 37, 41
Zanninotto, Prof. Gino 3, 115
Zias, Joseph 92-94
Zlotnick, Prof. Dov 94, 95
Zohary, Michael 28
Zugibe, Dr. Frederick 50, 55, 58, 93

SUBJECT INDEX

Abgar legends 101-117
Accelerated Mass Spectrometer (AMS) 159-161
acheiropoietas xvii, 103, 112, 116-117, 152
Acheiropoietas, Church of 134
age of Man of Shroud 6
Agony in Garden (see Garden)
aloes 87, 89
Arizona University Lab 162, 164, 169
A.S.S.I.S.T. 20
Athens (Shroud in) 128, 130
atomic decay 160
augur's wand (see *lituus*)
aura (of Jesus) 184-185
auto-radiograph 187, 189
bacteria on Shroud 17, 94, 172
beard 6, 47, 152
Besançon, shroud of 129, 209
binding strips (see *othonia*)
biofractionation 170
bio-plastic coating 172
bio-radiation 184
Blachernae Palace 123, 126, 127
blood:
  angles of flow 59
  blood and water 61, 63, 66, 166
  blood before image 66, 178
  bloodtype AB 67
  blood DNA 67, 68
  degraded/older 65, 68
  serum (separation) 66, 166
  human/male/primate xvi, 65, 68
  bloodstains 2
  human globulins 66
  halo effect 66
  positive vs. negative 5, 34, 66
  broken flow of 9
  venal and arterial 66, 67, 166
braid (see ponytail)
brush strokes, lack of (see directionality)
Bucholeon Palace 111, 113, 121, 126, 134
burden of proof 67
burial attitude 8, 9, 64
burial: primary 74, 75
  secondary 74, 75

burial of Jesus-theory 84-86
burn holes 4
Cadouin, shroud of 209
calcium carbonate 9, 44, 70, 78, 79
California test 174-5
camel hair 68
capillary action, lack of 156
cap of thorns (see thorns)
Carbon-14 xviii, 19, 31, 33, 46, 67, 94, 118, 142, 157, 159, 190
carboxylation 170
Catacombs (art) 29, 150
Cathedral of St. John Baptist 143
cave tombs 75-78
cellulose, degradation and dehydration of 15, 157, 180, 183
chaffing wounds 64
Charlemagne, shroud of 209
cheir (hand) 58
chin-band (see *sudarium*)
cloning 68
Cloth of Oviedo 91, 92, 207
cloth-body distance 177, 182
Code of Law (Jewish) 73, 89
coins (see *leptons*)
conspiracy theory 166
Constantinople xvii, 7, 22-23, 25, 30, 71, 93, 99-100, 111-115, 118-121, 123, 125-128, 130, 133-134, 136, 138, 140-141, 154, 193
Constantinople, sack of 125, 126, 133
contaminants on Shroud 165, 167-168
coronal discharge 42-43, 46
corruption, lack of (see decomposition)
cotton fibers 13, 14
Council of Nicea 111
crown of thorns (see thorns)
crucifixion, practice of 49
crucifragium 60-62, 64
Crusades (see Fourth Crusade)
D'Arcis Memorandum 129
decomposition, lack of 3, 12, 29, 70, 88, 181
dematerialized body of Jesus (see glorified body of Jesus)
deo (binding process) 81
digital enhancement 39, 46

directionality, lack of 156, 177
dirt (see *travertine*)
document of release 85
Dominum Flevit cemetery 74
doubled-in-four (see *tetradiplon*)
dyes, lack of 156, 177
Edessa xvii, 20, 22, 30, 70, 99-103, 107-109, 112, 114, 118, 131, 146-148, 151, 191
entulissa (see enveloped)
enveloped (in Shroud) 80, 83
Epitaphioi 134, 154
Essenes 74, 86
Exactor mortis 52
face-cloth (see *sudarium*)
fever, post-mortem 182, 212
Fifth Gospel xvi
fingerprints on heel 85-86
Fire of 1532 xviii, 3, 4, 141-142
Fire of 1997 142-143
fire model 169
flagrum 3, 52, 53
floral images 9, 19, 21, 25, 26, 29, 87, 89, 96
fold-marks (see raking light test)
forgery theory 24
four circles 154-155
Fourth Crusade xvii, 120, 121, 123
fractionation (see biofractionation)
Garden of Gethsemane 51, 55, 63, 80
glorified body of Jesus 90
Golgotha 55, 61, 75
Gossypium herbaceum 13, 14
gradalis 122
Grail xvii, 122, 135, 137
haematidrosis 63
Hagia Sophia (Constantinople) 123
Hagia Sophia (Edessa) 108, 109
half-life (atomic) 160
halos 184
handkerchief 147
hasta (spear) 62
hasta veliaris (short spear) 62
heel (dirt on) 59
height of Man of Shroud 7, 8
herringbone (see weave)
Himation 110, 117
Hiroshima 186-187
Holland cloth backing 4
Holy Grail (see Grail)
horizontal vs. vertical 105, 178

Hospitallers 131
Hungarian *Pray* Manuscript 154-155
Image of Edessa xvii, 22, 102-103, 105-106, 108, 111, 113-115, 147-149, 150, 154
images of Jesus (6th Cent.) 148-149, 153
inert gases 143
infrared light 6, 156, 178
inverse ratio (see cloth-body distance)
iron-oxide theory 179
Jehohanan 60, 62, 93
Jerusalem 118, 132
Julia *lepton* 38, 44
keriai 81, 84
Kirlian Aura 43, 183-185, 189
Knights Templar (see Templars)
Lamentation Scenes 119
lance wound 61, 62, 64
lepton coins 9, 33, 35, 36, 44, 70, 86, 204
Letter of Abgar 101, 102, 104, 120
limestone (see calcium)
Lirey, Church of 128, 130
litter (burial) 85-86
lituus 36, 37, 40, 44
locks (see side-locks)
loculi (*kochim*) 79
mafia (Shroud) 138-141
Mandylion 29, 30, 103, 105-106, 109, 116-117, 120, 149
material traces 16
Medieval image theory 43-44, 68-70
microchemistry 156, 178
mildew (see mold)
mineral coating 24
miracles xvii
Mishnah 9, 14, 73, 82
mites xvi, 19, 21ff, 31, 44, 70
mixing of kinds 15
MK80 Mass Spectrometer 170
moist secretion 112, 115-117
mold 11
Monastery of Daphni 128, 153
Monastery of St. Catherine 153
muscle, microscopic 211
mustache 6, 47, 152
myrrh 87, 89
nails: type 3
   efficacy of 60
   wrist vs. palm 57, 58
naked (Jesus as) 69, 75, 98, 123, 155, 180
natron on Shroud 17

natronocuccus (see natron)
natural formation 10
necropolis 74
negative images 5, 34, 44, 70
neutron-flux theory 190
Ossilegium 76
ossuaries 60, 75, 76
othonia 81, 82, 84, 85, 155
outline, lack of 6, 156, 177-178
Outremer 131
Oviedo (see Cloth of Oviedo)
Oxford University 162, 164
oxidation of cellulose 15, 157, 180, 183
painting, not a 145, 156, 177
Pantocrator Icon 30, 153
Parzival 135
patches on Shroud 142
patibulum 55, 56, 64
penetration, lack of 156, 177
peridedeto (bound about) 84
Perlesvaus 135
Pharos, Chapel of xvii, 112-114, 117,
    121, 126, 127, 134
phylactery (see *tephillin*)
physical outline (see outline)
pigment, lack of 44, 146, 177
pigtail (see ponytail)
Pilgrim's Medallion 129
pilum (javelin) 62
plumbatae 53
Polarized Image 41, 42, 46, 153
pollen on Shroud 9, 19ff, 31, 44, 70,
    96, 100, 103, 112
  on back of Shroud 79
  on Cloth of Oviedo 91
ponytail 7, 47
prayer box (see *tephillin*)
preponderance of evidence xvi, 67,
    165, 191
pressure sensitive, image not 182
Qumran 74, 86
radiation 177, 183, 184, 186, 190
  as heat or light 177, 180, 186, 189,
    190
  of Jesus' body 188
raking-light test 107
red crosses, Templars' 132, 135
Renaissance image theory 43-44, 68-70
Resurrection theory of image forma-
    tion 15
retting process 11, 180

rigor mortis 166
saliva 52
Sandia Laboratory 33
Sanhedrin 51, 52
saponaria 11
saturation, lack of 156, 177
scorch 2, 15, 142, 157, 180, 187, 189,
    190
scutella lata 122
sedile 49
selvedge 1, 2, 170
Semitic male xix, 7, 47
sepia color 2, 15, 157, 180
Sheol 76
Shroud, physical description of 1, 2
side-locks 7
side-strip (see selvedge)
signature of crucifixion 50, 61, 64
silence of N.T. 97, 98
Silent Witness xvi
silk backing 4
silver (on Shroud) 142
sindon xvi, 75, 78-80, 82, 86, 110, 121,
    123, 127, 146
soapweed (see struthium)
solidus coin 30, 154
sovev 89
Space of Destot 58
Spas Nereditsa fresco 154
stipes 55, 60
straw-yellow (see sepia)
struthium 11
S.T.U.R.P. xviii, 22, 23, 39, 45, 107,
    155-156
style, lack of artistic 180
sub alas 62
sudarium 82, 83, 86, 90, 91, 127, 207
surface phenomenon 4, 15, 177, 182
syndoine 126, 127
Templars xvii, 7, 131, 135-137
Templecombe 137-138
Temple of Solomon 132
tephillin 9
tetradiplon 104-107, 115-117, 147
Teutonic Knights 131
textile, Shroud as 10
thorns:
  cap of 3, 54, 64
  crown of 54
three-dimensional image xvi, 33-35, 45,
    70, 178

Threnos (see Lamentation Scenes)
thumbs, missing 58-59, 154-155
titulus 61
travertine argonite 44, 56, 59, 70
trellis pattern 116, 117, 147
tremisses coin 154
trial-by-fire 4
True Cross, relic of 125, 127
Turin Commission 12
ultraviolet light 6, 156, 178
ultraviolet radiation 186
Urfa (see Edessa)
Vaporgraph theory 181-182
Veronica 146
Vignon markings 151-152
Volckringer Effect 182, 184, 185

VP-8 Image Analyzer (see three-
dimensional image)
warrior monks (see Templars)
washing of body 88
(also anointing with oil) 88
water-stains 3, 142
weave (of Shroud) 1, 13, 155
weave anomalies 37, 39, 43, 45, 83
weight of Man of Shroud 8
widow's mite (see *lepton*)
wool 15
wrapped (see enveloped)
X-ray fluorescence 156, 178
yad (hand) 58
Zurich, Federal Polytechnic Institute of
Technology 161-162, 164